D1486745

SECRETS OF THE BIBLE

SECRETS OF THE BIBLE

from the editors of

With an Introduction by
Neil Asher Silberman

HATHERLEIGH PRESS
New York • London

Secrets of the Bible
A Hatherleigh Press Book

Hatherleigh Press
5-22 46th Avenue
Long Island City, NY 11101
1-800-528-2550

Library of Congress Cataloging-in-Publication Data

Secrets of the Bible / [from the editors of] Archaeology Magazine ; with an
introduction by Neil Asher Silberman ; contributions from Richard Horsley ... [et al.].
     p. cm.
  Includes bibliographical references.
  ISBN 1-57826-172-4
  1. Bible--Antiquities. 2. Bible. O.T.--History of Biblical events. 3.
Excavations (Archaeology)--Middle East. 4. Middle East--Antiquities. 5.
Palestine--History--To 70 A.D. 6. Shrines--Palestine. 7. Church
history--Primitive and early church, ca. 30-600. I. Archaeology magazine.
  BS621.S45 2005
  220.9'3--dc22

                            2004018871

ISBN 1-57826-172-4

Project Credits

ARCHAEOLOGY Staff
Publisher: Phyllis Pollak Katz
Editor-In-Chief: Peter A. Young
Executive Editor: Mark Rose

Hatherleigh Press Staff
President & CEO: Andrew Flach
Publisher: Kevin Moran
Managing Editor: Andrea Au
Art Director & Production Manager: Deborah Miller
Assistant Editor: Alyssa Smith
Cover Design: Calvin Lyte
Interior Design: Deborah Miller and Calvin Lyte
Indexer: Jessica Stasinos, Pegasus Indexing

ABOUT THE ARCHAEOLOGICAL INSTITUTE OF AMERICA

The Archaeological Institute of America (AIA), publisher of ARCHAEOLOGY Magazine, is North America's oldest and largest organization devoted to the world of archaeology. The Institute is a nonprofit educational organization founded in 1879 and chartered by the United States Congress in 1906. Today, the AIA has nearly 10,000 members belonging to 103 local societies in the United States, Canada, and overseas. The organization is unique because it counts among its members professional archaeologists, students, and many others from all walks of life. This diverse group is united by a shared passion for archaeology and its role in furthering human knowledge.

Contents

Part II:
READING BETWEEN
THE LINES OF THE BIBLE

Part III:
THE RISE OF CHRISTIANITY

Part IV:
THE HOLY LAND TODAY

ARCHAEOLOGY AND THE WORLD OF THE BIBLE

by NEIL ASHER SILBERMAN

In recent years, dramatic archaeological discoveries have cast important new light on some of the Bible's deepest and most intriguing mysteries. A vast and constantly growing array of buried inscriptions, artifacts, and ancient city ruins unearthed by archaeologists digging throughout the Lands of the Bible and indeed throughout the entire Mediterranean region have provided surprising new evidence about the origins of the People of Israel and the rise of Christianity—and about the historical realities that underlie the scriptural narratives of such famous biblical figures as Abraham, Moses, David and Solomon, Jesus, and Paul.

As the articles and illustrations in this book clearly show, archaeology has become an essential tool for understanding the world of the Bible. Painstaking excavations at biblical sites, together with the twenty-first-century technologies of radiocarbon dating, remote sensing, satellite imagery, wide-ranging surveys of surface remains, and the intriguing new field of archaeoastronomy have revolutionized our understanding of the peoples, events, and societies described in the Bible's timeless historical narratives, law codes, poetry, prayers, and prophetic works.

Readers will discover for themselves how the study of archaeological sites in Israel, Palestine, Jordan, Lebanon, and neighboring regions provide unique perspectives on the related, yet differing civilizations of the Canaanites, Phoenicians, Philistines, and other ancient Near Eastern peoples who appear so prominently in the text of the Old Testament. Even the question "Who were the Israelites?" has yielded up some unexpected insights about the process by which an ancient highland population known as "Israel" emerged on the historical stage and developed over centuries, contributing its unique monotheism and biblical faith to the world.

The New Testament has likewise provided its fair share of historical mysteries and has inspired an intense archaeological search. The quest to find physical traces of the lives and

BIBLICAL TIMELINE

The exact dates for events are open to interpretation. In ARCHAEOLOGY, we have followed the preferences of those scholars authoring individual articles and have consulted with several to create this overview of the historical framework of the Holy Land.

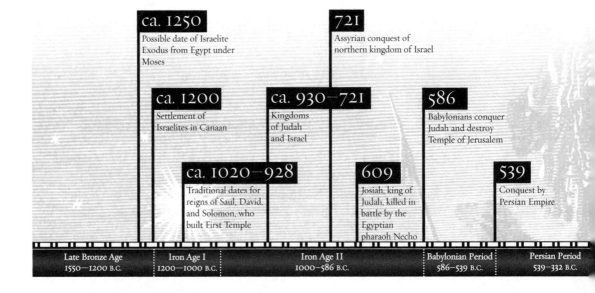

ca. 1250
Possible date of Israelite Exodus from Egypt under Moses

ca. 1200
Settlement of Israelites in Canaan

ca. 1020–928
Traditional dates for reigns of Saul, David, and Solomon, who built First Temple

ca. 930–721
Kingdoms of Judah and Israel

721
Assyrian conquest of northern kingdom of Israel

609
Josiah, king of Judah, killed in battle by the Egyptian pharaoh Necho

586
Babylonians conquer Judah and destroy Temple of Jerusalem

539
Conquest by Persian Empire

| Late Bronze Age 1550–1200 B.C. | Iron Age I 1200–1000 B.C. | Iron Age II 1000–586 B.C. | Babylonian Period 586–539 B.C. | Persian Period 539–332 B.C. |

Biblical vs. Archaeological Events

KINGS	DATES	BIBLICAL ACCOUNT	ARCHAEOLOGICAL EVIDENCE
Saul, David, and Solomon	ca. 1025-931	Conquest of Canaan, building of the Temple in Jerusalem, building at Megiddo, Hazor, and Gezer	No evidence for conquest; Canaanite culture continues uninterrupted; no signs of monumental building in named cities
Ahab	873-852	Marries Jezebel, a Phoenician princess; builds House for the Baal at Samaria; confronted by the prophet Elijah	Main building phase at Samaria; Jezreel compound; Megiddo palaces; Hazor wall and gate; possibly mentioned in Tel Dan inscription
Jeroboam II (Israel)	788-747	Defeats Damascus; northern kingdom reaches its greatest extent	Large-scale building at Hazor, Gezer, and Megiddo; seal with Jeroboam's name found at Megiddo
Pekah (Israel)	735-732	Allied with Damascus against Ahaz, king of Judah; Assyrian king Tiglath-Pileser III conquers the Galilee and Jezreel Valley	Destruction of Israelite cities in the north
	721		Assyrians complete conquest of Israel
Hezekiah-Josiah (Judah)	727-609	Hezekiah rebels against Assyria, Jerusalem regained; Josiah killed by Egyptian pharaoh Necho	Jerusalem grows dramatically, with new wall; Siloam Tunnel and cemetery; Lachish fortifications; prosperity in the Beersheva Valley; Judah participates in large-scale olive oil production at Ekron
	586		Jerusalem falls to the Babylonians

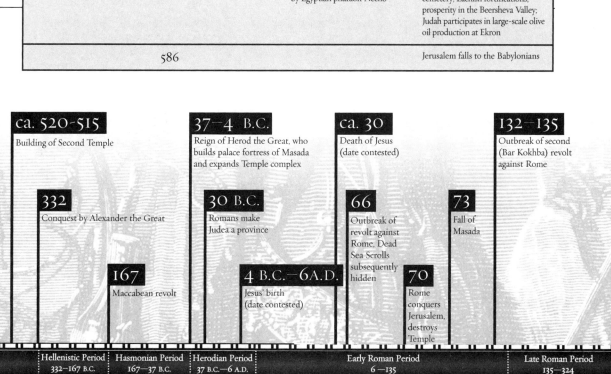

ca. 520-515
Building of Second Temple

37-4 B.C.
Reign of Herod the Great, who builds palace fortress of Masada and expands Temple complex

ca. 30
Death of Jesus (date contested)

132-135
Outbreak of second (Bar Kokhba) revolt against Rome

332
Conquest by Alexander the Great

30 B.C.
Romans make Judea a province

66
Outbreak of revolt against Rome, Dead Sea Scrolls subsequently hidden

73
Fall of Masada

167
Maccabean revolt

4 B.C.—6 A.D.
Jesus' birth (date contested)

70
Rome conquers Jerusalem, destroys Temple

Hellenistic Period 332–167 B.C.	Hasmonian Period 167–37 B.C.	Herodian Period 37 B.C.—6 A.D.	Early Roman Period 6 —135	Late Roman Period 135–324

acts of Jesus and the apostles has revealed the extent to which the religious message of the Gospels was a unique by-product of the Roman civilization in which it was born. In archaeological remains of Roman cities, farms, workshops, and places of worship, we can distinguish the long-forgotten social conditions of everyday life that gave rise to the symbols and doctrines of earliest Christianity. And the archaeological quest continues to reveal clues to the development of the Church itself—through the discovery of the earliest church structures and the Byzantine Empire's most imposing monuments.

Some of the new archaeological conclusions have sparked controversy and often bitter debate between scholars and believers. The lack of clear archaeological evidence for Joshua's conquest of the Promised Land (however vividly it is described in the Bible) has led some archaeologists to suggest that the ancient Israelites were not ethnically distinct invaders,

but originally members of the local Canaanite population, who established their new identity as part of a complex process of social change. At the famous biblical site of Hazor, however, a more traditional explanation of the conquest of the Promised Land has emerged. Readers can judge for themselves the weight of the relative evidence in this fascinating biblical archaeological debate about the Bible's value as a historical document.

The Dead Sea Scrolls are perhaps the most famous and enigmatic biblical archaeological finds of the last century and their general religious significance, possible social context, and meaning are explored by several of the contributors to this book. No less fascinating is the modern struggle for the physical possession of the ancient scrolls, which is deeply affected by modern Middle Eastern conflict and religious belief. This quest to stake a contemporary claim to antiquity continues even today.

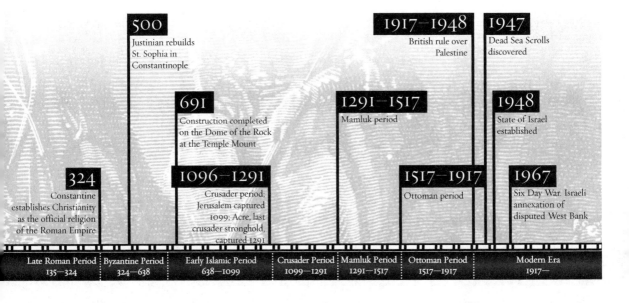

500
Justinian rebuilds
St. Sophia in
Constantinople

1917–1948
British rule over
Palestine

1947
Dead Sea Scrolls
discovered

691
Construction completed
on the Dome of the Rock
at the Temple Mount

1291–1517
Mamluk period

1948
State of Israel
established

324
Constantine
establishes Christianity
as the official religion
of the Roman Empire

1096–1291
Crusader period;
Jerusalem captured
1099; Acre, last
crusader stronghold,
captured 1291

1517–1917
Ottoman period

1967
Six Day War. Israeli
annexation of
disputed West Bank

| Late Roman Period 135–324 | Byzantine Period 324–638 | Early Islamic Period 638–1099 | Crusader Period 1099–1291 | Mamluk Period 1291–1517 | Ottoman Period 1517–1917 | Modern Era 1917— |

The Holy Land of the Bible, having gone through many hands and many names, re-emerged as Israel in 1948.

Jerusalem, site of Solomon's and Herod's Temple, now occupied by the revered Muslim shrines of the Dome of the Rock and the al-Aqsa mosque?

And what of the recent spectacular finds that purportedly provide the earliest archaeological evidence of Jesus and of the Temple of Solomon? The intrigue behind these finds and the charges and counter-charges about forgery, scholarly corruption, and hidden political motives connected with these astounding recent "discoveries" provide a true-to-life detective story from the world of biblical archaeology.

This book thus provides dramatic and wide-ranging glimpses at the ongoing archaeological search for the Bible. And while the diggers and recent finds from the Lands of the Bible may not have provided answers to all of the Bible's mysteries, they have utterly transformed how we look at this ancient, sacred text. In that light, the following chapters will provide readers with an exciting and vivid introduction to the great discoveries already made—and an appreciation of the many great biblical archaeological discoveries still to be found.

Indeed, modern politics and controversy are never entirely absent from the archaeological search for the Bible, and readers will learn of the bitter controversies that swirl around some of the most famous biblical sites. Is the ancient mound of Megiddo really the site of the prophesied final battle of Armageddon, feared by many and eagerly awaited by die-hard apocalyptic believers? Who really owns the Temple Mount in

PART I:

THE ANCIENTS

THEIR KINGDOMS, TRADE, AND POLITICS

THE PHOENICIANS

RICH AND GLORIOUS
TRADERS OF THE LEVANT

by Patricia M. Bikai

The names of Phoenicia's maritime city-states are familiar to all students of ancient history, archaeology, and the Bible: Byblos in the north, Sidon, and, to the south, Tyre. Mention of the Phoenicians themselves raises images of seafaring traders traversing the Mediterranean, and of their colonies, especially Tyrian Carthage. Yet I recall a spring day in 1970, when James B. Pritchard sent two enthusiastic young graduate students to look for Phoenician remains on the surface of the tell of Sarept in southern Lebanon. The two of us, Bill Anderson and I, dutifully picked up sherds, and reported back to Pritchard that we had seen very few that was Phoenician. This was no surprise as very few people had seen much that was Phoenician in their homeland, Lebanon.

By the middle of this century, Egyptian, Palestinian, and classical archaeologists could argue the fine points of the results of hundreds of excavations in their respective areas, but relatively little was known about the Phoenicians. Why? Partly because of the chance of excavation, and partly because of prejudice.

Ancient Phoenicia was located on a narrow plain between the Lebanon mountain range and the Mediterranean Sea. On average the plain is only a mile wide. Now heavily populated and devastated by civil war, Lebanon offers few possibilities for excavation. Another geographical factor has made recovery of Phoenician cultural remains difficult. Because of the association of Phoenicians with seafaring, there is a tendency to focus on the maritime element of their geography. In fact, the mountains behind their coastal plain had an equal impact on Phoenician culture. It is easy to understand why, as there are few places on earth of such beauty as grandeur as the mountains of Lebanon. Some of the ancient literature (e.g., Ezekial 31:1–18) places Eden, the "Garden of God," in those mountains. The highest point, Qornet es Sauda—the "Black "Horn"—rises to over 10,000 feet a mere 15 miles from the seacoast. In the winter, the mountains are covered with snow (Lebanon probably means "white"), and in the spring, underground rivers erupt spectacularly from grottos in the high mountains. In antiquity, the mountains were heavily forested with the cedar for which Lebanon was famous.

While geography played an important role in Phoenician culture and religion, it has had an unfortunate secondary consequence in terms of archaeology. The mountains gave an abundance of wood, and the coastal plain is wet. Thus many Phoenician artifacts were made of perishable materials and were deposited in sites so damp that they did indeed perish. We have little of Phoenician architecture and statuary because much of it was made of wood, and we have little of their literature because it was written on leather and papyrus.

Other factors contribute to our lack of knowledge about the Phoenicians. For example, most of the early archaeological explorers of the Levant were preoccupied with Jerusalem and other biblical sites. Their ships might land at Tripoli or Beirut, but they usually made a quick trip down the coast to get to their real goal. Some visited Tyre on their way, but it was usually just to gloat on that city's pitiful state. In 1841, for example, Edward Robinson recalled the prophet Ezekial's curse of Tyre when he wrote "I continued my walk…musing upon the pomp and glory, the pride and all, of ancient Tyre…[which] has indeed become 'like the top of a rock, a place to spread nets upon!'…and the hovels which now nestle upon a portion of her site, present no contradiction of [Ezekial's] dread decree: 'Thou shalt be built no more!'" Phoenicia was, after all, the ancient world's evil empire, the home of Baal and Astarte, the archetypal "pagan" gods. Jezebel, the model of the "evil woman," was a princess of Tyre.

Indentification with ancient peoples—politically with Greece, religiously with Palestine—was a powerful motivating factor in early exploration and archaeology. As the Phoenicians had little or no constituency among European scholars, there was little interest in exploring Lebanon.

Prejudice was an even more sinister element in the neglect of the Phoenicians. William Smith's *History of Greece*, a standard nineteenth-century British school text, for example, concedes that while the Phoenicians gave the Greeks the alphabet, "...the Oriental strangers left no permanent traces of their settlement in Greece; and the population of the country continued to be essentially Grecian, uncontaminated by any foreign elements." Potent language such as "Oriental strangers" and "foreign elements" often appeared in texts relating to the Phoenicians because they were Semites. In European anti-Semitic circles, the Phoenicians were secondary targets, but targets nonetheless. Martin Bernal of Cornell University has argued that much of the denial of the achievements of the Phoenicians was dictated by that prejudice. Since they couldn't have accomplished anything of real merit, their cities were not deemed worthy of archaeological investigation.

The result was that only two small projects were conducted in Lebanon in the nineteenth century. In 1860, Ernest Renan, a French Semitic philologist, conducted some surveys and excavations at Tyre, Sidon, Byblos, and Arwad, enriching the Louvre in the process. In the 1880s, there was a German excavation at Tyre, the sole purpose of which was to find the tomb of Frederick Barbarossa, the German emperor who had died in 1190 while on a crusade. They failed in their search, but damaged the site in the process.

In this century there were excavations at Byblos by Pierre Montet, a French Egyptologist. Montet, digging in the 1920s, was interested primarily in Egyptian connections with Lebanon, and his excavations did not uncover any material of the great age of Phoenician expansion—the Iron Age. Subsequent excavations at Byblos, directed by Maurice Dunand, also failed to uncover any Phoenician remains. Sir Leonard Woolley's excavation at Al Mina in the 1930s uncovered what was probably a Phoenician trading post in northern Syria, but because of the quantity of Greek pottery there, it was interpreted as a Greek site. Also in the 1930s, Tell Abu Hawam, an ancient port near Haifa, was excavated under the British Mandate by R.W. Hamilton. Because no substantial collections of excavated Phoenician material existed to compare with the finds from Tell Abu Hawam, it was not recognized as a Phoenician city. So until the late 1960s, the Phoenicians were known mainly from chance finds, from a few excavations at their colonies around the Mediterranean like Carthage and Motya, off the coast of Sicily, and from what had been written about them by classical and biblical authors, hostile witnesses at best. In the 20 years since, there has been great progress, particularly at sites in the western Mediterranean. That progress was marked by a major exhibition in Venice in 1988, "I Fenici," which brought together hundreds of Phoenician objects for the first time. The exhibition highlighted Phoenician artistic and cultural achievements, showing that, because of prejudice and because of the chance of excavation, an important element in the history of the ancient Mediterranean has been overlooked.

At the end of the Bronze Age, ca. 1200 B.C., the decline of both Mycenaean Greece and of Egypt created a power vacuum in the eastern Mediterranean. Assyria, Persia, and classical Greece would not be major forces for some centuries to come. During the intervening years, the first centuries of the Iron Age, a center of activity developed that would lay the basis for much of history, and that center was Phoenicia. Quietly, indeed often secretively, the great port cities of Tyre, Sidon, Byblos, and Arwad started sending ships farther and farther into the Mediterranean and into the Atlantic and Indian Oceans in search of markets for their goods and in search of raw materials to make those gods. As by-products of those ventures, the Phoencians set in motion at least three processes which influenced the cource of Western history. First, they created long-distance trade routes and the navigational techniques necessary to use those routes. This further integrated the economy of the whole Mediterranean basin. Second, they spread their alphabet, that simple and effective tool that would become the basis of all written communication in the West. You are using it right now.

Finally, Phoenician Tyre founded Carthage and the dozens of other colonies that would one day challenge Rome in the Punic Wars, a tedious series of conflicts best remembered for the trans-Alpine assault on Italy by Hannibal and his elephants in 217 B.C. What is little remembered today that is the Carthaginians were masters of the sea, and their challenge to Rome forced that land-based kingdom out onto the water, resulting in a Roman empire that was considerably larger and more powerful than it otherwise would have been. The consequence of those three Phoenician accomplishments—the creation of economic linkage, the spreading of the alphabet, and the challenge to Rome—

was that by the time Rome crushed Carthage in 146 B.C., the West was unified along lines that we can recognize today, and it had an effective means of communication.

During the hundreds of years that they dominated the sea, the Phoenicians made enemies, the sorts of enemies that are inevitable when you are commercially successful. Homer described the Phoenicians as slippery and as swindlers. Isaiah called Tyre a whore. The Romans depicted the Carthaginians as treacherous. In the end the Phoenicians and the Carthaginians lost to those enemies and were completely crushed, militarily and culturally. Their modern descendants live in port cities from Tyre to Gibraltar and beyond, and the first attempts to recover the Phoenicians occurred in those old port cities, at first in Italy and Spain, then in Tunisia, Malta, Ibiza, and finally, but only relatively recently, in Cyprus and in Lebanon itself. The excavations in the western Mediterranean, however, have mainly yielded late material, from the seventh century onward.

In the late 1960s and early 1970s, there were several excavations which uncovered quantities of Early Iron Age material. The first major excavation exclusively devoted to the recovery of a Phoenician port in Lebanon began in 1969 at Sarepta under the direction of James B. Pritchard of the University of Pennsylvania. Sarepta was probably a satellite town of Sidon. The excavations there uncovered an industrial quarter, with 22 kilns used for manufacturing amphorae, and a small religious structure with benches on which offerings were placed. At Larnaca in Cyprus, Vassos Karageorghis, then director of the Department of Antiquities of the Republic of Cyrus, discovered part of what was probably Tyre's first major colony, Kition. The excavation, begun in 1962, exposed a large temple which was probably dedicated to the goddess Astarte.

My own involvement with the Phoenicians was due to the chance of being invited to join the project at Sarepta. By 1971, I was excavating at Tyre where intensive excavations had been going on since 1948, but these had uncovered only remains of the Roman era and later. In the fall of 1971, Phoenician levels were reached for the first time at the site. The Emir Maurice Chéhab, Director General of Antiquities of Lebanon and director of the Tyre excavation, asked me to direct the work on the Phoenicians.

The excavation began in the Roman levels and went down some 30 feet to bedrock. On bedrock, remains of the Early Bronze Age were found, and among the finds was a seal belonging to a minor official of the Egyptian court; he may well have been at Tyre to negotiate the purchase of cedar. The royal tombs of the Bronze Age at Byblos had already produced evidence for the close relationship between the port cities and Egypt as they were filled with gifts from the Pharaohs to the princes of Byblos. Additionally, a number of inscriptions in Egypt attest that relationship. The earliest known is from an Egyptian document of about 2600 B.C. recording that Pharaoh Snefru bought 40 shiploads of cedar. Lebanon has few natural resources other than cedar, and Egypt had to have large beams for her construction projects. This led to a symbiotic relationship between Lebanon and Egypt which profoundly affected the way the city-states on the coast would develop. It was not enough just to have the timber resource, the

Phoenicians also had to have an infrastructure capable of cutting and transporting the large trees. It also required navigational skills to move the timber down to Egypt; moving huge logs by sea is not the same as moving gold bars or even copper ingots. So the coastal Phoenicians developed the necessary organization and the skills. By 750 B.C., if not earlier, these skills would lead them to the Straits of Gibraltar and beyond, not as individual traders but as city-states organized into multinational trading companies.

In addition to timber, Phoenicia had abundant quantities of clean beach sand for glass-making and, in the sea, the shellfish Murex which could be used to dye cloth "Tyrian purple." It was on the basis of these commodities—wood, glass, and purple cloth—that the Phoenicians built their prosperity. Through trade, other commodities were quickly added. Ezekiel (27:12–24) says that Tyre was trading in gold, silver, iron, ebony, coral, precious stone, and rare spices. There is even a memory of that trade in the English language. The word cinnamon is Phoenician, as are probably the words cumin, coriander, crocus (for the spice saffron), myrrh, aloe, balsam, jasper, diamond, and sapphire—all luxury goods. These were apparently introduced into Greece with their Phoenician names and thence came to the English language. Another appropriate survivor is the dollar sign which came to us via Spain and Mexico. The two vertical lines through the "S" probably recall the legend of the two Phoenician columns that once stood at the Straits of Gibraltar—the "pillars of Hercules."

So while Greece was in the Dark Age and

Egypt was in political confusion, Phoenicia flourished. We have only a few texts from this period, but one of these illustrates how powerful and independent the coastal city-states became. Around 1100 B.C., a minor Egyptian official called Wen-Amon arrived in Byblos to purchase cedar beams. In the account of his journey, which has survived, Wen-Amon states that he had been robbed of his money, so the king of Byblos mocked him. In an earlier era, the king of Byblos would have extended credit to a representative of the Egyptian Pharaoh. No more!

Initially, it appears that the Phoenicians may have conducted their overseas trade directly, but single ships or even fleets arriving at irregular intervals could probably not meet the demand for goods. So in time, groups of permanent sales representatives were stationed at strategic points around the Mediterranean. They could receive shipments and store them and also purchase raw materials and warehouse those until a fleet came to pick them up. This ensured a constant flow of goods.

Because of that trade, Tyre became "rich and glorious" (Ezekiel 27:25), and there were relatively few wars. This may have led to unchecked population growth, a potential disaster for a people so land poor. Even after King Hiram I, the friend of Solomon, expanded the city in ca. 970 B.C., the island-city Tyre covered no more than about 40 acres. It is possible that the custom of infant sacrifice, which is so well known from Carthage and other colonies, developed as a social response to that problem. The biblical story of Abraham and Isaac is a condemnation of that practice. Perhaps to deal with overpopulation and also to further protect their far-flung markets, large-scale overseas colonization began. The first colony, at Kition in Cyprus, was founded no later than the ninth century B.C. Within a few hundred years, Phoenician colonies ringed the Mediterranean basin.

The most important colony, the one that would challenge both Greece and Rome, was Carthage in modern Tunisia. The traditional story of the founding of Carthage is that King Pygmalion of Tyre (821–774 B.C.) killed the husband of his sister, Elissa, in order to seize his wealth. Elissa, Jezebel's grandniece, fled with her husband's gold to what is now Tunisia. Once there she negotiated to buy a piece of land as large as the hide of an ox could cover and then cut a hide into tiny strips and surrounded a large hill with it. Thus was born Carthage (the "new city") which in turn founded her own colonies in the western Mediterranean. The Carthaginian empire gradually took over the role of the Levantine cities as those cities were swallowed up by the Babylonian and then the Persian and Greek empires. Carthage and the other colonies in the west remained independent until Rome defeated them in 146 B.C.

Until that defeat, the Carthaginians continued the exploration and expansion begun by Tyre nearly a millenium before. Trade networks stretched along the Atlantic coast both north and south of Gibraltar. Around 600 B.C. a group of Phoenicians probably even circumnavigated Africa, a feat that would not be replicated until Vasco da Gama's voyage in A.D. 1497–98, two millennia later. The Greek historian Herodotus (4.42) tells the story of that voyage but rejects it as a fable since the sailors claimed that they had "the sun on their right hand." In fact having the sun on the right—to the north—is a phenomenon of the southern hemisphere. Although there is as yet no confirmation of it in the British Isles, the story of a fifth-century voyage led by Himilco, probably to Cornwall, contains details that make it believable. There is yet another story from the same period of colonists led down the west coast of Africa by the Carthaginian Hanno. After planting colonies along the coast, some of the expeditionaries probably reached the vicinity of Sierra Leone and may have gone as far as Cameroon. It is interesting that even today many Lebanese, particularly those from the Tyre area, have strong economic links to that area of West Africa.

In recent years, research on the Phoenicians has blossomed. The tragedy of civil war in Lebanon has, of course, stopped work at the main ports, but current excavations at Ras el Bassit in Syria, Tell Dor in Israel, and Kition-Bamboula in Cyprus, are now flooding the literature with fresh information. The picture, however, is by no means complete. For example, there is an ancient tradition tha Tyre founded a colony at Cadiz in Spain as early as 1100 B.C., yet the earliest Phoenician material remains uncovered to date in Spain are from about 800 --. We don't know whether to believe the tradition or the present evidence, but reliance on our current knowledge can be misleading. Evidence for an early Phoenician presence in either Cyprus or Crete was lacking as recently as ten years ago. Two excavations since then, at Palaepaphos in southwest Cyprus and at Kommos on the southern coast of Crete, have uncovered Phoenician ceramics, including storage jars and jugs perhaps used to export wines and oils, from the early part of the Iron Age.

Their overseas exploits and the gradual recovery of the material traces of their voyages has been the focus of much research on the Phoenicians. From that evidence, however, we will never be able to reconstruct more than a part of their culture, for the Phoenicians were more than just good sailors and clever traders. It is an irony that almost none of the literature of the people who gave us the alphabet has been preserved. Fragments of their poetry have survived in, for example, the biblical Song of Songs and in the Psalms. The mountains are described as "a fountain that makes the gardens fertile, [a] well of living water" (Song of Songs 4:15). Even more evocative is the Phoenician poem embedded in Psalm 104 which speaks of the birds making their nests in the cedars which God planted and of the streams breaking out of the ravines. In that Psalm, the creator lives in a palace above the mountains—the thunder is his voice, that clouds his chariot, and the winds his messengers. Those are the Phoenician images that still survive in the religious consciousness of the west.

In the future, better excavation and conservation techniques may allow us to recover more from Phoenician sites than we have in the past. Those techniques may overcome the frustration of seeing, as I once did, a trace of dark carbonized material on the damp floor of a Phoenician building, wondering whether it was the remains of a long-ago dinner—or excerpts from one of those songs about the mountains.

A NATION OF ARTISANS

PHOENICIANS SUPPLIED THE MEDITERRANEAN WORLD WITH TRINKETS AND BAUBLES FOR THE MASSES, CARVED IVORIES, ORNAMENTAL GOLDWORK, AND GILT-SILVER FOR ARISTOCRATIC CLIENTS

by GLENN MARKOE

Trade is the word that springs to mind when one thinks of the Phoenicians, and it is precisely this element of merchandising that so clearly defines Phoenician art. For much of Phoenician art—especially what survives to us today—was intended for a foreign market. This is reflected in the broad geographic distribution of Phoenician goods, from Spain to Morocco in the west to southern Russian and Mesopotamia in the east. In fact, our definition of Phoenican art is based largely on finds from Phoenician colonies and from outlying regions that formed distant markets for Phoenician traders.

The preponderance of Phoenician goods found in outlying regions reflects a strong economic reality: the focus of the Phoenician sea trader and craftsman upon a foreign market or clientele. Craftsmanship and maritime trade were closely related for the Phoenicians. According to Alexandrian historian Philo of Byblos, the Phoenician craftsman-god Chousor was the inventor of the raft and the first of all men to sail.

As commercial traders and middlemen, the Phoenicians came to appreciate the economic potential of the export market. In a country largely devoid of natural resources, with the notable exception of timber, necessity dictated that manufactured goods play an important role in trade. In fact, the Phoenician economy seems to have been predominantly based on the export of finished products manufactured from imported materials and commodities. The prophet Ezekial, writing in the sixth century B.C., provides a detailed list of materials obtained by the Phoenicians from their far-flung training partners. Staples such as wheat, oil, and livestock and precious commodities, such as silver, iron, tin, lead, ivory, and ebony, were acquired in exchange for unspecified Phoenician merchandise. From other passages in the Old Testament and from contemporary Assyrian and Greek sources we learn more about these Phoenician wares: they consisted of decorated clothing and textiles, engraved and repoussé metalwork, and carved ivory and woodwork. Phoenician luxury goods in a variety of media have been found throughout the Mediterranean basin and beyond.

The clientele for the Phoenician crafts-man was diverse, ranging from the lower classes to the aristocracy. Manufactured goods were produced accordingly. Multicolored glass pendants and beads and molded faience amulets and trinkets were produced for the mass market. Phoenician glass pendants, formed of glass rods wound around a sand core, were distinctively shaped in the form of caricatured human and animal heads. Their popularity is attested by their frequent occurrence in tombs throughout the Mediterranean, especially in North Africa. They may have been a specialty of Carthage and its colonies. Faience, a silica-based frit which self-glazes when fired, was molded to form a seemingly infinite variety of charms, including scarabs and amulets in the form of Egyptian symbols and deities. The scarab form, as well as the technique of faience manufacture, was borrowed directly from the Egyptians. A Phoenician scarab can usually be distinguished by its simplified shape, its frequent use of glass paste in place of true faience, its inscriptions in the Phoenico—Punic alphabet, and, above all, by its use of pseudo—Egyptian motifs and hieroglyphs.

Some Phoenician attempts at imitation of Egyptian faience could be quite convincing. A case in point is the famous "Bocchoris" vase from Tarquinia, named after the 24th Dynasty Egyptian king whose royal cartouche is inscribed on the vessel. Opinions range widely on the subject of its authorship—is it an Egyptian original or a nearly exact Phoenician copy of one? Certain stylistic anomalies on the vase, together with the discovery of a nearly identical version in Phoenician style at Motya, a Phoenician island colony off the coast of Sicily, strongly suggest that the Tarquinia vessel was a Phoenician work.

Phoenician traders were renowned in antiquity for clever trinkets mass produced for wholesale consumption. The Greek poet Homer and the classical historian Herodotus both describe the arrival of Phoenician traders equipped with their bags of trinkets and baubles (Homer calls them *athyrmata*, or playthings). In addition to objects in glass, frit, and faience, a whole series of specialty items was produced from exotic materials, among them carved tridacna shells, sculpted amber, and painted and incised ostrich eggs. For practical reasons, cheaper and more readily available materials were often substituted for the expensive originals: carved bone instead of ivory, or colored glass paste inlays in place of semiprecious stones.

The royal or aristocratic market was, of course, the most lucrative one for the Phoenician merchant. Delicately carved ivories were highly prized by royalty. A whole series of such ivories was discovered in a storeroom of the palace of the Assyrian king Ashurnasirpal II at Nimrud, very probably booty from a Levantine royal residence. One of these, depicting a lioness attacking an African youth, shows the characteristic Phoenician use of colored glass paste inlays and applied gold leaf. A pair of ivory open-work panels depicting a sphinx and a sacred tree, or "palmette," in Egyptian style were found in a nobleman's tomb at Salamis on Cyprus. Designed as decorative ornaments for a wooden chair discovered in the tomb, they were almost certainly the products of a royal Phoenician workshop operating on the mainland. The famous repoussé bronze and gilt-silver bowls form another category of Phoenician luxury goods geared to a royal or aristocratic market. Examples have been found in royal tombs in Etrutia, Cyprus, and more recently, in Anatolian Phrygia.

Theme and subject matter were equally adapted to their audiences. Glass pendants with demon and satyr heads and the faience amulets in the shape of Egyptian gods and religious symbols clearly appealed to the tastes and religious preferences of the general populace. Carved ivories and repoussé silver bowls, on the other hand, incorporated themes and motifs associated with royalty or royal pursuits, such as the sphinx, lion, or falcon—symbols of Egyptian sovereignty—or lion hunts, sumptuous banquet scenes, and processionals.

Despite its diversity, the surviving material record constitutes only a partial picture of the total output of the Phoenician craftsman, for the two most abundant and marketable commodities, decorated textiles and carved woodwork, have not survived the passage of time. Homer, writing in the eight century B.C., tells us of the colorful woven textiles for which the Sidonian, or Phoenician, women were famous. Among the tribute recorded by the Assyrians from the Phoenician cities were "garments of brightly colored stuffs." These garments almost certainly included textiles colored with the coveted purple dyes for which the Phoenicians were renowned. The designs and decorative techniques, weaving or embroidery, employed on the textiles remain unknown to us.

Wood, particularly cedar and fir, was one natural resource not found wanting in ancient Phoenicia, and the timber trade was lucrative. From the ancient sources we know that the Phoenicians were renowned for their woodworking skills, and we can assume that this applied to fine ornamental relief work as well as joinery. According to the Old Testament, the Tyrian mastercraftsman Hiram, contracted to supervise the construction and decoration of Solomon's Temple in Jerusalem, was a skilled worker in wood as well as metal and stone, "trained in the art of fine engraving and design-working." The most direct indication of the Phoenician woodworker's skill may be found in the fine relief and openwork designs executed on Phoenician craftsman, closely associated. In his prophecy on Tyre, Ezekial's "ship of Tyre" is described as having a cedar cabin with an ivory throne-room, or pavilion, within. The majority of Phoenician ivories, like those from Salamis, were manufactured as inlays or ornamentation for wooden furniture—beds, couches, tables, thrones, chests, and the like. Tally marks in Phoenician script, often found on the backs of ivory panels, were written there to ensure that the panels were attached to such furniture in the proper sequence.

The ivory panels from Nimrud and Salamis emphasize an important aspect of Phoenician art: the strong Egyptian influence which pervades both style and subject matter. The adaptation, or reuse, of foreign, especially Egyptian, motifs has been traditionally identified as a hallmark of Phoenician art. This strong predilection for Egyptian themes and motifs reflects the commercial ties that Phoenicia enjoyed, in varying degrees throughout its history, with its powerful neighbor to the south. Attempts at the creation of an Egyptian royal style can be documented in ornamental goldwork found at Byblos in the Middle Bronze Age (ca. eighteenth century B.C.), long before the emergence of Phoenician art and civilization. Egyptian influence is particularly apparent in Phoenician art from the "classical" epoch, the eight and seventh centuries B.C. The gilt-silver Phoenician bowl from Curium on Cyprus is an excellent case in point. Its outer register faithfully reproduces a long-standing royal Egyptian theme—that of the victorious pharaoh smiting a group of entreating prisoners. The motif of a vanquishing Egyptian king who stands triumphant over his enemies is a venerable one in Egyptian art, extending as far back as the Early Dynastic Period (ca. 3100–2700 B.C.). Art of the New Kingdom, particularly the thirteenth and twelfth centuries, provides the immediate prototypes for the scene on the bowl.

The Curium bowl provides an excellent illustration of the diversity of artistic influences affecting Phoenician art. Its central medallion, for example, depicts a theme borrowed directly from royal Assyrian art: a four-winged genius or demon with a short sword slaying a rampant lion. As in the case of the victorious pharaoh in Egypt, the theme of swordsman and lion is an old one in the art of Mesopotamia and figures prominently in the iconographic repertoire of the Assyrian artist of the early first millennium B.C. This strong Assyrian element is characteristic of Phoenician art from Cyprus and underscores the strong political ties that existed between the island of Cyprus and the Assyrian state.

The Phoenician artists' receptivity to foreign influences from diverse quarters and their ability to adapt and combine motifs and traits from these separate sources is perhaps the single most identifying characteristic of Phoenician art. This very eclectic quality, however, complicates any attempt to categorize Phoenician art on the basis of style. In recent years, attention has been focused on differentiating Phoenician and North Syrian stylistic traditions. These studies have attempted to identify the strongly Egyptianizing features in the style, selection, and rendering of motifs in Phoenician art and to pinpoint the more northerly, i.e., Hittite and Mitannian, influences in the iconography of the North Syrian tradition. While the basic premise is clearly valid, the distinctions are not always quite as clear and consistent as one would like them to be.

The question of stylistic attribution, Phoenician versus North Syrian, is complicated by difficulties associated with pinpointing the precise source, or sources, of Phoenician artistic production. The latter problem stems from the geographic nature of the findspots of Phoenician art: the overwhelming majority of the luxury goods

ACCORDING TO THE OLD TESTAMENT, THE TYRIAN MASTER-CRAFTSMAN HIRAM WAS CONTRACTED TO SUPERVISE THE CONSTRUCTION AND DECORATION OF SOLOMON'S TEMPLE IN JERUSALEM

associated with the Phoenician tradition have been found *outside* of Phoenicia, in colonies and outlying regions in the Mediterranean basin and in isolated finds in the Near East proper. An excellent example is the large cache of repoussé bronze bowls discovered by Sir Austen Henry Layard in the palace of the Assyrian king Ashurnasirpal II at Nimrud. The hoard itself is not a homogenous unit but a composite of many different types and styles. The Assyrian findspot is clearly a secondary one; the cache of vessels probably represents war booty or tribute-/gifts collected by Assyrians sometime in the latter half of the eight century B.C. The precise source, or sources, of origin for these vessels are unknown. Many of these vessels were probably the work of a select number of Phoenician workshops operating in the major Levantine coastal centers.

The emergence of the Phoenician artistic tradition is also complicated by the paucity of material evidence. Earlier studies in the century tended to place its beginnings as far back as the Middle Bronze Age, or early second millennium B.C., based upon the discoveries at Byblos. According to current interpretation, however, Phoenician art and culture are considered an Iron Age phenomenon whose roots extend back to the preceding Late Bronze Age. Phoenician culture is associated with the reemergence of Levantine city-states after 1200 B.C., following the incursions of the Sea Peoples at the end of the Bronze Age. The literary tradition, preserved in the Old Testament and in contemporary Assyrian sources, points clearly to a flourishing craft tradition in the Phoenician Levant at the end of the second millennium B.C. Solomon's request to King Hiram of Tyre for a skilled Phoenician to supervise construction and decoration of his palace and temple underscores the esteem in which the Phoenician craft industry was held by the mid-tenth century B.C.

Ironically, the literary tradition does not find support in the archaeological record. With the notable exception of the famous sarcophagus of King Ahiram of Byblos, whose date remains the subject of controversy, no major Iron Age Phoenician artistic monument or artifact may be securely dated to the period prior to the ninth century. The Ahiram sarcophagus is a revealing document of Phoenician artistic expression. While its inscription may be securely assigned to the early tenth century B.C., the sarcophogus itself, if it derives from the tomb's initial burial context, may be considerably earlier. Here, a date in the first half of the twelfth century is indicated by the latest find—a fragmentary ivory plaque in a hybrid Canaanite—Mycenaean style depicting a bull attacked by a lion and a griffin. The main frieze on the sarcophagus depicts a procession of male votaries, led by an official, perhaps a head priest, toward an enthroned king seated with a cup and lotus flower in hand. This type of ceremonial scene is common in Phoenician art of the first millennium B.C., appearing on both bronzes and ivories. The theme may be traced back to the Late Bronze Age, as on the famous ivory sheath inlay from Megiddo. The lotus flower held by the king on the Ahiram sarcophagus and the sphinx-throne upon which he is seated point to the scene's interpretation as an allegorical representation of a king's rebirth or apotheosis after death. As is often the case in Phoenician art, the concept of the lotus as a symbol of the soul's rebirth is borrowed directly from Egyptian art and religion, where the flower symbolizes the god Nefertem, overseer of the soul's passage to the afterlife.

In its more durable stone medium and monumental scale, the Ahiram sarcophagus stands out in sharp contrast to the better known portable and exportable wares of the Phoenician craftsman. It was this very commercial market of the Phoenician artist, and his natural exposure to foreign influences through trade, that gives Phoenician art its distinctive identity.

A DYE FOR GODS AND KINGS

PHOENICIA'S MOST FAMOUS EXPORT IS STILL REGARDED AS THE COLOR OF ROYALTY

by PATRICK E. MCGOVERN

P urple, extolled by the poet Robert Browning as the "dye of dyes," has close associations with the Phoenicians. According to the Greek legend the dye was discovered by Melqart, king and deity of Tyre, when he and the nymph Tyros were strolling along the Mediterranean shore with their dog. Biting into a large sea-snail or mollusk, the dog stained its mouth purple, whereupon Melqart promptly dyed a gown with the new-found substance and presented it to his consort.

The legend may well retain a kernel of truth. The Mediterranean mollusk species (*Murex trunculus, M. brandaris,* and *Purpura haemostoma*), whose hypobranchial glands contain the chemical precursors for the purple dye, come into shallower water—especially along rocky shorelines such as that of Lebanon—to mate in the late spring. A dog biting into a shell would certainly come away with a purple mouthful. It is not difficult to imagine that ancient humans would be fascinated by the dye. Once having touched it and strongly colored one's hands, its use as a very fast, intense dye would have been soon appreciated.

The Phoenicians played the preeminent role in purple dyeing, and this is highlighted in the archaeological and historical record. Excavations at Sarepta (biblical Zarephath), located midway between Tyre and Sidon, have yielded pottery shards covered with a purple deposit from a thirteenth-century B.C. context. Chemical analysis of the deposit verified that it was indeed composed of molluscan purple (6,6′-dibromoindigotin). Moreover, the pottery shards were from storage containers of the well-known Canaanite jar type, used to store and transport goods throughout the Mediterranean. The jar fragments were found near a pile of crushed shells, primarily *Murex trunculus*. Here, then, was the earliest evidence for large-scale dye production.

Contemporaneous literary evidence, including the Amarna correspondence from Egypt, the Ugaritic archives at Ras Shamra in north Syria, and Linear B tablets from Crete, also indicates that fabrics dyed with purple were already important commercial items. Unfortunately, these texts provide no information about where the fabrics were dyed. The finding of shell middens on Crete, in particular, which pre-date the Sarepta industry by as much as 400 years, suggests to some scholars that the Levantine dyers learned their craft from the Minoans or, at least, that a number of sites in the eastern Mediterranean were engaged in dye production. Yet, thus far, no conclusive evidence, such as a dyed fabric or a dyeing installation from this period has been found on Crete or elsewhere in the Aegean.

In the succeeding centuries of the Iron Age, the Canaanite city-states on the Levantine coast dominated the purple dyeing industry. Even the names of these peoples—Canaanites and later Phoenicians—very likely derive from the ancient Semitic and Greek roots for "purple." To promote this industry, dye factories were set up at Phoenician colonies—most notably, along the coasts of Tunisia, Malta, Sicily, and Spain.

Despite the importance of purple dyeing, there are few references to it in Phoenician writings. This may indicate a desire to guard secrets about dyeing, or may simply reflect our very limited knowledge of Phoenician literature. Biblical texts (Ezekial 27:7, 16, 24; II Chronicles 2:7, 14) that incorporate Iron Age traditions are more informative about the involvement of Phoenician city-states, especially Tyre, in the industry. The use of purple in early Israelite religion (e.g., in the tabernacle curtains and the High Priest's vestments: Exodus 26:1, 31: 28:4–6; 39:1, 28–29; II Chronicles 3:14) shows considerable Phoenician influence, which was especially strong during the time of Solomon.

It is only in the time of the early Roman Empire that the dyeing process is first described. The most authoritative account is in the *Historia Naturalis* (book IX sections 60–65, chapters XXXVI–XLI) by Pliny the Elder, who wrote in the mid-first century A.D. He describes in marvelous

Jack Hazut, JHM Photography

Among the remains uncovered in the excavations of Ashdod, once a powerful Phoenician city, was a Hellenistic installation for extracting purple dye from murex.

detail how the mollusks were captured using baited wicker baskets; how the best time to capture the animals was after the rising of the dog-star, Sirius (possibly a veiled reference to the legendary dog?); how the gland was extracted and the extracts heated for ten days in a large tin vat with added salt and water, during which refuse organic materials were periodically skimmed off the surface, and the liquid tested for its dyeing properties; how double-dipping the wool was able to produce the "Tyrian color," and so forth. Considering the wealth of detail in Pliny's account, he most likely observed the process first-hand.

The purple was difficult to produce, and thousands of mollusks were needed to make an ounce of the dye, which was worth more than its weight in gold. It is no wonder then that purple became a mark of status (both religious and political) and wealth. One example of conspicuous display was the Tyrian purple sail of Cleopatra's ship at the Battle of Actium in the first century B.C. One hundred years later, Nero issued an edict that permitted only the emperor to wear purple.

The complex extractions and dyeing process as described by Pliny has often been understood as a vat process—a chemical reduction of the dye to a colorless compound, in which form it is more easily absorbed by textile fibers. Subsequent reoxidation by exposure to air yields the colored dye, which is now wash-fast. This procedure contrasts with direct application of the molluscan glandular secretions to the textile, followed by color development in the sun. Actual experiments following the recipes and procedures outlined by the Roman writer substantiate vat dyeing in this period. We do not know how early the vat process for purple dying was used. That the Sarepta dyeing facility was located in the midst of a large group of pottery kilns may not simply be coincidence or the result of an attempt to consolidate polluting industries—we know from classical writers that the purple dying created a horrendous stench. Rather, the kilns could have supplied heat to aid in the extraction process and the true vat-dyeing of the textiles.

Following the Islamic conquest of the Middle East in the early seventh century A.D., purple dying along the Levantine coast was greatly curtailed, not least because of the increasing availability of less expensive substitutes. Production of the molluscan dye ceased altogether after the fall of Constantinople in A.D. 1453. Eleven years later, Pope Paul II issued an edict instructing cardinals to substitute kermes, an insect-derived scarlet dye, for the royal purple the church had been using to dye its vestments.

EARLY IRON AGE GEOPOLITICS

CANAANITES, ISRAELITES, AND SEA PEOPLES VIE FOR SUPERIORITY

by ROBERT STIEGLITZ

Shortly after the year 1200 B.C., the land of Canaan was permanently transformed by upheavals. A bitter conflict arose over possession of the coastal plain and its flourishing harbor towns. The native Canaanites, freed from domination by Egyptians and Hittites, were now challenged by two groups of newcomers: the Israelites, and another confederation of tribes the Egyptians called "Peoples of the Sea."

The Philistines, one of the Sea Peoples, had successfully entrenched themselves in the south, between Jaffa and Gaza. That part of Canaan was henceforth known as *Peleshet*, our "Palestine." To the north, the harbor town of Dor was dominated by another tribe of the Sea Peoples as was the settlement of Akko. The Israelite tribes of Asher, Zebulon, and Dan had gained control of the hinterland between Akko and Tyre. The remaining Canaanites maintained their independence only along a narrow coastal strip north of Akko, an area called Phoenicia by the Greeks.

For Phoenician city-states, the ports of Arwad, Byblos, Sidon, and Tyre, were all active between 1200–1000 B.C., heirs to a long maritime history in the Bronze Age. Arwad and Tyre were small offshore islands, Byblos had been a main Egyptian port-of-call, but it was Sidon that took the lead in ushering in the Phoenician florescence of the Early Iron Age.

The final collapse of Egyptian power in Canaan was caused by the attacks of the Sea Peoples, who began their thrust toward Egypt about 1175 B.C. This onslaught, best known from its vivid description by Ramses III, must have devastated the Canaanite coast.

The accounts of late classical authors preserve a vague memory of these and subsequent events. Strabo states that refugees from Sidon refounded the island of Arwad. Justin records that the island of Tyre was also refounded by Sidonian refugees, one year before Troy was captured in 1183 B.C.

These late accounts suggest that while Sidon itself was affected by warfare, its people recovered, assuming hegemony over the Phoenician heartland. Homer used the term "Sidonian" as synonymous with "Phoenician" (*Iliad* 23.743–44). The Hebrews, too, preserved a similar meaning; in II Kings 16:31, the ruler of Tyre is called King of the Sidonians. In the biblical Table of Nations (Genesis 10:15–19), Sidon is named as the "first-born" of Canaan. Sidonian coins of

the Roman era still perpetuated the tradition that Sidon was the primary Phoenician metropolis.

An inscription of Tiglath-Pileser I (1114–1076 B.C.) records that this Assyrian emperor received the tribute of three major Phoenician harbors: Arwad, Byblos, and Sidon. Tyre is conspicuously absent from his list. The Sea Peoples may have destroyed Tyre by that time, but the city's absence from the inscription could also indicate that Tyre did not submit to the Assyrian army and remained independent. If Tyre indeed was destroyed ca. 1200 B.C., and then rebuilt by Sidonians—as recorded by Justin—it may well be that by the end of the twelfth century B.C. the island fortress was strong enough to withstand an Assyrian threat.

What is certain, as attested by the report of the Egyptian official Wen-Amon about 1075 B.C., is that Tyre, Sidon, and Byblos were all flourishing maritime centers in the period just after the reign of Tiglath-Pileser I. The Assyrian campaign in Phoenicia did not prevent these city-states from developing their maritime interests. There is evidence for the relative decline of Byblos in the eleventh century, but Tyre, Sidon, and probably Arwad seem to have attained substantial political and naval power.

The emergence of the Phoenicians, then, is linked to the decline of Egypt and could not sustain its hegemony over Canaan. When the Assyrian army of Tukuli-Ninurta I destroyed the once-dominant Hittite empire shortly before 1200 B.C., the Phoenician littoral was finally free from overlords. Tiglath-Pileser I temporarily disturbed the peace by campaigning on the

Levantine coast, ca. 1100 B.C., but this did not interrupt Phoenician enterprise. It is tempting to suggest that Assyria actually encouraged Phoenician maritime ventures. Assyria, a land power, could only stand to advance its imperial aims from a successful Phoenician maritime monopoly in the Levant. We find, as Wen-Amon relates in some detail, that the Phoenician kings had established very profitable shipping companies, which dominated the Levantine maritime trade in the eleventh century B.C.

By the end of the eleventh century, two new factors assumed primary importance in early Phoenician history. Tyre became the leading maritime center, eclipsing its mother-city Sidon, and King David succeeded in breaking the military power of the Philistines and the Aramaeans. An alliance between Tyre and Jerusalem was central to the emerging geopolitical environment. The commercial focus of Phoenician maritime activities was no longer just limited to trade, but now included colonization. The age of the Phoenician expansion into the Mediterranean world was truly under way.

PANTHEONS OF GODS

MEAGER PHOENICIAN SOURCES
SUGGEST A COMPLEX RELIGION

by RICHARD J. CLIFFORD

eligion pervaded all aspects of Phoenician culture. The gods and their powers were believed to be a constituent part of the world; and the temple was viewed as a civic as well as a religious institution. Chosen by the gods to rule, the king prayed to his own dynastic god and to other gods on behalf of his city-state. Judging by their proper names, commoners might venerate gods different from the king's; different cities honored different gods.

Unfortunately, the details that would help us better understand Phoenician religion are lacking. More than 6,000 Phoenician and Punic inscriptions have been recovered, but they generally do little other than mention deities and rituals; there are no prayers, god lists, or mythologies that we can use to reconstruct the Phoenician religious system. Religious texts found in excavations at Ugarit-written around 1200 B.C., prior to the flowering of the Phoenician city-states—and *The Phoenician History* of Philo of Byblos supplement the meager Phoenician sources.

Each Phoenician city-state appears to have favored certain deities and had distinctive religious practices. There were, however, strong common elements. The pantheon of a city could be invoked separately from the chief gods, e.g., "the assembly of the holy gods of Byblos, the whole assembly of the sons of god." Baal could be alternately a title, "lord," or a specific deity such as Baal Saphon, Baal Hammon, Baal of Tyre or Sidon. Phoenician gods were often linked to a place, usually a mountain or a spring, marked as sacred by a striking natural feature; hence the Baals of mountains, Amanus, Saphon, Lebanon, Carmel. At least three cities worshiped dying and rising gods: Eshmun of Sidon (Greek Asklepios), Adonis of Byblos, and Melqart of Tyre (Greek Herakles).

The most notorious feature of Phoenician an Punic religion was child sacrifice. Recently, revisionist interpretations of this practice have been proposed: such sacrifices, it is argued, were exceptional and exaggerated by hostile writers; the *tophet*, or cemetery, was a cemetery for children dead of natural causes dedicated to the normally benign Tanit and Baal Hammon; the biblical rite of "passing through fire" really meant passing between fire, an initiation rite rather than a sacrifice. Recent excavation at the Tyrian colony Carthage, however, has brought forth massive evidence against such

revisionism. As many as 20,000 urns containing infant and animal bones were buried over a period of 600 years. Some urns held only animal bones, whereas others held bones of both animals and children, or of children alone. All were cremated.

The religion of each city was distinctive. The people of Tyre—the most powerful city in the early period—worshiped Melqart, whose name means "king (*milk*) of the city (*qart*)." King Hiram of Tyre in the tenth century built temples for Melqart and Astarte. A second-century inscription from Malta is dedicated "to our lord Melqart, lord of Tyre." Further dedications to Melqart are found in (possibly) Tyrian outposts in Cyprus, Carthage, Sicily, Sardinia, Malta, and Spain. Despite this prominence, one should not conclude that Melqart is the head of the Tyrian pantheon. The seventh-century treaty between the Assyrian king Esarhaddon and the king of Tyre places not Melqart but *Bayt-il* (probably another name for the high god El) and his consort at the head of the Tyrian pantheon. Treaties invariably put the chief gods of a region in first place. This treaty shows the priority of El, and the inscriptions show the dynastic prominence of Melqart.

Sidon, the leading city during the Persian period, worshiped chief deities different from those worshiped at Tyre, to judge by the extant inscriptions. These record dedications by several fifth-century kings to Astarte (called mistress and queen) and to Eshmun, the dying and rising god of Sidon, apparently dynastic gods. Also honored with temples are the gods Baal of Sidon and Astarte-Face-of-Baal. These inscriptions, and others found in lands linked to Sidon by treaty, convey an exalted notion of human kingship. The righteous king is a father and a mother to his people, assures boundaries and bestows peace, and makes peace with other kings.

Carthage, on the coast of North Africa, was the most famous colony of Tyre. Not surprisingly, Tyrian religion persisted at Carthage. The tophet has already been mentioned. Religious continuity is also attested by a second-century B.C. treaty between Carthage and Philip V of Macedon, recorded by the Greek historian Polybius and listing the official pantheon of Carthage. The treaty lists Baal Hammon and Tanit, in all probability El and Astarte (or Asherah). These are the chief deities of the mother city Tyre, according to the seventh-century Baal of Tyre treaty, mentioned above.

Conclusions about the pantheons of the major cities must be tentative. The treaties give the official hierarchy of two cities at a particular period, but these lists do not always coincide with divine dynastic patrons and the gods of popular religion. The triad often proposed for Phoenician cities: a protective god of the city, a goddess companion symbolizing the fertile earth, and a young god rising annually with the vegetation does not rest on good evidence.

LAST DAYS OF THE PHILISTINES

FINDS AT THE SITE OF EKRON MAY EXPLAIN THE SUDDEN DISAPPEARANCE OF THE PHILISTINES FROM THE COASTAL PLAIN OF CANAAN

by SEYMOUR GITIN

A round 1200 B.C., the Philistines—one of the Sea Peoples who stormed through the eastern Mediterranean basin exploiting the weakness of the Egyptian and Hittite empires—settled on the southern coastal plain of Canaan. In this fertile strip, which became known as Philistia, they developed into an independent political and economic power that soon threatened the existence of the indigenous Canaan city-states and the emerging Israelite nation. Numerous references in the biblical books of Samuel, Kings, and the later prophets tell of their ongoing conflict with the Israelites. Yet, at the end of the seventh century B.C., the Philistines suddenly vanished from the historical record, almost without a trace. The reason for their disappearance has long been an enigma, but recent archaeological finds in Israel have provided the evidence that may solve this ancient mystery.

The most eloquent testimony to the impending destruction of the Philistine culture is contained in an ancient papyrus letter discovered almost 50 years ago at Saqqara, the necropolis of ancient Memphis, south of modern Cairo. Written in Aramaic and dated to the end of the seventh century B.C., the letter contains the desperate plea of an certain King Adon, ruler of a Philistine city, probably Ekron, who begs his lord the pharaoh of Egypt to rescue him from the invading King of Babylon, whose forces are about to descend upon him.

According to scholars, Ashkelon was the first Philistine capital city to be conquered, in 604 B.C. The capital city of Ekron fell in 603, and Gaza and Ashdod were taken soon afterward. The destruction of these four cities, prior to the conquest of Jerusalem, is also mentioned in the oracles against Philistia in the prophetic books of Zephaniah and Jeremiah. Yet, while the textual evidence provides us with the setting and circumstances of the conquest of Philistia by the Babylonian king Nebuchadnezzar, it does not explain its disastrous finality. It does not explain why the Philistines, who had endured previous Egyptian, Judean, and Assyrian conquests, did not survive the Babylonian conquest.

Ongoing work at Tel Miqne in Israel, site of the city of Ekron, has sought an answer to this question. Located ten miles inland from the Mediterranean coast, on the border that separates the coastal plain from the hill country of Judah, Tel Miqne-Ekron

is among the largest Iron Age sites in Israel. Because it was never rebuilt as an urban center (as were other major Philistine cities like Ashdod, Ashkelon, and Gaza), the Philistine levels of Ekron have remained largely undisturbed. As a result, we have been able to excavate large areas of well-preserved Iron Age remains.

From its founding in the twelfth century B.C., the city of Ekron was a large, 50-acre metropolis. Although the reliability of biblical accounts remains in doubt, references to Ekron are made repeatedly in the books of Joshua, Judges, Samuel, and Kings. After its destruction at the beginning of the tenth century B.C., perhaps by the forces of the Israelite monarchy, Ekron's role as a major fortified city guarding the northeast frontier of Philistia was reduced. During the ninth and eighth centuries B.C., Ekron became a semi-independent fortress town of only ten acres, confined to the upper tel, with a mud-brick city wall and a massive 23-foot-wide mud-brick tower faced with ashlar masonry.

The events that stimulated Ekron's regeneration occurred in the last quarter of the eight century B.C., after the city was conquered by the Neo-Assyrian kings Sargon II in 712 and Sennacherib in 701. Under Assyrian imperial policy, Ekron became part of a new and enlarged political and economic common market. There is some striking visual documentation of the conquest in a detailed wall relief at Sargon II's palace at Khorsabad that depicts the Assyrian army laying siege to a city called *'amqar(r)úna*, the Assyrian name for Ekron.

In Neo-Assyrian annals, Sennacherib is

described as retaking Ekron from Hezekiah, the rebellious Judean king. The annals also refer to the prosperity of Ekron in the seventh century B.C. under its king, Ikausu, during the reigns of the Assyrian kings Esarhaddon and Ashurbanipal. Our excavations have revealed the basis for Ekron's prosperity. In the seventh century B.C., Ekron became the largest known center for olive oil production in the ancient Near East. The suddenness of its industrial growth is striking. On both the periphery and in the interior of the city, we found seventh-century buildings constructed directly over ruins of early tenth-century structures-clearly indicating how the new 85-acre city grew and expanded over areas long unoccupied.

We could distinguish four zones in the new city, each of which had a distinct function and a distinctive assemblage of artifacts. Outermost was the fortification zone, composed of a thick upper city wall extending for thousands of feet and a narrow lower city wall limited to one side of the city. These were separated in part by a 260-foot-long row of stables. The impressive elements of this defensive system include a large gate house connected to the lower city wall, a huge bastion in the southeast corner of the tel, and a four-pier city gate with flanking towers connected to the upper city wall.

REFERENCES TO EKRON ARE MADE REPEATEDLY IN THE BOOKS OF JOSHUA, JUDGES, SAMUEL, AND KINGS

In an economic sense, the most important sector of the city was the industrial zone, located in a belt that extended around the inner face of the upper city wall. It occupied 20 percent of the surface area of the city and had at least two major subdivisions, north and south, bisected by an east-west street. Although only three percent of the site has been excavated to date, we have so far identified 105 olive oil installations, mostly through extensive surface survey. With further excavations, it seems likely that this number could increase dramatically. The production capacity of the 105 installations has been estimated at 1,000 tons of oil annually, that is, 290,000 gallons requiring 48,000 storage jars each year. This enormous output equals one-fifth of Israel's current level of export production.

The typical oil installation building was a rectangular three-room structure. One room housed the oil installation itself, which usually consisted of two drum-shaped presses flanking a large, rectangular crushing basin. The olives were apparently first crushed with a stone roller in the rectangular basin; the finest of the oil was produced in this stage. The olive pulp was then placed in straw baskets, stacked on the presses, and topped with a flat stone. Pressure applied by a long wooden beam, anchored in a wall niche and weighted down with several stones, squeezed the remaining oil out of the pulp.

Each oil installation building, besides containing piles of olive pits, was filled with hundreds of restorable ceramic vessels and other artifacts, including at least one four-horned altar, found in one case in a niche. The altars, used for cultic rituals, were made of limestone blocks five to 66 inches in height and had triangular-shaped horns at each corner of their top surface. Generally, they fit the biblical description of the four-horned incense altar. The rooms of these buildings also contained numerous ceramic vessels connected with oil production, such as huge kraters with drainage holes, for the separation of various grades of oil; dozens of dipper juglets, including one of bronze, for pouring the oil; and a large number of storage-jar lids. One room also contained a cache of iron agricultural tools hidden in a pottery jar sunk into the floor.

Besides producing olive oil, Ekron's industrial zone also may have included production facilities for textiles. We have found hundreds of small, perforated and doughnut-shaped clay loom weights and stone soaking vats in several buildings.

The economic basis for the sudden expansion of commercial activity in seventh-century Ekron is to be found in the ideology of the era's great superpower, the Neo-Assyrian empire. The Assyrians, like the Babylonians who would arrive with their armies in the following century, conquered Philistia as a prelude to a direct attack on Egypt. Both Assyrians and Babylonians demanded tribute from the Philistine cities, but the Assyrians had a more long-term approach based on effectively exploiting the existing political structure and economic

potential of Philistia.

By transforming the Philistine cities into vassal states and replacing traditional dynasties with local leaders who owed their position to their Assyrian overlords, Philistia was effectively incorporated politically into the Assyrian empire. On an economic level, the Assyrians took control of the established commercial monopolies and greatly expanded international trade in the eastern Mediterranean basin, much of which came within their political sphere of influence.

Thus, with their administrative know-how, bureaucratic experience, and mastery of logistics, the Assyrians not only obtained secure and self-sustaining military and supply bases along the road to Egypt, but also reaped great economic benefits. This approach to empire brought peace and stability to the region for 70 years. During this *pax Assyriaca*, the cities of Philistia, in particular, experienced urban expansion and unparalleled commercial and industrial growth.

That prosperity can be seen throughout the various quarters of seventh-century Ekron. North of the industrial zone, we uncovered a densely built-up domestic quarter, distinguished by buildings, courtyards, and a roadway. Most important, we have also identified a zone deep within the inner city that apparently was the residential neighborhood of Ekron's most powerful religious and political leaders. The finds in this area contrasted sharply with those in the domestic and industrial zones. The houses here were spacious residences with interior courtyards. This area also produced the highest percentage of decorated and fine wares found anywhere on the site. Among them were local red-slipped and burnished bowls, Assyrian-type and imported East Greek vessels, and two caches of jewelry.

Yet the commercial prosperity that brought about the urban renaissance in seventh-century B.C. Ekron did not last. We could distinguish a later stage, toward the end of the seventh century, during which olive oil production was dramatically scaled down. Many oil installations were abandoned; in some cases, they were dismantled and reused for other purposes. For example, stone presses and perforated weights were used in the construction of walls.

We believe that the beginning of this rebuilding and consolidation took place around 630 B.C., when the Assyrians withdrew from Philistia and the region came under Egyptian political hegemony. This superpower realignment set the stage for the ultimate struggle between Egypt and Babylonia, the rising power to the east, for control of Philistia.

In wresting Philistia from Egypt, the Babylonians brought about a radical shift in the world in which Ekron had prospered. And that shift was directly tied to the Babylonian's distinctive ideology of empire. The Babylonian imperial interest was only partly focused on collecting tribute from conquered territories in Philistia (and elsewhere). Its main goal was to control the land bridge to Egypt, a necessary requirement for the invasion of that country; and the often harsh implementation of this goal brought destruction to the Philistine cities, as well as to some Phoenician trading centers, like those at Al Mina and Suckas. The economic

effect in both Philistia and Phoenicia was devastating; beyond the vast cost in human and material loss, the Babylonian empire short-sightedly lost a rich source of taxes and tribute.

In our excavations at Tel Miqne-Ekron, the signs of the great Babylonian destruction were unmistakable. The massive fortification system were breached and destroyed; entire building complexes were toppled; industrial installations and private residences, and all of their contents, were set to the touch and buried under a thick blanket of ash and collapsed mud-brick and stone structures. The fact that the Babylonians did not refortify the city or even restore Ekron's oil industry tends to support our conclusions that the harsh and erratic nature of Babylonian imperial policy was one of the main reasons why the Philistines did not survive as a political entity beyond the Babylonian conquest.

There were, in addition, some cultural developments that have been gaining momentum over a long period that would seal the fate of Philistine Ekron. While basic elements of material culture like architecture and pottery forms at Ekron developed from earlier Philistine traditions, customs, and techniques related to language, script, cult, weights and measures, technology, and industry were gradually borrowed from surrounding cultures over the course of several centuries. By the late seventh century B.C., this process of cultural assimilation may have severely diluted the coherence and vitality of Ekron's Philistine heritage.

Although the Philistines may have maintained a distinctive language (or at least dialect) in this period, some of the letter-forms in the 16 inscriptions we discovered at Ekron are quite similar to those of Old Hebrew and Phoenician scripts. As for language, the use of the divine name Asherat (as opposed to the form in which the goddess' name appears in the Bible, as Asherah) reflects a Phoenician tradition, as does the word *mqm*, for sanctuary. The letter *tet*, a sign used in connection with tithing, reflects a Hebrew-language tradition, and the use of three horizontal lines to indicate the number 30 is known only in Phoenician and Aramaic. Finally, the names of the Ekron kings mentioned in the Assyrian annals

reveals a surprising linguistic diversity. The royal name Padi is West Semitic, while the name Ikausu, another king of Ekron in this period, may be Indo-European.

Outside cultural influences are also apparent with regard to Ekron's cult. The four-horned incense altars are the most conspicuous class of cultic objects. Thirteen were found, with at least one in every excavated building. Yet, while four-horned altars have not been found at any other site in Philistia or Judah in this period, they are known in previous centuries in Israel and Judah and represent a major Israelite or Hebrew cult tradition—as do the inscriptions mentioning the goddess Asherat or Asherah, the use of a central sanctuary, and the custom of tithing. Excavated votive objects include Judean-type figurines, as well as examples displaying Egyptian and Phoenician stylistic influences; Assyrian palace-type cups and goblets; and a Hathor-type sistrum, a music instrument used in Egyptian cult.

Weights and measures at Ekron were also part of a tradition common to Judah and Philistia in this period; they included shekel and *beqa'* weights, as well as the common liquid measure *bat*, which we have calculated as equaling 32 quarts. Technology in construction, including the use of stone as the major building material, and the four-pier gate plan are common features in Judah and Philistia. Finally, Ekron's major olive oil industry featured the extensive use of the 50-quart capacity press, which was adapted from the earlier, smaller, and less efficient press used in the Iron Age Israelite olive oil cottage industry.

Gustave Doré

David slaying the Philistine giant Goliath.

All these finds–of language, script, cult, commerce, and technology–indicate that by the end of the seventh century B.C. late Philistine life at Ekron was heavily impacted by other cultures and highly adaptive in its specialized practices. In fact, it is possible to conclude that within the established political and geographic unit defined by the texts as Philistia, Philistine culture had become so flexible and so highly pluralistic that its earlier unique cultural core had been lost.

This adaptability is the dynamic that contributed to Philistia's, and specific Ekron's, survival as a distinct cultural entity for 600 years, until the Babylonian conquest. Hebrew University Assyriologist Hayim Tadmor described this phenomenon when he wrote more than 25 years ago, based on the textual evidence alone, that: "Caught between the Assyria and Egypt, the rich Philistine cities developed a particular flexibility, continually adapting themselves to the fluctuating political situations?— Thus, they had the capacity to endure."

The evidence from our excavations at Ekron support Tadmor's conclusions, but also suggest what happens when a city-state becomes too flexible—when it becomes so expert in adapting to external cultural influences that it loses its own cultural core, that is, the essence that makes it special and able to endure as a separate entity. Such a state, however, collapses when struck by a physical blow as destructive as the one the Babylonians leveled against Philistia. Lacking the cohesiveness to survive as a unique entity, the culture seems to vanish from the archaeological record.

For the people of Ekron, the Babylonian conquest was more than a horrible military disaster. It was a blow from which the Philistine culture could never recover. Once the traditional boundaries of Philistia and its cities had been destroyed, their populations either dispersed or deported, the Philistines, including the Ekronites, lacking a preserving cultural dynamic, were easily assimilated into the cultures that remained.

There can be many reasons for the collapse of a society. The textual and archaeological evidence suggest a model that can help to explain why the Philistines disappeared from history following the Babylonian conquest, a model which also illustrates the dynamics of history itself. King Adon's desperate plea to his lord pharaoh of Egypt is as eloquent a testimony to those dynamics, as it is to the last days of Philistia.

EKRON IDENTITY CONFIRMED

A UNIQUE ROYAL INSCRIPTION OFFERS CLUES TO EARLY PHILISTINE HISTORY, NAMING FIVE KINGS MENTIONED IN THE BIBLE

by SEYMOUR GITIN, TRUDE DOTHAN, *and* JOSEPH NAVEH

An inscription carved into a limestone slab found at Tel Miqne, 23 miles southwest of Jerusalem, confirms the identification of the site as Ekron, one of the five Philistine capital cities mentioned in the Bible, and offers intriguing clues about the origin of the city and its rulers. The inscription is unique because it contains the name of a biblical city and five of its rulers, two of whom are mentioned as kings in texts other than the Bible. The only such inscription found in situ in a securely defined, datable archaeological context, it has far-reaching implications for our understanding of the history of Ekron and

Philistia. It also strengthens the identification of Ekron with 'amqar(r)úna, a vassal city-state recorded in Assyrian texts of the seventh century B.C., when the Bible is relatively silent on Assyrian domination of Philistia and Judah.

Located on the boundary of the Philistine coastal plain and the Judaean hills, Tel Miqne was first identified as ancient Ekron in 1957 in a survey by the Israel Department of Antiquities. Since 1981, the site has been investigated by the Albright Institute of Archaeological Research, Jerusalem, and the Hebrew University of Jerusalem.

Tel Miqne was founded in the twelfth century B.C. by the Philistines, a tribe of the Sea Peoples, raiders from the Aegean and central Mediterranean who had swept through the Levant and into the Nile Delta before being halted by Ramesses II, eventually settling along the coastal plains of the eastern Mediterranean basin. Ekron's earliest phases of material culture reflect Aegean traditions, including Mycenaean monochrome pottery, megaron-type architecture, and cultic installations such as circular hearths. A large urban center until the beginning of the tenth century B.C., it was destroyed, by either the Egyptians or Israelites, after which a smaller city arose that blended local Philistine cultural traditions with Judaean and Phoenician influences. In 712 B.C. this city was conquered by the Assyrian king Sargon II. For a short time, beginning in 705 B.C., it came under the control of Hezekiah, king of Judah. A third city was founded after Sennacherib's 701 B.C. campaign against the rebellious rulers of Phoenicia and Palestine, which reestablished Assyrian dominance over the area. It

became the largest olive oil production center yet known from the ancient world. The Assyrians withdrew ca. 630-623 B.C. as their empire declined, and Egypt briefly established control over the region. In 603 B.C. the city was sacked by the Babylonian king Nebuchadnezzar.

The inscription was found in the Babylonian destruction debris of a 186-by-124-foot structure, known as Temple Complex 650, in the elite zone on the site's lower tel. The design of the complex is based on that of Assyrian palaces. It has a courtyard, around which rooms are grouped, and a narrow throne room or reception hall, which separates the courtyard from a large, rectangular, cultic room or sanctuary. The entrance to the sanctuary was flanked on the inside by large stone vats, perhaps for ablutions. At the far end of the room was a stone pavement onto which the inscription had fallen. Consisting of 72 letters in five lines, it reads,

> The temple which he built, 'kyš? (Achish, Ikausu) son of Padi, son of Ysd, son of Ada, son of Ya'ir, ruler of Ekron, for Ptgyh his lady. May she bless him, and protect him, and prolong his days, and bless his land.

(Italics indicate the pronunciation of a name is uncertain. The name Achish is a reading based on its appearance in the Bible; Ikausu is based on Assyrian texts.)

The inscription records the dedication of the temple by Ikausu, son of Padi, both of whom Assyrian records refer to as kings of Ekron. Padi is mentioned in annals of

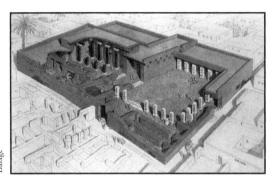

Balage

The royal inscription was found in a columned room, upper left, of this temple complex at Ekron. A jar from a storeroom, center left, was inscribed with a dedication to the god Ba'al and one of Ekron's kings.

Sennacherib in the context of the Assyrian king's 701 B.C. campaign. He also appears in a royal clay sealing of a cloth sack, recording that in 699 he delivered a light talent (about 67.5 pounds) of silver to Sennacherib, possibly as a tax payment. Ikausu is listed among 12 coastal kings who carried building material to Nineveh for the palace of Esarhaddon (680–669 B.C.) and in a list of kings who participated in Ashurbanipal's first campaign against Egypt in 667.

The kings Ysd, Ada, and Ya'ir, forefathers of Ikausu in the inscription, are otherwise unknown. The name Ikausu is interesting in that it is the only non-Semitic name among those of the eighth- and seventh-century Philistine kings mentioned in the Assyrian records. It may be related to the word Achaean, meaning Greek. That Padi gave this name to his son, or that his son adopted the name, may be further evidence of the Philistines' Aegean origin.

The name of the goddess Ptgyh is also non-Semitic. She is perhaps an unknown Philistine or Indo-European deity, apparently not an insignificant one if she was the patron of the dynasty and city. Perhaps the people of Ekron identified her with the Semitic deity Asherah, known from inscriptions on two jars found at the site.

Chronologically, the list of Ekron's rulers from Ya'ir to Ikausu suggests a dynastic period that probably lasted from the eighth through most of the first half of the seventh century. This provides an historical context for the site's archaeological record and a basis for establishing when the temple complex was built. It is reasonable to assume that Ikausu's reign began at or around the time that he is first mentioned in the annals of Esarhaddon; the inscription supports a date for the construction of Temple Complex 650 no later than the first quarter of the seventh century B.C., which is consistent with the stratigraphic data.

The inscription also furthers our knowledge of Philistine writing. In the seventh century these people wrote in a script adopted from Judah to which they introduced local cursive elements. The writing of the Ekron dedication, however, does not seem to belong to the cursive Hebreo-Philistine script-most letters could be Hebrew or Phoenician but apparently are in a local script. Its specific affinities to Phoenician may be the result of trade connections between Ekron, the major olive oil-producing center, and Tyre and Sidon, two of the great Phoenician commercial seaports.

Another dedication was discovered this past summer during the postexcavation restoration of the hundreds of storage jars found in a side room of Temple Complex 650. Inscribed on one of the jars, it reads, "for Ba'al and for Padi." The contents of the jar were probably a payment of cultic taxes to the god Ba'al or for service to the king Padi. The inscription reflects a formula known from Assyrian documents specifying the responsibilities of Assyrian citizens and underscores the cultural influence exerted on the city of Ekron by Assyrian imperial rule.

WHO WERE THE ISRAELITES?

RECENT DISCOVERIES SUGGEST THAT THE MILITARY CONQUEST OF THE PROMISED LAND AS DESCRIBED IN THE BOOK OF JOSHUA SIMPLY NEVER HAPPENED

by Neil Asher Silberman

The story of the Israelite's conquest of the Promised Land has long been an article of faith wherever the Bible is widely read and respected. For centuries, familiar scenes of the Israelite tribes crossing the Jordan River and encircling the walls of Jericho with their blasting trumpets have been vividly described in fire-and-brimstone sermons and solemn hymns, and depicted in heroic paintings and other works of art. Yet a new generation of archaeologists working in Israel has come to challenge the scriptural account in a manner that might seem heretical to some. Their survey, excavation, and analysis of finds from hundreds of Early Iron Age settlements in the rugged hill country of the West Bank and Galilee have led them to conclude that the ancient Israelite confederacy did not arise in a divinely directed military conquest from the desert but through a remarkable socio-economic change in the lives of a few thousand herders, farmers, and villagers in Canaan itself.

Today's archaeologists are certainly not the first to challenge the Book of Joshua—its historical reliability has been a matter of dispute for more than two centuries. At issue are the Book's first 12 chapters, which describe how, after the death of Moses in the wilderness, Joshua, his chosen successor, led the Tribes of Israel across the Jordan River to conquer the powerful Canaanite cities of Jericho, Ai, Gibeon, Makkedah, Libnah, Lachish, Eglon, Hebron, Debir, and Hazor in quick succession. By destroying these cities and exterminating or otherwise driving the pagan Canaanites from the land, the Israelite tribes fulfilled their God-given mission and each received a parcel of the conquered territory. These allotments became permanent territorial divisions in the later Israelite and Judean kingdoms, and the force of tradition is so strong that tribal names are still used for many administrative districts of modern Israel. Yet the precise identity of those conquering tribesmen—and the nature of their conquest—remains one of the most persistent riddles of biblical archaeology.

Miracles and Metaphors

As far back as the eighteenth century, many European scholars, relying more on reason than on reverence, began to question many of the miraculous details in the Exodus and Conquest narratives. Noting the implausibility of the sudden parting of a body of water as large as the Red Sea, the survival of two million wandering Israelites in a scorching desert for 40 years subsisting on *manna*, or the sudden stopping of the sun above the city of Gibeon so that the Israelites could complete their conquest in daylight, biblical scholars turned to naturalistic explanations. Unpredictable riptides, unusually nutritious tamarisk sap, and the gravitational effects of a passing comet were invoked to explain these biblical events. Even more important was the tendency to see the Israelite conquest as an instructive metaphor, phrased in the progressive vocabulary of the times. In 1829, the English historian H.H. Milman noted "the remarkable picture" that the story of the conquest of Canaan presented "of the gradual development of human society." With the arrival of the Israelites, Milman explained that "the Land of Milk and Honey began to yield its fruits to a simple, free, and pious race of husbandmen."

Invaders from the Desert

The nineteenth-century archaeological exploration of Egypt, Sinai, and Palestine moved the Israelite conquest from the realm of social metaphor to that of vivid historical fact. The decipherment of Egyptian hieroglyphics provided substantiation for biblical references to the "store cities" of Pithom and Ramesses, where the Israelites reportedly labored in captivity. Even more telling was the discovery of the name "Israel" on a commemorative stele of the late thirteenth century B.C. On this monument, Pharaoh Merneptah boasted of his triumph over this hostile group. Ironically, the tools of prehistoric archaeology, used in Europe in the nineteenth century to attack the credibility of the Book of Genesis, were put to use in Palestine in the twentieth century to defend the Book of Joshua. Though no indisputable physical proof was ever found of the Israelite's exodus and wandering in the desert, European, American, and Israeli archaeological teams interpreted the thick destruction levels of charred beams, collapsed walls, and smashed pottery blanketing the Late Bronze Age levels at ancient Canaanite cities as evidence of concerted military attacks by the advancing Israelites. The discovery of poor squatters' hovels and silos built in the ruins of the once mighty Canaanite cities seemed additional proof of the triumph of primitive semi-nomads over the city folk. Earlier doubts about the historical reliability of the biblical narrative were therefore confidently brushed aside by scholars like William F. Albright of the Johns Hopkins University and Yigael Yadin of Hebrew University in Jerusalem who ascribed the violent destruction and subsequent occupation of the conquered Canaanite cities in the late thirteenth century B.C. to arriving Israelite warriors, perhaps even led by an historical figure named Joshua—just as the Bible said.

There were, however, differences between the archaeological evidence and details of the biblical story. At Jericho, for instance, repeated, intensive excavations uncovered no trace of a city wall or destruction level at the supposed date of the arrival of the Israelites. At Yarmuth, Arad, and Ai (cities all specifically mentioned as being conquered), surveys and excavations found no trace of thirteenth-century B.C. occupation. While supporters of the biblical narrative initially suggested that these inconsistencies were minor, the discrepancies grew wider as the years went on. With the increasing precision of pottery dating, it became clear that the destruction of individual Canaanite cities occurred at various times over more than a century—far longer than even the longest concerted military campaign. Even more damaging was the realization that in many cases the ruined Canaanite cities lay desolate and abandoned for many decades before their occupation by new settlers. And in recognizing the relative slowness of the transition, a new theory of Israelite origins was born.

Peaceful Immigrants

In the 1920s, two German scholars, Albrecht Alt and Martin Noth, suggested a radically different explanation for the Israelite "conquest." Relying on ancient Egyptian records rather than biblical tradition, they suggested that the Israelite settlement of Canaan was the result of gradual immigration, not a unified military campaign. In particular, they based their reconstruction on evidence from the fourteenth-century B.C. Tell el-Amarna Letters, a collection of diplomatic correspondence between an Egyptian pharaoh and various Canaanite princes. These cuneiform tablets, which were discovered by chance in Middle Egypt in 1887, were filled with vivid reports of the chaotic political situation in Late Bronze Age Canaan, and frequently mentioned the activities of a restive and rebellious group called *'apiru* on the frontiers of the settled land.

While Alt and Noth followed earlier scholars with their equation of *'apiru* with "Hebrews," they went much further in assessing the term's historical significance. On the evidence of the Amarna Letters, *'apiru*/Hebrews were already present in Canaan and hostile to the Canaanite rules more than a century before the estimated date of the Israelite conquest. Alt and Noth theorized that the ancient Israelites, like the modern Bedouin settling down on the desert fringes of Palestine in the early twentieth century, must have been pastoral nomads who slowly filtered into the settled land from the desert and, after a long period of uneasy coexistence with the population of Canaan, overran and destroyed the Canaanite city-states.

This "peaceful immigration" theory gained influential supporters, and for many years seemed the best explanation for the growing body of archaeological evidence. In the early 1950s, Israeli archaeologist Yohanan Aharoni believed that he had found conclusive proof for the Alt-Noth theory in the Upper Galilee. There, he discovered a group of small, unfortified settlements in the traditional territory of the tribe of Naphtali that, he suggested, represented the arrival of an early wave of *'apiru* or "proto-Israelites." And after the 1967 war, throughout the West Bank—in the traditional tribal territories (and new Israeli administrative districts) of Manasseh, Ephraim, Benjamin, and Judah—the theory of peaceful immigration was seemingly bolstered as other archaeologists located the remains of approximately 250

more Early Iron Age herdsmen's enclosures, hilltop hamlets, and unfortified villages whose architecture and artifacts were much simpler than those found in the Canaanite cities of the preceding Late Bronze Age.

In 1978, Adam Zertal of the University of Haifa began the most painstaking survey of sites connected with the Israelite settlement of Canaan, in his exploration of the 800-square-mile territory of the tribe of Manasseh in the northern West Bank. Carefully recording the locations and relative dates of 136 Early Iron Age sites in the region, Zertal also collected information on each site's topography, geology, available water sources, and soil quality. Never before had so much environmental information been correlated with remains of Early Israelite sites. When he listed the scattered sites in chronological order, Zertal detected evidence of a gradual population movement from the eastern desert fringe into the interior valleys and finally to the hills *during* the Early Iron Age, suggesting progressive ecological adaptation from herding to grain-growing to intensive terrace agriculture. Through this process of economic intensification, he contended, the ancient Israelites came in from the desert and, abandoning their wanderings, inherited their Promised Land.

Pastoralists and Farmers

The ecologically based picture of "peaceful immigration" had its problems-some would say even a fatal flaw. Like the more militant "unified conquest" theory, it presumed that in the thirteenth century B.C., a discrete ethnic group of semi-nomads had entered

The wide-spread domestication of the camel took place after the Bible records the wandering of the Israelites in the desert, causing a problem for those who thought the Israelites were full-fledged nomads who invaded Canaan.

Canaan. This theory further suggested that the material culture of this group was far more primitive than that of the native Canaanites. The Israelite conquest of Canaan, whether by sudden military campaign or gradual infiltration, was therefore placed in the timeless, often violent conflict between Middle Eastern farmers and nomads-between "the Desert and the Sown."

This neat historical reconstruction, however, was based on some outdated ideas about Middle Eastern pastoralism. The first and most important of these was the nineteenth-century belief that throughout antiquity the Syrian and Arabian deserts contained vast numbers of turbulent nomads who periodically invaded and ravaged the settled land, a theory apparently spawned by romantic images of the Muslim Conquest with flashing scimitars and thundering camels. By the 1960s, however, there was a growing consensus among anthropologists that the great deserts had been unable to support more than a handful of pure nomads before the widespread domestication of the camel around 1100 B.C. Since this development took place *after* the Israelites were already presumably in Canaan, a "bedouin invasion" seemed an unlikely explanation for their arrival. Far more probable was that the Israelites were not pure nomads but rather primarily sheep- and goat-herders, pastoralists who roamed with their flocks-not in the midst of the desert but on the fringes of the heavily populated, settled land.

So if the Israelites' lonely desert origins were only a mirage, what of their hostility to the peoples of Canaan whom they had supposedly driven from the land? When anthropologists working in Central Asia, the Middle Euphrates Valley, and North Africa began to study the economic links between pastoralists and farmers, they discovered how closely the two groups are bound together. Since the summer grain harvest throughout much of the Middle East coincides with the drying up of grazing lands on the desert's edges, the natural movement of pastoralists and their flocks toward the well-watered agricultural regions brings them into contact with the settled population. There, the pastoralists may be hired as seasonal agricultural workers and their flocks may be allowed to graze in and fertilize the stubble of the harvest fields. In some cases, as with the modern Agedat people in the Middle Euphrates Valley, pastoralists and farmers may be members of a single community whose nomadic members wander off to the desert steppe in the winter, while the more sedentary members stay behind to prepare and plant the community's fields.

This pastoral/agricultural society was apparently common in the ancient Near East. In a study of the cuneiform archives of the Middle Bronze Age city of Mari, also on the Euphrates, John Luke of the University of Michigan convincingly demonstrated that the ancient records did not differentiate between populations of settled farmers and wandering pastoralists; the distinction was, instead, between those peasants who tended animals and peasants who tended crops. The situation in ancient Canaan was probably not much different. "Israelite" pastoralists and "Canaanite" peasants would have been members of the same Canaanite society.

Peasant Rebels

Israelites from Canaan? The thought clashes with everything we've been taught to believe. Yet in the 1960s, based on this understanding, a fascinating new theory of the Israelite "conquest" of Canaan arose. George Mendenhall, a feisty biblical scholar and one of John Luke's teachers at Michigan, rejected both the "immigration" and "conquest" theories of Israelite settlement. For years he had claimed that the rise of the Israelite religion and tribal confederacy could be explained solely on the basis of internal social developments in Canaan. As early as 1947 he had reviewed the evidence of the Amarna Letters and insisted that the 'apiru, long identified as invading Hebrews, were not an ethnic group at all but a well-defined social class.

Mendenhall argued that the Late Bronze Age city-states of Canaan were organized as highly stratified societies, with the king or governor at the top of the pyramid, with princes, court officials, and chariot warriors right below him, and the rural peasants at the base. The 'apiru were apparently outside the scheme of organization, and they seem to have threatened the social order in a number of ways. Besides being pastoralists on the fringes of the settled land, they sometimes also served as mercenaries for the highest bidder and, when that work was not forthcoming, some 'apiru actively encouraged the peasants to rebel. This social unrest, Mendenhall asserted, was not a conflict between nomads and a settled population but between the rural population and the rulers of the city-states. The Amarna Letters are filled with reports of famine and hardship and the increasingly onerous extractions by the kings. It was no wonder, noted Mendenhall, that the *'apiru* had great success in stirring up the peasants and that many Canaanite royal cities were destroyed at that time. "There was no real conquest of Palestine in the sense that has usually been understood," he wrote in 1970. "What happened instead may be termed, from the point of view of the secular historian interested only in socio-political processes, a peasants' revolt against the network of interlocking Canaanite city-states."

At the heart of Mendenhall's "peasant revolt" theory was a novel explanation of how the Israelite religion began. Mendenhall maintained that the *'apiru* and their peasant supporters could never have united and overcome Canaanite feudal domination without a compelling ideology to unify and inspire them. He believed that their worship of a single, transcendent god—Yahweh—was a brilliant response to the religion of the Canaanite kings. Instead of relying on a pantheon of divinities and elaborate fertility rituals that could be performed only by the king and his official priesthood, the new religious movement, Mendenhall believed, placed its faith in a single god who established egalitarian laws of social conduct and who communicated them *directly* to each member of the community. The hold of the kings over the people was therefore effectively broken by the spread of this new faith. And for Mendenhall the true Israelite conquest was accomplished-without invasion or immigration-when large numbers of Canaanite peasants overthrew their masters and became "Israelites."

Mendenhall did not deal with the archaeological evidence directly, but biblical scholar Norman K. Gottwald, who accepted and expanded Mendenhall's theories, confronted it. While Mendenhall had merely dismissed all talk of semi-nomads in the hill country, Gottwald believed that the Early Iron Age sites discovered there were, in fact, Israelite. He theorized that the remote frontier and forest regions were naturally attractive to the members of an independence movement who had fled from the more heavily populated, and more closely controlled, cities of the coastal plain to establish a new way of life. Adherents of the "peaceful immigration" theory had explained that the simplicity of the artifacts in the Early Iron Age villages was due to the Israelite's primitive, semi-nomadic origins. Gottwald, however, countered by suggesting that the absence of luxury goods was evidence of the breakdown in the high-status trade that had been carried on exclusively by the Canaanite nobility.

The "peasant revolt" theory of Israelite origins had obvious rhetorical power in the 1970s, a time of modern national liberation movements and the Third World insurgency. Yet it, too, had its shortcomings-chief of which was that it simply did not fit the accumulating archaeological evidence. Through the 1980s Adam Zertal's explorations in the territory of Manasseh were complemented by major new surveys in the Galilee and in the territories of the tribes of Ephraim and Judah further south. Unfortunately for the supporters of the peasant revolt theory, no evidence could be discerned for a major demographic shift from the coastal cities toward the hill country. The area of unoccupied hills immediately to the east of the coastal plain apparently experienced no intense wave of settlement during the Early Iron Age. Even more important, the pattern Zertal discovered in Manasseh seemed to apply to other parts of the hill country as well. The earliest of the new settlements were clustered far to the east, in the grazing lands of the desert fringe. And their characteristic sprawling layout of rustic structures surrounding a communal animal pen was dramatically different from what might have been expected from city-bred Canaanite peasants who headed out to establish independent farmsteads on the frontier.

Invisible Israelites

Though rejecting the idea of a peasant revolt, the conquest story that has emerged in recent years may be the most revolutionary version of all. It is framed as an epic struggle—not between Israelites and Canaanites, pastoralists and settled populations, feudal lords and rebellious peasants, but between the human populations of Canaan and a changing economic environment. Israel Finkelstein of Tel Aviv University, who directed the survey of the territory of Ephraim, has gone far beyond the conventional chronological limits imposed by the biblical story in crafting a new reconstruction of events. Having traced settlement patterns and ecological adaptation in the hill country of Canaan over hundreds of years, Finkelstein is convinced that the demographic revolution of the Early Iron Age can no longer be seen in isolation. In fact, he

believes that the phenomenon of Israelite settlement is intimately connected to developments that began half a millennium before.

As recent archaeological surveys have indicated, the hill country of Canaan was thickly settled and dotted with fortified cities, towns, and hamlets in the period beginning around 1750 B.C. Yet the surveys also showed that around 1550 B.C., toward the end of what is called the Middle Bronze IIC period, the settled population in the hill country declined dramatically. During the succeeding Late Bronze Age (1550–1200 B.C.), while the large cities along the coast and in the major valleys continued to flourish, more than 90 percent of the permanent settlement sites in the hill country were abandoned and the few surviving sites became much smaller in size. But that is not to say that the hill country of Canaan was empty. Far from it. According to Finkelstein, the people who would later become Israelites were already there.

His basic argument, put simply, is that the model of pastoral nomads settling down and farming, long regarded as the main avenue of human progress, was always something of a two-way street. While Enlightenment thinkers and early-twentieth-century archaeologists pointed to the economic and social conditions that prompted pastoralists to become farmers, they neglected to think about the kinds of conditions that might encourage the reverse. Such was precisely what happened among the Canaanite population of the hill country, according to Finkelstein, at the end of the Middle Bronze Age. Population pressure, competition for scarce agricultural land in this rugged region, or perhaps even political change in the administration of the Canaanite city-states caused a shift in the balance between farmers and pastoralists. A large portion of the population of the hill country gradually abandoned their villages. While some may have gone to the coast to find work, toiling in the fields and orchards, others—perhaps the majority, according to Finkelstein—may have adopted a new, wandering way of life.

These hill-country farmers-turned-herdsmen (almost invisible to archaeologists when compared to populations that built permanent houses) were able to establish a stable, alternative way of life on the desert fringe. For two or three centuries they lived in symbiosis with the settled populations of the large cities along the coasts and in the major valleys—presumably to trade milk, meat, wool, and leather for agricultural produce. It was only when the Canaan city-state system finally broke down completely and its agricultural surplus evaporated in the great upheavals of the thirteenth century B.C. that the life of the hill-country Canaanites shifted again.

Sometime shortly after 1250 B.C., far to the west in the Aegean, a combination of political, climatic, and economic factors brought an end to the power of the Mycenaean kingdoms—and this dramatic collapse disturbed the delicate balance of economic and political power in the entire eastern Mediterranean world. In an era of social, political, and economic disaster, the elaborate rituals of diplomacy and exchange of luxury goods that had legitimized the rule of hundreds of Bronze Age princes, kings,

priests, and warlords throughout the region simply could not be maintained. The economic life of the cities was disrupted. The scattered pastoralists in the hill country of Canaan could no longer depend on the periodic markets in the coastal and valley cities—where they had grown accustomed to trading their sheep and goats for grain. Those cities could now hardly support their own inhabitants; the pastoralists were left on their own. When the first clans of wandering herders began to choose unoccupied hilltops for permanent settlements—and started to clear nearby fields in preparation for planting—they became what archaeologists might call Early Israelites.

The finds from the hundreds of Early Iron Age settlements in the hill country can be seen as evidence of this social process: architectural forms, pottery vessels, and even a few cult objects reflect the slow crystallization of a new, settled culture on the fringes of Canaanite society. No massive immigration from the outside is necessary to explain the sudden establishment of these Israelite settlements. New methods of estimating ancient population through studying site size and the economic carrying capacity of the land have also helped place the Israelite settlement of Canaan in a more reasonable perspective. While the Book of Exodus relates that the Israelites fleeing Egypt numbered 600,000 warriors (bringing the incredible total to more than two million), recent archaeological assessments suggest that the Israelite population at the beginning of the Early Iron Age—which may indeed have included a small number of refugees from Egypt—probably did not exceed 20,000 souls.

Thus, the founding fathers of the Israelite nation can now be seen as scattered groups of pastoralists living in small family groups and grazing their flocks on hilltops and isolated valleys in the hill country of Canaan, reacting in their own way to the far-reaching social and economic changes that swept over the entire eastern Mediterranean world. Whether they possessed a unique, monotheistic religion—whether it was inspired and first articulated by refugees from Egypt—these are questions that are simply impossible to determine on the basis of current archaeological evidence. What seems almost certain, however, is that the story of the bloody conquest of the Land of Canaan as a unified military campaign led by a single, divinely directed leader was woven together centuries later—an anachronistic saga of triumph on the battlefield, crafted and compiled by loyal court poets anxious to flatter the later Israelite and Judean kings.

Who Were the Israelites?

This new understanding of Israelite origins as a socio-economic transformation is not really a religious challenge. It is a fulfillment of one of the most time-honored traditions of the West. For wherever the biblical faith has spread across the globe, the image of the Tribes of Israel conquering their Promised Land has been a medium of self-reflection as well as an episode of sacred history. For the seventeenth-century English Puritans, Canaan was the rolling hills and forests of New England. For the Boer settlers of South Africa, the Promised Land was the rich farmland of the Transvaal, with its own indigenous Canaanites. And the self-affirming visions continued throughout the nineteenth and twentieth centuries, as Western scholars formulated vivid images of manifest destiny, evolutionism, sociological analysis, and, now in the 1990s, hardheaded reflections on demographic pressure and economic change. Yet the historians of each age do not merely deceive themselves into believing that what is familiar is true. Generations of scholars are drawn to the problems of most immediate relevance to their society, viewing the ancient Israelites through an ever changing sequence of lenses. Each generation's reinterpretation of the biblical story has deepened historical understanding by addressing contemporary concerns.

"The crystallization of the People of Israel in their land," Finkelstein recently wrote, "was not a unique or miraculous event that occurred to a unique or peculiar people, but part of a wider, familiar phenomenon shared by many peoples appearing for the first time on the historical stage." In some earlier epochs, the suggestion that the Israelites, in their struggle to adapt and survive, were no different from hundreds of other groups throughout history would have earned its author a public stoning, or excommunication at the least. Yet one era's heresy is often another's article of faith. That's perhaps why in our own late-twentieth-century society—torn apart by economic stress, burdened with belated ecological awareness, and astounded by sweeping political changes—the new social explanation of Israelite origins can be seen as our generation's powerful and distinctive variation on a timeless biblical theme.

PART II:

READING BETWEEN THE LINES OF THE BIBLE

DIGGING IN THE LAND OF THE BIBLE

OUR UNDERSTANDING OF THE ISRAELITES, CANAANITES, AND OTHER BIBLICAL PEOPLES HAVE BEEN TRANSFORMED BEYOND RECOGNITION

by NEIL ASHER SILBERMAN

What can Bronze Age tombs and Iron Age citadels tell us about the Bible? How can archaeology help us better understand the wisdom of Solomon, the brute power of the Philistine armies, or the lure of the Promised Land? Early efforts to dig up landmarks and relics, to "illustrate" the Bible, have given way to meticulous excavations, regional surveys, and statistical analyses aimed at clarifying the social, economic, and environmental factors that shaped the biblical kingdoms of Israel, Judah, Phoenicia, Ammon, Moab, and Edom. Indeed, it is fair to say that biblical archaeology's most important achievement in the past half-century has not been a string of spectacular discoveries of ancient artifacts and architecture illustrating scriptural stories, but a far more demanding examination of the unique forms of nation-hood, cult, and kingship that arose among this small group of Near Eastern Iron Age societies.

Few places offer a richer field for archaeological exploration than the Land of the Bible, a conveniently vague term that is often used to describe the area of modern Sinai, Israel, and Jordan. As a vital bridge between Africa and Asia, this narrow strip of land between the Mediterranean Sea and the Syrian desert has always had a strategic importance out of propor-tion to its size and wealth. Egyptians, Assyrians, Baby-lonians, Persians, Greeks, and Romans all coveted it, intent on pacifying and taxing its population and securing its vital trade routes. The millennia-long struggle between would-be conquerors, home-grown kings, and local peoples has left a vivid legacy in the form of biblical tales of holy wars and national destiny and a rich archaeological mosaic of village ruins, tombs, temples, palaces, and crumbled forti-fications.

The efforts of dozens of expeditions and countless individual scholars, as well as

THE MILLENNIA-LONG STRUGGLE BETWEEN WOULD-BE CONQUERORS, HOME-GROWN KINGS, AND LOCAL PEOPLES HAS LEFT A VIVID LEGACY

important discoveries in other parts of the ancient world, have greatly expanded the archaeological story in recent decades. In the upper Jordan Valley, at the site of Ubediya, chipped-stone handaxes and choppers resembling artifacts from Tanzania's Olduvai Gorge provide the first evidence for the presence of *Homo erectus* in this region about a million years ago. In the cool darkness of the caves of the Galilee and Mount Carmel, prehistorians have investi-gated long sequences of human occupation debris. The levels dated to 40,000 B.C. contain remains of both Neandertals and anatomically modern humans, *Homo sapiens sapi-ens*. These finds suggest that the two human groups coexisted, at least temporarily. Elsewhere in the country, clusters of mud-brick houses at sites like Jericho in the lower Jordan Valley and 'Ain Ghazal in the Jordanian highlands have provided evidence of the familiar mix of cereal farming, herding, and horticulture that became the basis of Near Eastern village life as early as 9000 B.C. Perhaps the most impressive finds have come from the tells or city mounds of the Bronze Age (3300–1200 B.C.). Perched high above the surrounding farmland and circled by impressive earthen ramparts, these cities included palaces, storehouses, and tem-ples. Excavations at tells like Hazor,

Megiddo, Lachish, Beth Shean, and Gezer have revealed a highly structured, almost feudal culture that later biblical accounts would identify as that of the violent, idolatrous Canaanites.

The discovery of the Canaanite past began shortly before the turn of the century and continued with the great expeditions of the University of Chicago and University of Pennsylvania Museum at Megiddo and Beth Shean in the 1920s and 1930s, whose objective was the uncovering of extensive city plans rather than individual artifacts. Discoveries in Egypt, the Aegean, Mesopotamia, and Asia Minor were essential to placing the Canaanite city-states in their historical and cultural context. After World War II, with the refinement of the chronology of the Mycenaean civilization and the publication of the cuneiform archives from Mari on the Euphrates, archaeologists working in Israel, Jordan, Syria, and Lebanon were able to integrate the evidence of urbanization and cultural change with that of historical developments in the Bronze Age Mediterranean world. Today, Canaanite society's far-flung cultural links are evident in trading patterns throughout the Mediterranean, the sharing of artistic styles from Greece and Egypt, and the increasing dependence on an integrated system of international economics and diplomacy. Scholars still debate the cause of the massive social disorder, military conflicts, and economic upheaval that swept across the eastern Mediterranean around 1200 B.C. Some attribute the collapse of the Canaanite city-states to climatic change, excessive taxation, or invasion. Yet whatever the cause, the cultural and political landscape of the

Bronze Age Mediterranean world was changed forever. The succeeding Iron Age would witness the rise of the small, independent kingdoms known from biblical texts.

The Bible tells of many peoples in Canaan and the surrounding territories: Israelites, Jebusites, Amorites, Ammonites, Hittites, Horvites, and Philistines, among others. In recent decades archaeologists have tried to distinguish the characteristics of many of these regional groups. The most stunning example is the rediscovery of the Philistines. In settlements and cities along the southern coast of Israel, particularly at the four identified sites of the Philistine "pentapolis"—Ashdod, Ekron, Ashkelon, and Gaza (the location of the fifth, Gath, is still a matter of debate)—scholars have unearthed a range of crafts, architectural remains, fortifications, and even a few examples of an undeciphered script that provide clear cultural connections to the Aegean world. With the disintegration of the Mycenaean centers on the Greek mainland, a wave of settlers from the Aegean apparently made their way to the fertile lands of the eastern Mediterranean coastal plain. Egypt was powerless or unwilling to stop them. The Canaanite city-states, long dependent on Egypt for commerce and military protection, could not withstand the threat.

In uncovering the evidence of the Philistine past, and that of related immigrant groups farther north along the coast, archaeologists have done far more than illustrate a culture mentioned in the Bible. They have begun to analyze the far broader cultural relationships and demographic links that existed throughout the Bronze Age between the Canaanite, Egyptian, and Aegean worlds.

Critical to our understanding of biblical history is a new theory about the origin of the Israelites. Genesis speaks of Abraham's long migration from Ur to Canaan, and Exodus and Joshua describe a military invasion of Canaan by Israelite tribes freed from slavery in Egypt. Yet the archaeological picture points to no sudden invasion around 1250–1225 B.C., the postulated time of the beginning of the Israelite settlement. While some Canaanite cities mentioned prominently in the biblical account of the conquest, like Hazor, do indeed bear signs of hostile action and an intense conflagration, others, like Jericho and Ai, do not seem to have been occupied in that period at all. More significant is the phenomenon first perceived by teams of archaeologists from Haifa and Tel Aviv universities, who surveyed the central highlands of the West Bank in the years immediately after the 1967 war. In the tribal territories of Ephraim and Menasseh, traditionally identified as the core of the Early Israelite settlement in Canaan, they mapped and studied the remains of dozens of rustic hilltop villages that sprang up in this previously sparsely populated region around 1200 B.C. With their material culture an eclectic mix of lowland Canaanite tradition and innovative terrace agriculture on the steep, rocky hillsides, the inhabitants of these villages seem to have carried on old rituals and worshiped old Canaanite gods, at least initially. Whether these new settlers were pastoralists suddenly settling down to a sedentary way of life or peasants already accustomed to farming,

their villages seem to be evidence that the first people of Israel were not some phantom band of desert nomads but participants in a profound social transformation within Canaan itself.

At a time when the Bronze Age city-states of the Mediterranean were falling apart, these settlers, probably never amounting to more than a few tens of thousands, were building a new society in the hills. Centuries later, Israelite bards would telescope the events, transforming what archaeologists have recognized as a gradual recrystallization of settled life after the Bronze Age collapse into a great literary epic of conquest. Indeed, at sites like Tell Beit Mirsim, Shiloh, and Beth Shemesh, the initial rustic villages of the earliest Israelite period can be seen developing into towns. While biblical scholars debate how much historical fact lies behind the stories of Saul, David, and Solomon, archaeologists have noted intensified building activity, craft production, and regional trade in the late eleventh and throughout the tenth century B.C., precisely when, according to the chronology of the Bible, these monarchs would have ruled. While there is no indication that any Israelite king ever held sway over a realm that stretched from Sinai to the Euphrates, as Solomon is supposed to have done, the early kings of Israel were charismatic tribal leaders who began the process of forging a national identity. Similar developments were occurring throughout the Near East and Mediterranean. Far to the northwest, the major city-states of Greece were forming. Egypt was in temporary decline, but the Phoenician trading cities of Byblos, Sidon,

Gustave Doré

An artist's rendition of the building of Solomon's Temple in Jerusalem, the first of the religious buildings to be erected there.

presumed site of the Solomonic Temple and palace lying beneath the plaza of the Dome of the Rock and al-Aqsa mosque complex, extensive excavations conducted to the south, down the spine of the steep Ophel slope, by Yigal Shiloh of Hebrew University in the 1970s and 1980s uncovered the only residential structures in Jerusalem securely dated to the period of the biblical kings. Outside Jerusalem, impressive administrative centers from the time of the Israelite rulers have been uncovered at Megiddo, Hazor, Beersheva, and Arad, to name a few. While controversy rages over whether certain fortification systems and city gates should be dated to the time of Solomon or after the division of the kingdom into Israel and Judah, the monumental public works, Phoenician-inspired decorative arts, seal impressions, and a growing number of early Hebrew inscriptions offer a rich body of data with which to reconstruct the economic, political, and social development of the Israelite monarchies.

Yet it was only in 1993, at the site of Dan, excavated by Avraham Biran of the Hebrew Union College in Jerusalem, that the first nonbiblical evidence of the historical existence of the Davidic dynasty was discovered. Inscribed in archaic Aramaic letters on a broken basalt stele was a ninth-century Aramaic king's boastful recording of his triumph over a "king of Israel" and the "House of David." Other inscriptions found earlier in Jordan and Mesopotamia had mentioned Israel and Judah, but never before had the name David been identified. Almost immediately, a bitter scholarly debate erupted, with those who dispute the validity of biblical history

and Tyre were expanding their commercial connections and would soon establish colonies on the North African coast. Across the Jordan River, the kingdoms of Ammon, Moab, and, later, Edom were developing into distinctive societies, and the Arameans were establishing a kingdom in Syria. Far to the east, the Assyrian Empire was rising, soon to cast its shadow over all.

This is the world of the Old Testament, a complex patchwork of kingdoms, ethnic confederations, commercial alliances, and rising military powers, all jockeying for position and power in the post-Bronze Age world. Although digging is forbidden at the

Sodom and Gomorrah Update

Two geologists think they know how the infamous biblical cities of Sodom and Gomorrah were destroyed. Graham Harris and Tony Beardow argue in the Quarterly Journal of Engineering Geology *that the land near the Dead Sea on which the cities may have stood literally liquefied in an earthquake, swallowing them up ca. 1900 B.C. Another similar event, in which loosely packed, waterlogged soils liquefy under seismic force, destroyed an area of nearly 30,000 square miles in China in 1920. Harris and Beardow admit that the "analysis of a past earthquake event, especially one for which there is a lack of data, or even credible eyewitness accounts, is difficult," particularly "when the event is speculative and occurred in the dawn of history." But they suggest that a tidal wave caused by the earthquake might have stranded a large block of salt on shore, inspiring the tale that Lot's wife, ignoring God's command not to look back at the burning cities, was turned into a pillar of salt. Few scholars are likely to belive this hypothesis. "This is Noah's Ark stuff," says* ARCHAEOLOGY *contributing editor Neil Asher Silberman. "The real challenge for biblical archaeologists today is not to search for long-lost cities, but to understand why the ancient Israelites formulated these powerful myths."*

by ANDREW L. SLAYMAN

translating the Dan inscription in various ways that would eliminate the reference to David.

Even though scholarly infighting continues, a striking picture of the rise of Israelite society has emerged in which archaeological evidence in some cases flatly contradicts biblical assertions. For example, the common occurrence of female fertility figurines and private offering altars at sites throughout the area of the kingdoms of Judah and Israel indicates the existence of a popular cult of healing and fertility alongside the official, royal cult of the Temple of Jerusalem.

In 1966, American biblical archaeologist W.F. Albright described his field in almost impossibly broad terms—extending from the Stone Age to the Middle Ages and from the Straits of Gibraltar to India. There is something to be said for his intentional exaggeration, because, as excavation and study of material culture intensifies around the world, boundaries neatly demarcating where one ancient civilization ended and another began are harder than ever to establish. Fifty years ago, the famous story of the Queen of Sheba's visit to Jerusalem was dismissed by most historians as a folktale. Now with the continuing excavation of the cities, temples, and caravan stops of the south Arabian kingdoms, the possible historical basis for that story has been recognized. While archaeology cannot verify the visit of a particular ruler, it may be able to develop a deeper kind of historical reliability. In the tombs, pottery forms, and architecture of the Bronze and Iron Age societies of the eastern

Mediterranean are the raw materials with which archaeologists can reconstruct the economic, social, and political forces of which the Bible speaks so eloquently.

Many challenges to the study and preservation of the region's rich archaeological heritage lie ahead. The continuing threat of nationalistic exploitation of selected sites and monuments imperils free and open discussion of their historical meaning and poses a risk to those remains considered less significant to modern nations. No country in the modern Middle East is completely innocent of such archaeological chauvinism; each sees itself as a chosen people in a promised land. It can only be hoped that regional cooperation will promote a broader view. Religious fundamentalism and sectarian strife also severely limit archaeological work; the respectful, scientific study of human remains, assigned by local governments to the purview of religious authorities, has been brought to a halt. Runaway industrial development is a longstanding threat. Perhaps the most insidious danger to the archaeological record is its very attractiveness to the public. As long as common antiquities can be bought and sold as souvenirs and more precious pieces fetch astronomical prices in the auction houses of London, New York, and Geneva, the long chain of plunderers, middlemen, dealers, and collectors stretching from the poor villages of Jordan and the West Bank to the penthouses of Manhattan will continue to eat away at the region's finite archaeological resources.

That is not to say that the next 50 years will not be marked by even greater archaeological breakthroughs than those we have witnessed in our own time. The departments of archaeology in Israel, Jordan, and now in the territories administered by the Palestinian Authority are training new generations of scholars who are more closely attuned to archaeological trends and methods in other parts of the world and are committed to uncovering their nations' archaeological heritage. Among biblical scholars, archaeology has become an essential source of data, both for those who see the Bible as a reliable historical source (at least in its broad outlines) and for those who believe it to be a literary creation whose historical basis is contradicted by the archaeological finds. Every summer, dozens of excavations throughout the region have drawn eager participants, and archaeological institutions, such as the American Schools of Oriental Research, have expanded their involvement with local universities, antiquities departments, and national museums.

Biblical archaeology is always in the process of transformation, providing a means of historical self-reflection for the modern

> ## MANY CHALLENGES TO THE STUDY AND PRESERVATION OF THE REGION'S RICH ARCHAEOLOGICAL HERITAGE LIE AHEAD

populations of the region, and offering Jews, Christians, and Muslims insights into the background of familiar scriptural events, localities, and themes. The spiritual importance of biblical archaeology, however, can be easily overestimated. No amount of tangible proof of ancient kings and prophets will ever be enough to convince nonbelievers of the Bible's power, and no potsherds or city gates are necessary to shore up the faith of true believers. Archaeology's real contribution has been, and will continue to be, the recognition that our biblical heritage is drawn from a complex mosaic of cultures, ideologies, and economies, and that some of our most profound spiritual and cultural traditions were forged in the vibrant diversity of this ancient Near Eastern world.

THE BURNING OF HAZOR

CHARRED RUINS OF A LATE BRONZE AGE PALACE MAY YIELD THE HISTORICAL TRUTH BEHIND THE BIBLICAL ACCOUNT OF THE CONQUEST OF THE PROMISED LAND

by NEIL ASHER SILBERMAN *and* ABRAHAM RABINOVICH

Towering above a sharp bend in the highway leading toward Israel's northern border, Hazor commands a view of the Huleh Valley, the sources of the Jordan River, and the slopes ascending to the Golan Heights and Mount Hermon. For hundreds of years Hazor was one of the most important cities of Canaan, controlling a rich, well-watered agricultural hinterland and standing guard over a vital trade and military route linking the Nile Valley with the urban centers of the Tigris and Euphrates valleys far to the northeast.

The ancient ruins have held a special place in the history of biblical archaeology, for they are among the largest, richest, and most impressive in Israel, covering more than 200 acres. Described in the Book of Joshua (11:10–13) as the head of the Canaanite city-states, Hazor is said to have been the site of one of Joshua's most important victories in the Israelites' conquest of the Promised Land. It is also mentioned in connection with the battles of the Israelites led by Deborah and Barak against "Yabin, king of Canaan, who reigned in Hazor" (Judges 4–5) and is described as one of the Canaanite cities rebuilt as royal administrative centers by Solomon (1 Kings 9:15). Hazor is the only Canaanite town (in Israel) mentioned in the eighteenth-century B.C. royal archives of Mari, a large city on the Euphrates, where it appears repeatedly as an important center with extensive trade and diplomatic links to both Mari and Hammurabi's Babylon. In addition, correspondence between the king of Hazor and the pharaoh Akhenaten is preserved in the fourteenth-century B.C. royal archive from Amarna, Egypt. Hazor thus provides scholars with an excellent opportunity to place biblical events within the wider history of the ancient Near East.

Over the years, finds from the site have justified the enormous effort invested in its excavation. Yigael Yadin's expeditions to Hazor, from 1955 to 1958 and again in 1968, financed by Baron James de Rothschild and staffed by virtually every senior archaeologist in Israel, uncovered evidence of nearly continuous occupation from 3000 to 350 B.C., the Early Bronze Age to the Persian period. The most spectacular finds

emerged from the Middle and Late Bronze Age (2000–1200 B.C.) levels: temples, palaces, and massive fortifications of the Canaanite city.

The Yadin expedition also found evidence for the sudden, violent destruction of Canaanite Hazor. On the tel's acropolis and throughout the city below, it uncovered debris from a conflagration believed to have taken place in the thirteenth century B.C., when the city's once-impressive Bronze Age fortifications had apparently gone out of use. Yadin claimed that this destruction was evidence of the Israelite conquest of Hazor. The Yadin expedition also uncovered architecture and other finds from the later periods of Hazor's history, during the initial Israelite settlement in the twelfth century B.C., and under the reigns of the Israelite kings of the tenth through eighth centuries B.C. From the twelfth century on, settlement at Hazor was restricted to the acropolis, where Yadin identified a monumental, six-chambered gate and city wall as part of Solomon's tenth-century rebuilding program.

Yadin investigated only a tiny portion of the enormous mound, but his finds and their interpretation have fascinated biblical archaeologists ever since. Shortly before his death in 1984, he hoped to return to excavate the principal Canaanite palace, located on the acropolis. His goal was to find a royal archive of cuneiform tablets that might include a record of events in Canaan immediately preceding the arrival of the Israelites.

A new expedition to Hazor—the Selz Foundation Hazor Excavations in Memory of Yigael Yadin—sponsored by the Hebrew University of Jerusalem in conjunction with

Madrid's Complutense University and the Israel Exploration Society, took up the challenge in 1990. Project director Amnon Ben-Tor of the Hebrew University, while a student, participated in the 1950s excavations. In reopening the mound, he unavoidably opened up for reexamination Yadin's major findings, particularly his association of Joshua with the city's destruction. By concentrating his efforts on the main Canaanite palace and on structures at the northern edge of the acropolis, Ben-Tor has unearthed new evidence of the city's splendor and violent destruction, as well as the

An artist's rendering of the walls of Jericho falling down, as Joshua and the Israelites began their invasion of the land of Canaan.

Gustave Doré

later periods of its history under the Israelite kings.

Interest in finding an archive remains strong. Texts about Hazor's economy, politics, and foreign relations in the decades, or even centuries, leading up to the city's destruction would provide information about the history and culture of Hazor that scholars can now reconstruct only roughly from pottery and other artifacts. Archives were a standard feature of palaces in ancient Near Eastern cities the size of Hazor, and there is strong evidence that one will be found at the site. A number of tablets have been found scattered over the surface of the tel and buried in destruction debris. They include fragments of a bilingual Sumero-Akkadian dictionary and of a mathematical text with multiplication tables, clearly pointing to the existence of a scribal school. Others are legal and economic documents, some of them datable by language and style to the eighteenth century B.C. (Middle Bronze Age) and the fourteenth century B.C. (Late Bronze Age), suggesting the possible presence of two archives.

Like Yadin before him, Ben-Tor hopes to find an archive within the walls of the massive Canaanite palace complex. Eight years of excavation there have uncovered a raised outer courtyard surrounded by massive retaining walls, and a large chamber, dubbed the throne room by the excavators, reached from the courtyard through a monumental entrance with two decorative pillars. Although the palace's full dimensions are still unknown, its eastern facade is at least 130 feet long, its thick mud-brick walls preserved in some places to a height of more than eight feet. The structure's layout is nearly identical to that of a Bronze Age palace at the site of Alalakh, in southern Turkey, where cuneiform archives have been found. The floors of the inner chambers of the Hazor palace appear to have been made of wood, an extraordinarily expensive material in this region. Other finds include five cuneiform tablets; cylinder seals; ivory objects; bronze swords, armor, and figurines; and a basalt statue of a Canaanite god. It is the largest such statue ever found at a biblical site in Israel; its surviving portion, from neck to feet, measures more than four feet.

That this palace may have been the residence of the local Canaanite dynasty—perhaps even of King Yabin recorded in Joshua and Judges—is suggested by the discovery of cuneiform tablets at Mari mentioning a king named Ibni-Addu, an Akkadian variant of Yabin. A partially preserved name of a king on a broken tablet found at Hazor also begins with Ibni.

Whatever the relationship between the biblical Yabin and the historical Ibni-Addu, or their association with the site, there is unmistakable evidence that the palace and the entire city were destroyed by fire sometime in the late fourteenth or early thirteenth century B.C. The conflagration not only demolished all

> HEADS WERE BROKEN OFF SEVERAL OF THE STATUES OF CANAANITE KINGS AND DEITIES AND OF EGYPTIAN RULERS FOUND BOTH ON THE ACROPOLIS AND IN THE LOWER CITY

the main structures of the city, but buried them in a three-foot-thick layer of blackened ruins and ash. So intense was the blaze in the palace, which contained large amounts of wood and many storage jars filled with oil, that the bricks of its walls were vitrified, indicating the heat must have exceeded 1,100 degrees Celsius. "These were not just isolated fires," notes Ben-Tor. "You hit this burnt layer everywhere you dig." Heads were broken off several of the statues of Canaanite kings and deities and of Egyptian rulers found both on the acropolis and in the lower city. Ben-Tor is convinced that these instances of intentional defacement prove that the city's destruction was the result of hostile action, not accidental fire.

The account of the conquest of Hazor in the bible reads, "And Joshua turned back at that time and took Hazor and smote its king with the sword, for Hazor formerly was the head of all those kingdoms. And he put to the sword all who were in it, utterly destroying them; there was none left that breathed, and he burned Hazor with fire" (Joshua 11:10–11). In a later verse (10:13), the narrative notes the uniqueness of these events: "None of the cities that stood on mounds did Israel burn, except Hazor only; that Joshua burned." The destruction level, Yadin wrote in

Hazor: *The Rediscovery of a Great Citadel of the Bible* (1975), "is doubtless to be ascribed to the Israelite tribes, as related in the Book of Joshua."

In recent years, some scholars have begun to question whether Yadin's discoveries at Hazor justify his conclusion. Biblical scholars, archaeologists, and historians continue to debate whether Joshua and the Israelite tribes—explicit references in the Bible notwithstanding—had anything to do with the destruction of Hazor. Critics argue that the biblical account is a mythic saga written centuries after the events it describes. In searching for alternative explanations for the destruction, various scholars have suggested that it was the work of the Egyptians, rival Canaanite city-states, or the Sea Peoples from the Aegean, who were marauding along the eastern Mediterranean coast at about this time.

"Yadin believed Hazor was destroyed about 1230 or 1220 B.C., according to ceramic dating that was accepted 40 years ago," says Ben-Tor. "We know more about ceramics now, and I very much suspect that the dating could be earlier. If it were somewhat earlier it could still be Israelite, but the earlier you go the less the chances of that." A number of samples of charred wood and other organic remains have been carbon dated, but most apparently come from furnishings of a ca. 1800–1600 B.C. stage of the palace. A single olive pit has yielded a date of about 1300 B.C.

If the destruction took place in the early part of the thirteenth century B.C., the Egyptians could be responsible. One possible candidate is Pharaoh Seti I, who, in an inscription describing his military campaign against Canaan ca. 1300 B.C., claimed to have destroyed Hazor. Another possibility is that Ramses II could have conquered the city, either on his way northward to Syria before the Battle of Kadesh in 1275 B.C. or on his return to Egypt afterward. Yet Ben-Tor believes that the intentional smashing of statues at Hazor, particularly those of the Egyptian kings, makes these possibilities unlikely. He also dismisses the likelihood of destruction at the hands of a rival Canaanite city-state because of the apparent absence of nearby cities powerful enough to attack Hazor. As for the Sea Peoples, Ben-Tor notes that not a single sherd of their distinctive decorated pottery has been found in the city, which is much further inland than the sites they are known to have conquered. That leaves the Israelites. It is ironic to Ben-Tor that of all the candidates for the city's destruction, the only group credited by the Bible has been so stubbornly rejected in recent years. The discovery of an archive at Hazor might pinpoint the date of the city's destruction, or provide information about the historical situation in Canaan in the years immediately preceding the Israelite settlement.

Scholars generally accept Yadin's finding that the first people to settle in the ruins of the Late Bronze Age city were Israelites. Pottery and dozens of storage pits dug throughout the site, typical of many early Israelite settlements, places like Tel Dan, Tell Beit Mirsim, and Izbet Sartah, support this view. There is no evidence for substantial structures, suggesting the earliest Israelite inhabitants of Hazor lived in tents or huts. Two main scholarly theories have arisen to challenge the historical basis of Joshua's conquest. In the 1930s, German biblical scholars Albrecht Alt and Martin Noth suggested that the Israelite conquest was not a single, lightning military campaign but a slow infiltration of seminomadic people from the desert. In the 1960s and 1970s, American biblical scholars George Mendenhall and Norman Gottwald dispensed with the idea of an invasion altogether, arguing that the appearance of the first Israelites was the result of a gradual social transformation within Canaan itself. They proposed that long-oppressed Canaanite peasants and herders began to establish independent villages in the sparsely populated hill country far from the major cities. The new life-style gradually adopted by these people—herding and terrace farming in small, self-sufficient communities—became the basis of Israelite society and nationhood.

Ben-Tor believes the destruction of Hazor, specifically mentioned as unique in the Book of Joshua, may have been different. How a ragtag army of Israelites—poorly equipped, at least by the standards of Late Bronze Age city-states, and accompanied by families—could ever have conquered a large city like Hazor does not trouble him. "For one thing," he notes, "we have found no evidence that the city's fortifications were being maintained at the end of the Late Bronze Age. The cities of Canaan in the thirteenth century B.C. had been subject to oppressive Egyptian rule for 300 years and were squeezed dry. To put this in perspective, Yadin always pointed to the example of the conquest of Palestine by the Muslims in the seventh century A.D. They were Bedouin. They came out of the desert

with fervor and captured what we refer to as cities of the Byzantine Empire. But what was that empire? Just a collection of cities that had lost their will to live."

There is evidence that Hazor was already in decline at the time of its destruction. In addition to the apparent neglect of the city's fortifications, some of the finely carved basalt orthostats that had lined the bottom of the walls of the palace had been removed and reused elsewhere in the complex. There is also evidence of a sudden concern for security. Along the northern edge of the acropolis, a large public staircase that had given access to the lower city was rather crudely blocked with stones. The threat, from whatever source, proved real, as the thick thirteenth-century destruction level attests.

The history of Hazor in the following centuries is much less clear. "We don't know exactly what happened during the next 200 years," says Ben-Tor. "We have only a single archaeological layer covering this span, and it is so thin and unimpressive that it cannot possibly account for 200 years." Yadin suggested that Hazor was occupied by Israelites in the twelfth and eleventh centuries B.C. and rebuilt in the tenth century B.C., during the reign of Solomon (ca. 965–928 B.C.), as reported in 1 Kings 9:15. On the basis of finds from the new excavations, Ben-Tor has refined that chronology, suggesting that there is an occupation gap at the site. It is difficult, however, to determine whether that gap occurred immediately after the destruction of the Canaanite city or after an initial occupation by Israelite settlers.

If Ben-Tor has sometimes found Yadin

in error, he has more than once strongly supported his former teacher's judgments, some of which Yadin based more on intuition than hard evidence. In recent years, many of the same scholars who have challenged the historical basis of the tale of Joshua's conquest have contended that the narratives set in the tenth century B.C.—the time of David and Solomon—are religious and national myths, not reliable historical accounts. They suggest that the monumental architecture long ascribed to Solomon should be dated to later stages of the Israelite monarchy, in the ninth or eighth centuries B.C. Ben-Tor strongly disagrees. Using more sophisticated techniques of pottery typology and stratigraphic analysis than were available in Yadin's time, Ben-Tor has confirmed that the six-chambered gate and attached city wall, which Yadin identified as Solomonic, should indeed be dated to the period of Solomon's reign.

Ben-Tor believes the finds from Hazor prove that the tenth century, the very time of Solomon's reconstruction of "the wall of Jerusalem and Hazor and Megiddo and Gezer" (1 Kings 9:15), was a period of significant building in the city. Although archaeologists have not located the Solomonic wall of Jerusalem, six-chambered gates nearly identical to the one at Hazor have been uncovered at Megiddo and Gezer. Because of their similar plan and tenth-century date, they have long been attributed to Solomon. "I am not a historian or a biblical scholar, so I cannot take part in the discussion concerning the history of the composition of the Old Testament text," says Ben-Tor. "But as an archaeologist I can say

that the earliest Iron Age fortifications we have at Hazor date from the tenth century and were not built by nomads or temporary settlers, but by some kind of central authority. I cannot say for sure who that central authority was, but I maintain that the burden of proof is on those scholars who want to kill the traditional theories."

More than a decade of excavations by Yadin and now by Ben-Tor have raised as many questions as they have provided answers about Hazor's history and the events described in the Bible, but the questions are becoming more pointed and the answers more learned. This summer, excavations on the acropolis will continue, and as more rooms of the Canaanite palace are uncovered, hopes remain high that an archive will at last be discovered, perhaps containing detailed chronicles that will put many modern scholarly debates to rest. Few sites in the Near East can boast as long and rich a history as Hazor, and none holds out such a tantalizing prospect of revealing the historical truth behind the biblical account of the conquest of the Promised Land.

THE STAR OF BETHLEHEM

WAS IT A CELESTIAL EVENT, A SUPERNATURAL PHENOMENON, OR A STORY MADE UP BY MATTHEW?

by ANTHONY F. AVENI

No matter how many times Matthew's story is told, the question remains: What exactly was this star? There has been no shortage of explanations. According to one count, 250 major scholarly articles on the subject were published in the first three-quarters of the 20th century alone. Let me run down the short list of nominations: It may simply have been a bright star, a supernova (an old star which, in a gravitational death spasm, blazes forth for a few months before gasping its last breath of nuclear energy), or a recurrent supernova (the same, except that several hundred years generally intervene between spasms). Some believe it was a constellation, more portentous than a single star, or a bright comet; Halley's has been mentioned. Others say the great luminary was really two comets, a meteor shower, or a fireball (a colossal meteor visible only in a small part of the world). A few have nominated the aurora borealis (northern lights). There are those who contend the star should have been called the Planet of Bethlehem—Venus hovering over the horizon or transiting the surface of the sun. Combinations of sky phenomena have been suggested, including a conjunction of two or more planets, a planetary conjunction plus a comet, or eclipses of Saturn and Jupiter by the moon. The zodiacal light, a reflection of sunlight off interplanetary particles in the plane of the planets' orbits, has been cited, as have UFOs. A second category of explanation avoids the necessity of scientific accountability by positing a theophany, an aura of light surrounding God, a supernatural radiance. A third category raises the possibility that the star is neither chronological nor literal and that identifying it either naturally or supernaturally serves no purpose, that it is "just a story."

Which of these explanations one opts for depends on who is asking the question-astronomer, theologian, or historian-and what constitutes meaning for each in the historical framework in which he or she makes the inquiry. Those who propose explanations subject to natural law come largely from the sciences. They scour planetary tables and ply astronomical software in quest of unusual phenomena that they interpret literally to fit Matthew's descriptive phrases like "long seen," "in the East," and "stand over," weeding out those cosmic events they find inconsistent with scriptural clues.

Origen, a third-century gnostic, records the first attempt to give such a naturalistic account of the Star of Bethlehem. He wrote in A.D. 248, "We think that the star which appeared in the east...is to be classed with the comets which occasionally occur, or meteors, or jar-shaped stars." Such transient phenomena, difficult if not impossible to anticipate, were thought to have a bad influence on political affairs because they disturbed the order of the heavens. "When beggars die, there are no comets seen; the heavens themselves blaze forth the death of princes," said Shakespeare's Calpurnia to Julius Caesar on that fateful morning of the Ides of March. Recently, classicist John Ramsay and physicist Lewis Licht have documented through Chinese written sources that such a portent, almost universally taken to be evil, did indeed appear in Roman skies during the spring of 44 B.C., the year of Caesar's assassination.

Among modern proponents of natural explanation is the astronomical historian David Hughes. The scenario he opts for is accepted by most contemporary seekers of natural phenomena and is the one that I, too, find most convincing. Celestial events figure prominently in the Zoroastrian millennial cosmology that enjoyed a revival during the stable Roman rule of the first century B.C. A forerunner of Christianity, Zoroastrianism predicted a cyclic war between the forces of light and darkness. The end would come with the triumph of light, which would be followed by the day of redemption, punishment of the wicked, and the installation of the one true god. Repeated planetary conjunctions were thought to represent the beginning of successive eons that made up this cyclic world history. Hughes cites a triple conjunction (three close visual passes in a row) of Saturn and Jupiter in the constellation of Pisces in 7 B.C. and places the birth of the historical Jesus around October of that year. The Magi or magoi, a Middle Eastern tribe skilled in sorcery according to Herodotus, would have been recognized by Matthew as competent astrologers intimately familiar with the sky, who would have been aware that the conjunction was about to take place. A cuneiform text excavated at Sippar, a town north of Babylon known for its school of astrology, records calculations and predictions of the event. Familiar with Jewish tradition, the Magi would have known that Jupiter was a lucky star and that Pisces had a strong astrological association with the Jews. Fish were the sign of redemption and would later become a well-known symbol for the Savior, and the sun moves into Pisces between winter and spring, thus contrasting the end of an old cycle with the beginning of a new one. Hughes argues that these circumstances would have given the Wise Men ample cause to make the 550-mile (three- or four-month) journey west to honor the newborn king. Moreover, the three close passages of the two planets were spread conveniently over seven months from late May to early December, the first pass perhaps serving as a warning that something momentous was about to happen, the second as a sign to get moving, and the third as an indication that they were nearly there.

Other scholars have suggested that after

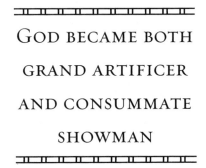

GOD BECAME BOTH GRAND ARTIFICER AND CONSUMMATE SHOWMAN

Christians came to believe Christ was the Son of God, they would have looked for a celestial event to connect with his birth—a bit like our relating Comet Hale-Bopp to the death of Princess Diana. Fascinated by a close conjunction of Jupiter and Saturn in 1603, Johannes Kepler, a founding father of modern astronomy, was among the first to back-calculate the 7 B.C. conjunction. (A Jewish astrologer from Baghdad, Masha-allah, anticipated Kepler's discovery by 900 years.) Though he believed the planetary conjunction heralded the coming of Christ, Kepler felt the biblical star itself was divine. In the autumn of 1604, one of the greatest supernovae of all time blazed forth. Here, Kepler thought, was an explanation for the star, the grandest of all celestial phenomena to announce the birth of the Savior! With a touch of the unpredictable, its miraculous yet scientifically documentable aspects satisfied across the board. God became both grand artificer and consummate showman, as theologian Kim Paffenroth has said.

Natural explanations like Kepler's often combine sky events; the triple conjunction of Jupiter and Saturn might have focused the Wise Men's eyes on the west, but perhaps a comet caused them to begin their journey. Another scenario cites comets that blazed forth in 5 B.C. and 12 B.C. The latter has been traced to an appearance of Halley's Comet, known to have recurred at 76-year intervals as far back as 240 B.C., but this is thought by most to be a bit too early to fit biblical history. Christ was likely born between 7 B.C. and A.D. 4, though we cannot be sure. Various historical events sharing the stage with Christ's birth, such as Herod's death and Augustus' tax decree, lie along a decade-wide time band. This uncertainty makes it hard to tie Christ's birth to a specific celestial event. For example, a Venus-Jupiter conjunction in 3–2 B.C. is also compatible with the acceptable dates.

There seems little room for miracles in today's way of thinking, but the case for a supernatural event beyond all scientific analysis remains plausible at least to some. Can we second-guess the Creator? Why should a believer even be tempted to look for a scientific explanation? Had God been so pleased he could have created a heavenly event for any purpose. Ah, but the ruler of the universe is frugal, runs the counterargument. Surely he would rather have made use of cosmic arrangements he had already fixed in the firmament to deliver his message. Penetrating the mind of God is no mean task! No wonder scientists find the miracle explanation theologically weak when perfectly natural phenomena occurred that can account for all the historical information.

It is humanists who stress the mythic and theologians the miraculous. "A miracle is simply what happens in so far as it meets people who are capable of receiving it, or are prepared to receive it, as a miracle," wrote theologian Martin Buber. When we try to dismantle an omen in search of its underlying causes, Buber argued, we can lose sight of the meaning it was intended to convey to the true believer who experienced the sign. Historians have tried to reconstruct the natural events that gave rise

to the story of Moses' parting of the Red Sea. What combination of wind and water, they ask, could have created an unusually low tide in a shallow bay at just the right time to permit the Israelites to escape pharaoh's pursuit? But, say theologians, the tides in the Gulf of Aqaba are irrelevant to the far more important question of how the children of Israel interpreted whatever happened. For those who followed the Way, that event became an abiding pillar in the edifice of their coming into being as a people.

If the story related by Matthew is "just a story," that does not mean it is devoid of truth and meaning. Following theologian

Gustave Doré

The wise men guided by the Star of Bethlehem.

Raymond Brown, Paffenroth explains the famous reference in the gospel as midrash, a method for arranging truth through story as old as the Talmud. Quite distinct from reporting a cosmic happening, natural or otherwise, midrash serves to illustrate a religious teaching. In Paffenroth's view, the star narrative is a story that reveals what the writer of Matthew's gospel felt to be the truth about a man taken to be Christ. Following the style of the times, he simply was not concerned with historical literalism, or at least not as concerned as we are. The narrative of Christ's infancy is really a story about the good news of salvation, literally the gospel, and only that. We should not be concerned with reading Matthew's gospel in any other way, lest we do violence to his account.

Why seek omens in the stars? Ancients the world over watched the skies diligently and noted the way the stars and planets functioned together like a well-ordered society. Inquiring into the animate wills of celestial bodies helped understand their range of powers, their personalities. While the Advent Star retains a central place in the story, once we try to reach out and touch that star, like the rainbow's end, it vanishes before our eyes. Like searching for unicorns, the quest for the Star of Bethlehem may tell us more about what lies in ourselves rather than in our stars.

DIALOGUE WITH THE FIRMAMENT

ANCIENTS THE WORLD OVER READ IN THE CYCLING STARS TALES OF THINGS TO COME

by ANTHONY F. AVENI

An oft-missing element in comprehending the story of the Star of Bethlehem is the vital role that astrology played in ancient beliefs about the natural world. Even today astrology is an accepted practice: a 1997 poll found that 37% of Americans believe in it-up from 17% in 1976. The doctrine linking celestial events to earthly activities—"as above, so below"—influenced all levels of society, from nobility to peasantry, and all forms of activity, from politics and science to medicine and agriculture. Rome at the time of nascent Christianity was no exception.

The Roman historian Livy writes,

> A nine-day observance was held because there had been a shower of stones in Picenum, and because lightning bolts, appearing in many places, had scorched the clothes of many persons by a slight blast of heat. The temple of Jupiter on the Capitol was struck by lightning. In Umbria, a hermaphrodite about 12 years old was discovered, and by order of the soothsayers was put to death. Gauls who had crossed the Alps into Italy were expelled without a battle.

Whence this belief that our destinies are determined by the denizens of heaven? What accounts for the holding power of an ideology so alien to the rationally schooled mind? To begin with, there really is logic of a sort to the belief that what happens in the sky relates to what takes place here in the sublunar realm. It goes like this: The ocean's tides correlate with the positions and phases of the moon, even with the sun, as any careful observer of nature will note. Many marine species breed according to lunar as well as solar cycles, and who will deny the female menstrual schedule its lunar appointment?

Anyone who lives in a low-tech world close to the vagaries of nature can see that what happens on terra firma is mirrored in more pristine fashion in the sky. As day turns into night and winter becomes summer, a multitude of life forms alternate from one extreme to the other. Flowers bloom and die. Animals hibernate, awaken, reproduce, then hibernate again. Our own lives cycle between wakefulness and sleep. We experience good times, bad times, then good times again. Ordered celestial movement, from slow Saturn at the top of the perceived layers of heavenly spheres to the fast-moving moon at the bottom, is replicated in the hierarchy of ancient states, from kings and nobles at the summit of the social heap to peasants at its base.

Given such celestial metaphors for change and hierarchy, the sky becomes life's logical role model. The movement of stars and planets is, with few exceptions, predictable. No wonder the Greeks thought the heavens were made of quintessence, that divine crystalline fifth element found only in the world above. Aristotle draws the line of cosmic perfection above the moon where, he says, stars move "rank in rank, the array of unalterable law." Humanity, according to Aristotle, lives here below in the microcosm amid the dregs of the universe, part of the cold heavy sediment that by virtue of its weight sank to the center. Our only link to the divine celestial realm resides in sympathetic forces to which we must attune both senses and soul for our betterment.

King or peasant, when you lived in a harsh world full of nasty surprises you needed to summon whatever means you could to gain a foothold on the future. To allay your anxieties, you had to peek through seams in the fabric of time to inquire of the great beyond, "Will my armies hold the gate? Will my child be born healthy? Will I have enough bread to feed her?" Mathematicians skilled at computing time and place, astrologers were also ideal facilitators. They were a part of the royal court, their knowledge handed down generation upon generation, faithfully and meticulously. Those of high ambition might have worked their way up the hierarchy by practicing on merchant clients and commoners in the city centers. Cuneiform texts dating from the first few centuries B.C. suggest that the astrologer was no less certain of what he was up to than today's laboratory physicist who, having assembled his equipment and with a prayer that it all works, flicks the switch to begin the experiment. One Babylonian sky priest of yore wrote in his diary,

O Pleiades, Orion and the dragon,
Ursa major, gout star and the bison,
—In the lamb which I am offering
Put truth for me.

What was this artful practitioner looking for in his dialogue with the firmament, and what meaning did it have? All calendar keepers are concerned with charting the cycles of time. Assessing the basic rhythms of the celestial bodies, therefore, took first priority. Observational records of the moon's cycles were kept, which yielded the seasonal cycles of the sun. Our week probably has its origin in the market cycle, its seven basic units derived from a combination of the quarter moon cycle and the seven visible planetary deities that ruled each day in turn.

The visible planets, "wanderers" as the Assyrians called them, were carefully followed across the 12 constellations of the zodiac. Swift Mercury was Nebo, a prophet because he stayed close to earth and repeatedly dipped down, ears open, into the human realm. Venus was Ishtar, the goddess

of love who dallied with the sun god, periodically descending with him into the netherworld to pursue a lustful affair. And Jupiter (the Babylonians called him Marduk) was king of the gods, symbolizing justice by virtue of the middle or moderate course he pursued between slower-moving old man Saturn (Ninib) and fiery Mars (Nergal), god of war.

Parts of the sky were believed to correspond to regions of the earth: the northern part of the heavens to Akkad or Babylonia, the southern to Elam, the western to Syria and Palestine, the eastern to Assyria. Where a planet appeared, how long it stayed its course, and where it made its cyclic retrograde (backward) motion all offered grist for the "when-then" statements written in cuneiform by the attentive astrologer: "When Venus disappears in the west then there will be slaughter in Elam," or "When Venus is fixed then the days of the king will be long and justice will reign." Infrequent and therefore harder to predict, close encounters of the planets were especially powerful. These happenings were not thought to be the result of an inalterable set of causal laws, as we might suppose; rather they were considered voluntary acts in an animate cosmos possessing the same sort of intellect as that of any mortal on earth.

A nova or "new star" flaring into daylight visibility for a few weeks offered a celestial metaphor for sudden change. A solar eclipse, when the moon covers the sun and darkness reigns in daytime, often held multiple meanings. An ancient Chaldean prediction reads, "When an eclipse begins on the first side and stands on the second side there will be a slaughter in Elam"; but things are not necessarily bad: "When an eclipse happens in the morning watch...[with] a north wind blowing the sick in Akkad will recover." Once enough such events were observed to pick out a pattern, the edge went to the astrologer; thus, "On the 14th an eclipse will take place; it is evil for Elam... lucky for the king."

This faith in foretelling the future by inspecting events in a cosmic domain that paralleled terrestrial affairs penetrated Hellenistic astronomy from the east after the age of Alexander. In the third century B.C., a Babylonian priest taught the history of his culture on the Greek island of Cos, and a century later Babylonian astrological texts were read by the Stoics. In the Greco-Roman world cosmic events applied as much to the affairs of commoners as kings. We owe our word horoscope-from horoscopus, meaning "I observe the hour," or literally "I watch what rises"-to the democratic Greeks. Everyone had a right to know the future. The nativity horoscope, upon which much modern astrology is based, predicts the general patterns of your future based on an examination of celestial bodies popping over the eastern horizon at the time and place of your birth. The more that social reality denied cosmic predictions, the greater the

IN MEDIEVAL ASTROLOGY, THE STARS WERE BELIEVED TO RULE THE BODY, WHILE GOD GUIDED THE SOUL

astrologer's effort to reenvision and revise the rules. The driving force of astrology and astronomy lay in creating models yielding ever more precise calculations to predict future astral events.

By Roman times astrology was "the only knowledge deserving the name of science," as Dutch historian of astronomy Anton Pannekoek put it. Almanacs of planetary positions and predictions in Greco-Babylonian style were abundant in an empire open to influence from the cultural periphery. A celestial globe is recorded among the treasures brought to Rome from Sicily by the third-century B.C. consul Marcellus. The first-century A.D. Farnese Atlas in the National Archaeological Museum in Naples pictures only the figures and not the component stars of the constellations (astrologically important effects were thought to emanate from entire constellations), the whole of the sky resting on the shoulders of the world bearer.

Early Christians, however, debunked astrology. St. Augustine's fourth-century *Confessions* is rife with stories alluding to astrologers' illusory claims and insane rituals. Opposition arose not because there was anything inherently wrong with astrology, but simply because the Greek philosophers who practiced it were considered pagans. Nonetheless there were aspects of the doctrine that omens come from the stars that appealed to many early sects, such as truth by revelation and the dialogue between priest and client. This led to compromises; in medieval astrology, for example, the stars were believed to rule the body, while God guided the soul. Christians appropriated those aspects of astrology along with the attending celestial imagery that supported their doctrine. "Astrology is now the science of the stars of Christ," wrote the early Christian philosopher Tertullian. As believers were weaned from pagan polytheism, the planets became intermediators who announced the intent of God but were never allowed to act contrary to his will. Decked out in the new garb of Christian morality, the pagan sky gods survived. Ecclesiastics transformed the old Mercury, swift and sentient, into an angel-like zephyr who blew away the low-lying clouds that hide our souls from heavenly grace. Perhaps most famous of all the old wanderers, Venus would become the image of Christian love portrayed in great works of Renaissance art, such as Botticelli's *Primavera* and Titian's *Sacred and Profane Love*.

Such a religious system carried over into the celebration of festal dates. In A.D. 273 the emperor Aurelian officially designated December 25 the Roman winter solstice (literally solar standstill) festival. This was the Birthday of the Unconquered Sun (Dies Natalis Solis Invicti), so called because of what actually happened in the sky on that occasion. This feast signaled the time when the old sun god Mithras-Apollo would not vanish on his southward winter course but instead remain and achieve victory over darkness. This was a pivotal time, when the sun started back on its course toward humanity, bringing an end to the menace of dwindling daylight hours and with it warmth and longer light. Believers realized that the light from heaven, though subject to diminution, was nonetheless eternal. After Constantine legalized Christianity in 313, it did not take long for this feast to be adopted as the celebration of the Dies Natalis. Today the lighting of the Christmas tree and the burning of the Yule log (from *hiaul* or *huul*, Old English for wheel or sun) are distant remnants of rituals in which celebrants beckoned the holy lights in the sky to return.

THE HISTORY AND LEGENDS OF MASADA

CONTROVERSY SURROUNDS HEROD'S FORTRESS, WHERE THE ZEALOTS MADE THEIR LAST STAND AGAINST THE FORCES OF ROME

by MARK ROSE

The magnificent palace-fortress of Masada is famous for the last stand of the Zealots in A.D. 73, three years after the fall of Jerusalem to the Romans. A massive plateau rising above the Judaean Desert and over-looking Dead Sea, Masada's potential was recognized by Herod the Great (r. 37–4 B.C.), who built the Western Palace, an administrative building, pool, and cisterns atop it in ca. 35 B.C. He expanded the complex in the mid-20s, enlarging the Western Place and constructing the North Palace, with its three terraces descending the cliff face, a royal bath house, complex of storerooms, and more cisterns.

Mythmaking at Masada

Masada has loomed large in the Israeli national consciousness as a symbol of resistance since the 1960s, when celebrated archaeologist Yigael Yadin first excavated the hilltop fortress near the Dead Sea. Yadin's interpetation of the site seemed to confirm the account of the siege as recorded by the first-century A.D. historian Josephus, who says that Jewish rebels committed suicide rather than surrender to Roman troops in A.D. 72-73. This interpretation has often been challenged, most recently by sociologist Nachman Ben-Yehuda, dean of social sciences at Hebrew University, in Sacrificing Truth: Archaeology and the Myth of Masada (Amherst, NY: Humanity Books, 2002). Building on his largely unnoticed 1995 book, The Masada Myth: Collective Memory and Mythmaking in Israel (Madison: University of Wisconsin Press), Ben-Yehuda draws on extensive personal interviews and transcripts of Yadin's staff meetings during the excavation to argue that the archaeologist crafted from Masada an ideology of heroic resistance by freedom fighters that he believed was in the best interest of the newly created state of Israel.

Ben-Yehuda is most devastating when he analyzes the way Yadin treated archaeological field data after it was uncovered. While transcripts often reveal Yadin's objective skills in weighing the evidence, they also show how quick he was to advance interpretations with a clear political agenda. This was especially true in respect to discussions surrounding the absence of bones for nearly all the 960 so-called suicides. When other caches of human bones found far away from the purported suicide site were honored as the remains of Jewish martyrs and reburied with a state funeral, Yadin did not intervene, despite his early misgivings that the dead were Roman soldiers. Ben-Yehuda not only provides alternative ways of understanding the archaeological data but places Yadin's systematic and heavy-handed control of the data and its authorized significance within the larger framework of the sociology of knowledge as well as the history of Zionism.

As a former student of Yadin, and one who stood in awe of his towering presence and commanding knowledge, I don't find it easy to deal with so negative an assessment of him as a man of science. On the other hand, in reflecting on Yadin's role in Israeli society as statesman, warrior, and molder of ideas, one can only be impressed at the vision he had of Israel; Masada offered an opportunity for him to bolster a nation's inner strength with a lesson from history that was full of compelling if not gripping images from an archaeological site that is one of the glories of the Roman period in ancient Palestine. As a former volunteer at the excavation site, I recall that the medallion we all received at the end of our work was inscribed with the words "Masada shall not fall again," the essence of Yadin's interpretative narrative.

by ERIC M. MEYERS

The final phase of Herod's Masada was the addition, ca. 15 B.C., of a massive casemate wall with 27 towers that extended 1.29 km around the plateau's summit.

After Herod's kingdom was absorbed into their empire, the Romans maintained a garrison at Masada. With the outbreak of Jewish revolt in A.D. 66, during reign of Nero, the Roman contingent was surprised and slaughtered by rebels known as Zealots or Sicarii (after a type of knife). Nero sent the generals—and future emperors—Vespasian and his son Titus to suppress rebellion. The story of the revolt is recorded in *The Jewish War* by Flavius Josephus. One of the Jewish leaders at the outset, Josephus surrendered to Vespasian. His account, which is not always reliable, details atrocities by the Zealots and Romans both, but favors the latter. The Zealots occupied Masada throughout the revolt, and increased numbers after the fall and sack of Jerusalem in A.D. 70. To Herod's palace complex they added ritual baths (*mikvehs*), a synagogue, and domestic features.

In A.D. 72, the Roman governor Flavius Silva sent the Tenth Legion to eliminate the thousand or so holdouts at Masada, which was the last center of resistance. The Romans built eight camps around the base of Masada and laid siege to the Zealots, who were led by Eleazar Ben-Yair. Eventually, in spring of A.D. 73, the Romans breached the fortress wall, only to find that most of the 960 defenders had taken their own lives rather than be captured. The Roman camps, a seven-mile-long wall they built to encircle Masada, and the siege ramp they built up against the side of the fortress, all remain today. The final occupation of Masada, a small Christian monastery of Byzantine times, has left the ruins of a church at center of the site.

Archaeological work at Masada began in 1955–1956 with a survey by the Israel Exploration Society. Excavations were carried out from 1963 to 1965 under the direction of Yigael Yadin. After leaving the Israel Defense Forces (he was chief of staff) in 1952, Yadin studied archaeology at the Hebrew University of Jerusalem, becoming head of its Institute of Archaeology in 1970. His interpretations of the remains were used to transform Masada

into a powerful symbol in Israel (young soldiers go there at the beginning of their training to affirm their allegiance to the country). But some of Yadin's ideas have been challenged. For example, with Yadin's acquiescence the Israeli government gave one group of skeletons a state funeral on the supposition that they represented some of the Zealots. However, photographs taken of the bones during excavation seem to show fewer individuals than the 25 Yadin said were present. Furthermore, pig bones were found together with the human bones. Given Jewish dietary prohibitions on pork, it is likely that the skeletons are of Roman soldiers. Recent excavations, during the 1990s, by Ehud Netzer of Hebrew University's Institute of Archaeology recovered a decorated reception hall and a 2,000-year-old dump in which were food remains (nut and egg shells, dates, and olive pits) and discarded bits of cloth, basketry, and wooden tools.

In 2002, Masada was added to UNESCO's list of World Heritage Sites. But its future is not unclouded. In the winter of 2003–2004, heavy rains damaged the fortress, necessitating temporary repairs and a round of permanent treatments that will cost an estimated at $2.2 million. Nature isn't the only adversary the site faces. If the region stabilizes politically, the number of visitors to Masada could reach 1.25 million by 2010, putting pressure on the monuments through physical wear and tear as well as alteration of the landscape through the greater infrastructure required to handle the crowds. And not all visitors are respectful. In fact, in December 2003, souvenir hunters helped themselves to part of a newly restored fresco.

DIGGING AT ARMAGEDDON

A TEAM OF ARCHAEOLOGISTS EXCAVATES MEGIDDO, IDENTIFIED AS THE LOCATION OF THE APOCALYPTIC BATTLE BETWEEN THE FORCES OF GOOD AND EVIL IN THE BOOK OF REVELATIONS

by NEIL ASHER SILBERMAN, ISRAEL FINKELSTEIN, DAVID USSISHKIN, *and* BARUCH HALPERN

No archaeological site in the world is so strongly associated with cosmic disaster as Megiddo, a prominent tel in northern Israel identified by many historians and theologians as the earthly location of Armageddon, the scene of the final, apocalyptic battle between the forces of Good and Evil at the End of Days in the Book of Revelation. Prophecies of judgment and destruction aside, archaeologists have been drawn to Megiddo for more than a century by the possibility of uncovering the streets, fortifications, palaces, and store-houses of a royal city that is mentioned eight times in the

Bible. The evidence they have uncovered attests its status as one of the most important and strategically sensitive cities in the ancient Near East. In 1992, an expedition from Tel Aviv University in partnership with Pennsylvania State University and other institutions resumed large-scale excavations there to explore more of Megiddo's ancient urban plan, refine the chronology of its rise and fall, and clarify its role in biblical history.

Located on the great highway between Egypt and Mesopotamia at the outlet of a narrow pass through the Carmel Range, Megiddo has a 6,000-year history of continuous settlement and is repeatedly named in the ancient archives of Egypt and Assyria. Time and again, battles between great empires that decided the region's fate were fought there. Biblical accounts of the ancient clashes at Megiddo that remained vivid long after the site was abandoned may underlie its apocalyptic mystique.

The new methods of excavation and scientific testing now being applied at Megiddo are offering archaeologists a chance to reevaluate how city, state, and empire interacted and occasionally collided, and how such events were interpreted in biblical accounts. The current expedition is specifically interested in Megiddo's economic and political prominence. Clues now being found at six locations scattered across the 25-acre surface of the tel include artifacts, architecture, and animal and plant remains. In addition, patterns of agricultural settlements have been identified in the area around the tel. Together, they offer a fascinating picture of state-formation and social evolution in the Bronze Age (ca. 3500–1150

B.C.) and Iron Age (ca. 1150–600 B.C.) that does not always mesh with the biblical descriptions of Megiddo's history.

The first expedition to Megiddo, at the end of the nineteenth century, was sponsored by Kaiser Wilhelm II. Directed by German engineer-architect Gottlieb Schumacher and deeply influenced by the methods of Heinrich Schliemann at Troy, the excavators drove an enormous trench through the middle of the tel and laid bare a complex of massive buildings. Small finds included a magnificent carved seal bearing the name Jeroboam—the first artifact recovered from an archaeological dig to be associated directly with an ancient Israelite king.

In the 1920s and 1930s, a large expedition from the Oriental Institute of the University of Chicago undertook a more systematic examination. With substantial funds provided by John D. Rockefeller, Jr., the expedition's senior staff worked year-round at the site and lived in an elegant stone dig house (now the site's visitor center). In 14 years of excavation, the institute team peeled away sections of 30 superimposed settlements and established the basic chronology of the city's history from the Neolithic (8000–4500 B.C.) to the Persian period (539–332 B.C.). In the early 1960s, Yigael Yadin of Hebrew University dug at Megiddo, focusing on the Israelite period (ca.1150–734 B.C.). His association of a massive city gate, fortification wall, and palace with the biblical description of King Solomon's rebuilding of the city (1 Kings 9:15) lent credence to the historical basis of that account, and to the biblical descriptions of a Solomonic empire extending from its capital in Jerusalem far to the north.

So why has a new expedition returned to Megiddo? Surprisingly, many of the most basic archaeological and historical conclusions about the city are now in dispute. Scholars are questioning the nature and date of the first fortified settlement (ca. 3100 B.C.), its destruction at the end of the Late Bronze Age (ca. 1150 B.C.), and even its supposed role as a district capital and royal administrative center during the reign of King Solomon.

The new expedition has collected evidence on the entire span of human occupation at Megiddo, from the establishment of the first walled settlement at the site to its last major city, the Assyrian center of the seventh century B.C. It shows the city's history was one of explosive development.

In a world of small villages and modest cult places, Early Bronze Age Megiddo grew rapidly. The first formal temple complex (ca. 3300–3100 B.C.), established in the initial phases of the Early Bronze Age, served the largest city that ever existed at the site. Throughout its monumental compound of altars, temples, and storerooms were vast deposits of butchered animal bones, evidence of the public sacrifices that may have marked the emergence of one of the first urban centers in this part of the ancient Near East. Although Megiddo was apparently largely abandoned ca. 2200 B.C. following the collapse of Early Bronze Age trade in the region, the sanctity of this first cultic area survived in later temple constructions and public altars were built on the same spot for millennia to come.

The site's strategic location, abundant water supply, fertile agricultural hinterland, and close contact with neighboring peoples such as the Phoenicians and Egyptians, enabled Megiddo to weather periods of unrest and economic contraction, becoming one of the most prominent cities of the region in the Middle and Late Bronze Age (ca. 2000–1150 B.C.). As the seat of a local dynasty of city-state princes, Megiddo was surrounded by high, beaten-earth ramparts—a defensive feature that can still be discerned in the steep tel slopes. Its prosperity is evident in the furnishings of its main palace, a cosmopolitan mix of Egyptian, Aegean, and Canaanite styles.

In the fifteenth century B.C., the wealthy and powerful princes of Megiddo joined a rebellion of Canaanite rulers against the military and fiscal demands of Egypt. The destruction of the alliance by Egyptian forces in the vicinity of Megiddo is narrated in detail by the chroniclers of Pharaoh Thutmosis III (1479–1425 B.C.) on the walls of the great Temple of Karnak in Upper Egypt.

The siege of Megiddo and its surrender to the Egyptians apparently did not diminish its influence. Subsequent diplomatic correspondence, preserved in the collection of clay tablets known as the Tel el-Amarna letters, was sent by Biridiya, the Canaanite prince of Megiddo, to the pharaohs Amenhotep III (1391–1353 B.C.) and Akhenaten (1353–1335 B.C.). It suggests that Megiddo retained its status even under direct Egyptian rule, one which apparently continued until the end of the Late Bronze Age.

Earlier scholars envisioned a sudden, violent end to this cosmopolitan era, possibly linked to the invasion of Canaan by the Israelites, or to the raids by Aegean Sea

Peoples along the Levantine coast. The Book of Joshua (12:21) specifically mentions the defeat of the king of Megiddo and the allotment of his territory to the tribe of Manasseh; Judges 5:19 describes a triumph by a coalition of Israelite tribes against the Canaanite kings: "The kings came and fought, then fought the kings of Canaan in Taanach by the waters of Megiddo."

According to interpretations of the new expedition to the site, however, the transition from Canaanite to Israelite eras may not have been clearly defined. While there is evidence in the palace area of destruction around 1150 B.C. (perhaps the result of a raid by Sea Peoples), the city seems to have been rebuilt shortly thereafter. The persistence of Canaanite artistic and architectural styles long after the establishment of Israelite settlements in the nearby hill country further suggests cultural continuity and the assimilation of Megiddo's Canaanite population into an ethnically diverse Israelite state.

Perhaps the most controversial aspect of the new expedition's investigations is the doubt it has cast on the once-unshakable evidence for the Solomonic rebuilding of the city—and perhaps on the historical character and geographical extent of the united monarchy of David and Solomon

THE WEALTHY AND POWERFUL PRINCES OF MEGIDDO JOINED A REBELLION OF CANAANITE RULERS AGAINST THE MILITARY AND FISCAL DEMANDS OF EGYPT

itself. The first book of Kings 4:21 describes Solomon's kingdom as extending from Sinai to the Euphrates. Although many biblical scholars now agree that the extent of Solomon's domain was much more modest, few have doubted that it reached as far north as Megiddo. Until recently, scholars generally agreed that Megiddo's six-chambered gate and adjoining city wall at the northern entrance to the city was commissioned by Solomon in the late tenth century B.C. as a part of the great building project mentioned in 1 Kings 9:15. It was further believed that at least one of Megiddo's Iron Age palaces was the residence of Baana son of Ahilud, Solomon's district governor, noted in 1 Kings 4:12. Scholars also suggested that it was only after the breakup of the united monarchy following the death of Solomon that Megiddo became part of the northern Kingdom of Israel, the kings of Jerusalem maintaining their rule only over the southern Kingdom of Judah.

Should these biblical accounts be taken at face value? There is now considerable debate regarding the precise date of Megiddo's massive constructions and how they fit into the city's history. Even the directors of the new expedition are not of one mind. Pennsylvania State University's Baruch Halpern, a co-author of this article, believes that the biblical description of Solomon's rebuilding of Megiddo is reliable, and that the famous six-chambered gate and several additional palace buildings were indeed constructed during the Solomonic era, which traditional biblical chronology dates to 967–928 B.C. The other excavation directors and co-authors, Israel Finkelstein and David Ussishkin of Tel Aviv University, disagree on the Israelite king to whom the gate and palaces should be attributed. They do agree, however, based on architectural parallels and pottery analyses, that the first great rebuilding of Megiddo took place after the establishment of the northern Kingdom of Israel and not under the united monarchy of David and Solomon.

This debate is still far from settled, yet its implications are far-reaching for modern understandings of biblical history. If the first major period of construction during the Israelite period at Megiddo took place after the time of Solomon, that king's legendary achievements as a builder and ruler over the entire land of Israel may require reassessment. The new expedition hopes to gather more evidence in the course of excavating a massive ashlar structure that was first located on the northern edge of the mound by the earlier Yadin expedition. This impressive building apparently was the residence of the royal governor of Megiddo during the earliest period of Israelite rule. The precise dating of this structure, to the Solomonic period or later, may offer scholars evidence that confirms or questions the biblical accounts of Solomon's extensive public

Gustave Doré

A scene from Revelation, where angels decend upon the beasts and the epic battle of Armageddon is waged. The narrator predicted this would take place at Megiddo.

works.

The current excavations and the intensive study of the area surrounding Megiddo highlight the considerable resources and economic capability of the northern regions of the land of Israel, especially during the period of the divided kingdoms of Israel and Judah (ca. 930–722 B.C.). While Israel boasted rich valleys, active trade routes, and cultural communication with neighboring Phoenicians, Arameans, Philistines, and Moabites, the smaller Kingdom of Judah covered an isolated area of rugged hill country. Its agricultural resources were limited and the herding of sheep and goats played a much larger economic role there.

Jack Hazut, JHM Photography

Located at Megiddo, the site of biblical Armageddon, this Iron Age granary dates to the ninth to eighth centuries B.C.

From a strictly archaeological standpoint it would seem unlikely that the poorer, more isolated southern capital of Jerusalem could have marshaled the resources and troops to extend its rule over the far richer north as early as the time of Solomon. Impressive constructions attributed to Solomon in the cities of Gezer, Megiddo, and Hazor were all in the territory controlled by the northern Kingdom of Israel. New evidence may suggest that the first true Israelite monarchy (with the fully developed state apparatus of administration and centralized planning) emerged not in Jerusalem but in the rich valleys and cities of the north, like Megiddo. The redating of the first monumental structures to a period

after the reign of Solomon may also suggest that the development of the first full-fledged Israelite kingdom occurred under the rule of northern kings like Jeroboam I, Omri, or Ahab, who are pictured as sinful, idol-worshipping villains in the biblical sources. The biblical accounts of the northern kingdom that are contained in 2 Kings were heavily edited and assembled by the priestly and royal scribes of the south probably no earlier than the seventh century B.C. Southern scribes may have given the credit for empire-building to the almost legendary King Solomon as a means of enhancing the reputation and geographical reach of Judah's Davidic dynasty.

There is a certain irony in viewing the

villains of the traditional biblical story as heroes of a new archaeological tale of political and economic development. Yet the contemporary records of the Assyrian Empire make no mistake about the prominence of Israel. While Judah is mentioned only in passing, the Assyrians clearly recognized Israel as a dangerous obstacle to their political control of the region. The so-called Monolith Inscription of the Assyrian king Shalmaneser III from the ninth century B.C. reports that Ahab, known from the Bible as the husband of the notorious princess Jezebel, contributed 2,000 chariots to an anti-Assyrian coalition at the Battle of Qarqar in Syria in 853 B.C. In terms of sheer numbers, this chariot force would certainly rank Israel as a formidable military power.

Indeed, the excavations at Megiddo, both those conducted more than a half-century ago by the University of Chicago and the present ones, have uncovered massive complexes of long buildings, uniformly divided down their lengths by rows of columns and roughly hewn stone troughs. Despite scholarly suggestions that these structures may have been used as storehouses or covered bazaars (as is indicated by the discovery of storage jars in similar buildings at other contemporary sites in Israel), their use at Megiddo as chariot stables under the kings of the Kingdom of Israel seems fairly clear, at least in their initial

THE KINGDOM'S RESOURCES PROVED INSUFFICIENT IN TURNING BACK THE ADVANCE OF THE ASSYRIAN EMPIRE

stages of use. No pottery or other finds were found within the structures, and the arrangement of the buildings around a large courtyard suggests an area for exercising horses. It is interesting to note that the kingdom was so well known for its chariotry skills that after its eventual conquest by Assyria in 722 B.C., Israelite chariot units were incorporated directly into the Assyrian army. In fact, by the eighth century B.C., Megiddo seems to have become a heavily defended royal citadel devoted almost entirely to military and administrative functions. The city's impressive underground water tunnel allowed its residents access to a nearby spring even under siege conditions; a massive, stone-lined silo may have served for the centralized distribution of grain or other provisions; the putative stables would have provided facilities for as many as 150 chariot teams.

The finds of monumental buildings, stables, and a sophisticated water system at Megiddo offer a complex new understanding of the history of the Kingdom of Israel and its sources of economic and military power. The archaeological evidence richly supplements the scattered biblical references to Assyrian-Israelite relations and the occasional mention in Assyrian records of the Kingdom of Israel's prominence. Ultimately, however, the kingdom's resources proved insufficient in turning back the advance of the

Armageddon, Megiddo, and the End of the World

...they assembled them at the place which is called in Hebrew Armageddon.
—*Revelation 16:16*

A final and conclusive conflict between the forces of good and evil. A widespread annihilating war. A vast conflict that is marked by great slaughter and widespread destruction. Dictionary definitions of Armageddon are vivid and grim.

How did such a frightening image of judgment and annihilation come to be associated with Megiddo? One possible answer may be that the late first- or early second-century A.D. author of the Book of Revelation, in reshaping the ancient Jewish apocalyptic tradition of a final battle between light and darkness, chose this particular locale for poetic and symbolic reasons.

The Valley of Mageddon, mentioned in the Book of Zechariah (12:11) and now known as the Jezreel Valley, was located at the edge of a broad valley where great battles had been waged and the fate of empires decided for thousands of years. Perhaps the empty, ruined city of Megiddo on its edge inspired reflection on the fierce struggles that had been waged there—and the ultimate conflict between Good and Evil that would come at the End of Times.

Most scholars theorize that the word Armageddon is a Greek corruption of the Hebrew Har-Megiddo, "the mound of Megiddo," yet it is unclear when the designation Armageddon first arose. Following the abandonment of Megiddo during the Persian period (539—332 B.C.), the small towns established to the south of the tel were known by other names. By the Middle Ages, Armageddon had become a purely biblical concept, unconnected—at least consciously—to Megiddo. Over the centuries, theologians and biblical commentators located Armageddon at places in the Holy Land as diverse as Mount Tabor, Jerusalem's Mount Zion, Mount Carmel, and the snow-covered Mount Hermon far to the north.

Fearsome scenes of final battles at Armageddon have been elaborated in artwork, poetry, and fire-and-brimstone sermons. These creative expressions of the end of the world had no tie to any particular ancient site until the fourteenth century, when the Jewish explorer and geographer Estori Ha-Farchi first suggested that the roadside town of Lejjun (an Arabicized form of its Roman-period name Legio) might be the location of biblical Megiddo. This identification was revived in the early nineteenth century by the American biblical scholar Edward Robinson, whose own travels in Ottoman Palestine convinced him that the location of the site meshed perfectly with Megiddo's description in biblical texts. Later explorers refined the identification by recognizing that the remains of the ancient city lay approximately one mile north of Lejjun at the mound of Tell el-Mutasellim, "the hill of the governor," which was named for the nearby estates of the Ottoman government. By that time, however, Armageddon had a worldwide significance quite distinct from the historical site that may have inspired the authors of the biblical texts so many centuries before.

Visitors are coming to Tel Megiddo in increasing numbers as the millennium nears, drawn both by the site's dramatic history and its apocalyptic mystique. The Israel National Parks Authority, in close coordination with the Megiddo Expedition and the Ename Center for Public Archaeology of Belgium, has undertaken a major new project in public interpretation. By the spring of 2000, an innovative on-site multimedia program utilizing virtual reality reconstructions of the excavated ruins will offer visitors to Megiddo a vivid perspective on the dramatic history that lies behind Armageddon's grim images.

by NEIL ASHER SILBERMAN

Assyrian Empire. At Megiddo, the arrival of the Assyrian conquerors is present in the archaeological record in the dismantling of the stables and the construction of impressive Assyrian-style palaces from which the rich Jezreel Valley was governed in the name of the Assyrian king.

It is at this point, after nearly 6,000 years of continuous history, that Tel Megiddo's archaeological history grows fuzzy. With the decline of the Assyrians, it apparently lost its position as a regional center. The once-great city fell into ruins and a small fortress was built on its northeastern edge to secure the vital road junction that had been a key to the city's prominence over the millennia.

For one final time, Megiddo would play a brief, but fateful, role in a clash of empires. In the spring of 609 B.C., the Judean king Josiah—hoping to claim control of the territory of the former Kingdom of Israel that the disintegrating Assyrian Empire had abandoned—rode northward to confront Pharaoh Necho II and a large Egyptian force. At Megiddo, by then little more than a crumbling, roadside castle, the last powerful heir of the House of David was killed in battle, as reported in 2 Kings 23:29: "In his days Pharaoh Necho king of Egypt went up against the king of Assyria to the river Euphrates: and King Josiah went against him; and he slew him at Megiddo, when he had seen him."

The death of Josiah at Megiddo had enormous implications. With the political hopes of the Kingdom of Judah dashed, expectations for the future of the Davidic dynasty shifted from military to metaphysical—to a messiah or savior who would return to earth to restore the House of Israel. This vision has been preserved in the vivid prophecies of the New Testament's Book of Revelation, themselves perhaps based on distant memories of invading Egyptian armies, Canaanite coalitions, and Israelite ambitions to control this important nexus of agricultural richness and vital overland trade routes. At Megiddo the current excavations continue to unravel the complex interconnections between apocalyptic myth, biblical legend, and the archaeological evidence of the city's long history.

PART III:

THE RISE OF CHRISTIANITY

SEARCHING FOR JESUS

EVIDENCE FROM EXCAVATIONS IN ISRAEL SUGGESTS A
MAJOR SPLIT IN FIRST-CENTURY JUDEAN SOCIETY
BETWEEN THE HIGH PRIESTHOOD AND ARISTOCRACY
AND THE IMPOVERISHED MAJORITY

by NEIL ASHER SILBERMAN

In the ancient cities and towns of Galilee and Judea
where Jesus of Nazareth lived his life, preached to his
followers, and was crucified by the Romans, a new generation of archaeologists and historians is radically altering
our understanding of early Christianity. Excavations are
yielding evidence of major economic and cultural changes
that swept the region during the early. Roman period. No
less important for a re-examination of the historical roots of
Christianity are the many Dead Sea Scroll documents
released within the past three years that, in combination with
evolving New Testament studies, offer surprising insights into

the cultural context and possible motivations of Jesus and his early followers.

Several studies of the life of Jesus-based in part on recent archaeological findings-have attracted national publicity and have sparked theological debate. The best known of the new Jesus scholars is John Dominic Crossan of De Paul University, whose books *The Historical Jesus: The Life of a Mediterranean Jewish Peasant* (1991) and *Jesus: A Revolutionary Biography* (1994) have expressed the main themes of the new research. Combining archaeological data on first-century Judea with recent anthropological studies of rural-urban tensions within Spanish, Greek, Cypriote, and North African village cultures, Crossan argues persuasively that the original teachings of Jesus were deeply affected by similar social stresses intensified by oppressive Roman rule. Richard Horsley of the University of Massachusetts, in his books Sociology and *The Jesus Movement* (1990) and *Jesus and the Spiral of Violence* (1993), goes even further in casting Jesus and his followers as radical political activists. Horsley, Crossan, and other prominent New Testament scholars depict the original Jesus movement as a popular response to economic and political oppression whose timeless message shines through the later layers of miracle stories, Christological imagery, and outright hostility to Judaism that were gradually woven into the New Testament texts.

The archaeological and historical re-examination of the birth of Christianity are part of a larger intellectual movement. Over the last century, scholars working in the Near East and the eastern Mediterranean have achieved striking successes in using material culture to provide alternative cultural and economic explanations for some of the Western world's most cherished myths. Underlying the epics of Homer, for instance, we can now see the outlines of Minoan, Mycenaean, and Dark Age Greek civilizations; in place of Egyptian legends and sacred stories we now have archaeological evidence of the gradual unification of Egypt and the rise of pharaonic power; in the shifting Early Iron Age settlement patterns of the land of Israel we now understand the Israelite conquest of Canaan as a dramatic demographic shift, not a concerted military campaign. Now early Christianity may be understood more fully from an archaeological and historical perspective, in the context of first-century Judean and Galilean society.

The Dead Sea Scrolls are among the most intriguing sources of evidence for a new understanding of early Christianity. Unlike the New Testament, which has undergone centuries of ecclesiastical editing, this huge cache of Hebrew and Aramaic texts, found in caves near the Dead Sea in the 1940s and 1950s, is the only contemporary manuscript evidence of religious thought from first-century Judea that is available to us. Consisting of some 800 separate documents—among them oracles, commentaries, legal codes, scripture, and speculations about the imminent arrival of a messiah—the scrolls offer an unparalleled opportunity for scholars to examine the beliefs of at least one group of Jesus' contemporaries.

Palaeographic dating of the Qumran texts in the 1950s suggested that the latest among them were copied, if not composed, in the first century A.D. A carbon 14 examination of selected Qumran texts in 1991 showed they ranged in date from the second century B.C. to the first century A.D., validating the possibility that at least some of the texts for which there are no earlier copies may be original first century compositions.

The excavations conducted in the 1950s at Khirbet Qumran, the site closest to the caves in which the scrolls were found, revealed the extensive remains of a communal settlement that was identified by the excavator, Father Roland De Vaux of the École Biblique et Archéologique in Jerusalem, as the wilderness retreat of the ancient Jewish sect of Essenes, probably established sometime around 125 B.C. Ancient descriptions of the Essenes stressed their piety, asceticism, and practice of baptism, which naturally aroused scholarly interest in their possible connection to John the Baptist, whose wilderness haunts along the banks of the Jordan River were within hiking distance of Qumran. Yet the interpretation of the site as an Essene monastery cut off from Judean society is now coming under serious attack. In a reevaluation of the pottery, glass, and architectural finds recovered in the original excavations, Jean-Baptiste Humbert, also of the École Biblique et Archéologique, and Robert and Pauline Donceel-Voûte of the University of Louvain have concluded that the site, at least initially, bears no distinctive "monastic" characteristics. They believe that it was originally established as an agricultural center for the cultivation and processing of the famous dates and balsam oil

of the Jordan Valley. Brief excavations at the site in late 1993 by the Israel Antiquities Authority (IAA) indicate that the site was founded as a fortress and trade depot in the late second or early first century B.C. by one of the Hasmonean kings.

The results of the recent IAA excavations and a reanalysis of DeVaux's original finds suggest that the use of the Qumran site as a communal, religious settlement may have begun at the end of the first century B.C. or early first century A.D. That places the intense literary and scribal activity at Qumran in the turbulent decades after the death of Herod in 4 B.C., when Judea was annexed by the Roman Empire, and when widespread political unrest and messianic agitation arose in both Judea and in the northern region of Galilee.

Some of the scroll texts made public in the past few years have called into question the traditional conception of the Qumran literature as the feverish speculations of an isolated fringe sect. With the recent publication of previously untranslated legal texts, messianic poetry, unique versions of biblical books, and scriptural interpretation, it is now clear that within this vast collection of writings are literary genres and religious traditions that were cherished by large sections of the Judean and Galilean populace. Conspicuous among these traditions was a distinctive brand of Jewish apocalypticism begun at the time of the later prophets, some 500 years earlier, and typified by a belief that the End of Days was approaching, a time when a messiah would arise to lead the righteous of Israel in a Holy War against the forces of Evil.

Scholars like Harmut Stegemann of the University of Göttingen, Devorah Dimant of the University of Haifa, Philip Davies of the University of Sheffield, and Lawrence Schiffman of New York University now suggest that much of the Qumran literature should be considered as expressions of wider trends in Jewish religious literature over centuries, not merely as the work of an isolated sect. According to Shiffman, "It is now becoming increasingly clear that the scrolls are the primary source for the study of Judaism in all its varieties in the last centuries before the Common Era." That new understanding is what makes the scroll's parallels to early Christian messianic terminology, baptismal ritual, and community organization so intriguing. Although few scholars have gone as far as Robert Eisenman of California State University in asserting that the earliest Christians were members of the community that produced the scrolls, and that the Qumran sect's Teacher of Righteousness was none other than Jesus' own brother James the Just, the study of the life of Jesus and earliest Christianity is increasingly being focused on their roots in Jewish apocalypticism and on the larger religio-political movement in first-century Judea whose purpose was to resist the cultural, political, and economic tyranny of Rome.

Although the first-century Jewish belief in the imminent dawning of the messianic age had many variants, particularly in the timing of the advent and even the identity of the messiah, the expectation of God's impending intervention in human history apparently provided a vast cross-section of the Judean and Galilean population with a religious rationale for open revolt against Rome in A.D. 66. "The growing power of messianism," writes Uriel Rappaport of the University of Haifa, "which was itself nourished by the state of affairs in Judea, is what eventually tipped the scales in favor of the radicals, against the moderates."

There are some indications that, particularly in Galilee, the rise of messianic expectations may have been linked to the painful, dislocating effects of economic change. On the northern lakeshore of the Sea of Galilee, just off the main road between Tiberias and the Lebanese border, is the traditional site of Capernaum, "the village Nahum," the small fishing community where, according to the Gospels, Jesus began his public ministry sometime around A.D. 28. Excavations conducted here during the past century have laid bare the outlines of the first-century town with its synagogue and blocks of residential structures reaching to the water's edge. At other places along the lakeshore the New Testament sites of Bethsaida and Gergesa have been identified, and in the muck of the receded waterline a well-preserved fishing dory from the early Roman period was recently found. Together with finds from Nazareth and the Galilean city of Sepphoris, these are all pieces of a vast archaeological puzzle in which patterns of ancient Jewish-Roman cultural, political, and economic interaction are beginning to emerge.

Until the last century, the most common images of the sea and rolling hills of Galilee had far more to do with faith than with topographical reality. Gradually, a first-hand knowledge of Galilean geography became an essential part of New Testament history and scholarship. An important first step was taken by the French historian Ernest Renan, who accompanied Napoleon III's invasion force to Lebanon in 1860. After carrying out brief excavations along the Phoenician coast, Renan traveled through the villages of southern Lebanon and Galilee. The result of this expedition was his own *Life of Jesus* (1863). However, Renan's still somewhat romantic impressions of the simple nobility of the modern Muslim and Maronite villagers deeply colored his descriptions of the birth of Christianity. Indeed, romanticized Middle Eastern peasant life remained the main motif of archaeological descriptions up to and including Franciscan scholar Bellarmino Bagatti's 1950s excavations beneath the Church of the Annunciation at Nazareth. Bagatti placed great importance on his discovery of first-century A.D. wells, granaries, and olive presses as evidence of Galilee village life. In the early 1980s, with the start of large-scale excavations at Sepphoris, three miles northwest of Nazareth, archaeologists gained a striking new perspective on the kind of society in which Jesus grew up.

Though Sepphoris is not mentioned in the gospels, it plays a prominent part in the first-century Jewish history of Josephus Flavius as a regional administrative and political center, lavishly rebuilt in the Roman style by Herod's son, Antipas, in A.D. 6. Excavations by James Strange of the University of South Florida, Eric and Carol Meyers of Duke University, and Ehud Netzer and Zev Weiss of the Hebrew University

have focused scholarly attention on the social and economic effects of the first-century Romanization of Galilee. Though only scattered potsherds and a few fragmentary walls have been discovered from the preceding Iron Age, Persian, and Hellenistic periods, the reign of Antipas as Roman client ruler over Galilee (4 B.C.–A.D. 39) brought with it the construction at Sepphoris of a gleaming marble theater and surrounding public buildings that were not merely architectural innovations, but powerful, pervasive symbols of the new, Roman way of culture, economics, and life.

The results of the excavations at Sepphoris have helped shape Crossan's quest for the cultural matrix of Christianity. In contrast to the idyllic landscapes of Renan, Crossan has created a world in which the looming power of Roman civilization is always present, influencing the political and religious message of Jesus of Nazareth. Utilizing the archaeological evidence from Romanized Sepphoris, Crossan depicts Jesus and the farmers, fishermen, and tradesmen of Galilee who became his followers not as Middle Eastern bumpkins, but as people fully exposed to cosmopolitan Roman civilization and empire—who consciously rejected it. Eric Meyers believes that Jesus of Nazareth knew and reacted passionately to Roman culture, "growing up along one of the busiest trade routes of ancient Palestine, at the very administrative center of the Roman provincial government."

But what was the nature of the interaction? Though Meyers and Strange suggest a vibrant syncretism of Jewish and Greco-Roman cultures, other scholars like Richard

Horsley suggest a tense and often confrontational relationship between the Galilean peasantry and the Roman officials and urban aristocracy. "The economic impact of Antipas' building programs following upon the heavy taxation of Herod," Horsley writes of the economic changes of the period, "would have left many producer-households heavily in debt." And although Herod Antipas—the patron of Sepphoris—is known from the gospels primarily as the tyrant who executed John the Baptist and who refused to become involved in the trial of Jesus, archaeology now suggests he played a far more pervasive role in the story of first-century Galilee. Inheriting the region from his father, with the blessing of the Romans, Antipas ruled it as his private fiefdom; his costly building projects at Sepphoris and his establishment of the lakeside town of Tiberias in A.D. 18 as the region's new capital enabled him to maintain ever tighter administrative control. Increasing taxation and economic centralization would certainly have had an enormous, negative impact on the lives of many Galilean townspeople, farmers, and fishermen.

Archaeologists working at Roman sites in Italy and Britain have observed that the linking of rural areas to the empire—through regional urban centers, Roman civic ceremonies, and the spread of Roman coinage-sparked an intensification of trade, an increase in cash-crop farming over subsistence, and the creation of vast, plantation-like estates. The work of Stephen Dyson near Cosa, Italy, in particular, has demonstrated the close connection between land-tenure patterns and economic and political change. Given Josephus Flavius' repeated reports of rural unrest and banditry in Galilee through the first century, it is likely that the social and economic changes of the early Roman period were not viewed favorably by everyone.

In light of what we now know about messianic ideology and first-century Romanization in both Judea and Galilee, it would not have been surprising that a non-conformist Galilean preacher would find it necessary to journey southward to confront the Forces of Darkness—Herodian aristocrats, corrupt priests, and Roman oppressors—in the temple city of Jerusalem. It is astounding how little was known about this ancient city until about 25 years ago. Like Galilee, there was always a fairy-tale quality about Jerusalem—a city filled with unforgettable characters and events. Although the topography of the city began to be studied intensively by European and American scholars in the nineteenth century, excavation opportunities were limited by local religious sensibilities to scattered probes in gardens and empty lots. After the 1967 Israeli takeover of the Old City, however, ambitious excavations were begun throughout the Jewish Quarter and on the western and southern sides of the Temple Mount. For the first time, extensive areas within the city walls were dug down to the levels of the Early Roman period.

As a result of these excavations, we know today that Jerusalem expanded enormously beginning in the Hasmonean period (ca. 165–37 B.C.). From its original location on a narrow ridge called the City of David, it expanded to encompass a western hill known as the Upper City. During the reign of Herod (37–4 B.C.) the Temple compound was extended and lavishly embellished by the construction of a massive platform, a huge sanctuary, and surrounding colonnades, making it one of the most impressive structures in the entire Roman world. The city's population swelled. By the time of the reign of Herod's grandson Agrippa I (A.D. 40–44), the outer fortification walls of the city encompassed an area that was not exceeded until the expansion of modern Jerusalem in the nineteenth century.

The question of Jerusalem's size and city walls was an important one for the first modern explorers, who attempted to determine the authentic location of Golgotha, the place of Jesus's crucifixion, and of the nearby tomb in which his body was reportedly laid to rest. For centuries pious Christians venerated a site within the Church of the Holy Sepulchre, built in the fourth century A.D. under the supervision of Emperor Constantine's mother Queen Helena—at a spot within the walls of Roman Jerusalem, which she reported seeing in a vision. It was only in the nineteenth century that some Protestant scholars voiced their skepticism about the Holy Sepulchre's historical reliablity, noting that in light of the strict Jewish purity laws, respected even by the Roman rulers, the authentic place of Jesus' execution and burial must have lain outside the city walls. In recent years, archaeological studies of Jerusalem's urban growth in the Early Roman period have indicated that the site of the Church of the Holy Sepulchre was indeed outside the city at the estimated time of Jesus' death, around A.D. 29.

The importance of the latest archaeological work in Jerusalem is, however, far more than a refinement of New Testament geography. As in Galilee, it has deepened our understanding of the social world of Jesus and his followers. In the rubble of the medieval Jewish Quarter of the Old City, the excavations of Nahman Avigad of the Hebrew University from 1969 to 1982 uncovered the ruins of elegant first-century A.D. villas. An inscribed weight found in one of the largest of the residences identified it as the home of the Kathros family, which was, according to the Talmud, one of the four most powerful priestly clans. The home of the High Priest Joseph Caiaphas, where Jesus was interrogated before being handed over to the Roman authorities for execution, may have been in this neighborhood, known as the "Upper City" in the description of Josephus Flavius. In 1990, an elaborate family tomb was discovered on the southern outskirts of Jerusalem containing an ossuary, a receptacle for bones, bearing the inscription "Joseph son of Caiaphas."

Many modern visitors are seduced by the elegance and material wealth of such homes in the Upper City, seeing them as evidence of a golden age of Judean history. That age was apparently golden for only a few. Historian Martin Goodman, in his book *The Ruling Class of Judea*, has convincingly linked the sudden material wealth of Jerusalem's high priesthood and Herodian aristocracy with the gradual disintegration of Judean society. Benefiting directly and disproportionately from the taxes and tithes flowing into the expanding temple city of Jerusalem, the priesthood and secular aristocracy were getting richer and the poor were becoming poorer, many even disenfranchised. Traditional land-tenure patterns of Judea were changing, and on the basis of a close reading of Josephus Flavius and rabbinic references, Goodman suggests that small family holdings were bought up by the aristocrats and priests, condemning their former owners to lives as tenant farmers or hired laborers.

Political agitation against the Romans and the Judean priesthood and aristocracy was inevitable. And the consequences were enormous, since, as Goodman puts it, the ruling class of Judea was "not capable of controlling the increasing expressions of social discontent, fueled by economic disparities, that afflicted the population over which they tried to rule." This seems to be the social context of Jesus' ministry and of the day-to-day lives of his followers. The coming Kingdom of God was no abstract spiritual concept, but a longing for a new order whereby the corrupt and the wicked would finally be punished for their sins, and the poor and the meek would inherit the earth. It was a message that almost certainly resonated among the majority of Judeans and Galileans, preached with passion and conviction by a number of would-be redeemers—Judah the Galilean, Athronges, Simon of Perea, John the Baptist, Jesus, an unnamed "Egyptian prophet," and the zealot leader Menachem, son of Judah, to name only a few mentioned by Josephus Flavius.

Distant echoes of that first-century rage against a corrupt aristocracy can be perceived even in the much later rabbinic literature. The elegance and the wealth uncovered in the excavations of the House of Kathros in Jerusalem's Upper City was apparently paid for by the misfortunes of others. In a lamentation against the corrupt Temple priesthood, a passage in the Talmud reads: "Woe unto me because of the House of Kathros, woe unto me because of their reed pens for they are high priests and their sons are treasurers and their sons-in-law are temple overseers and their servants smite the people with sticks."

Archaeologists often tended to concentrate on the most impressive and elaborate structures of every period, and this has certainly been true of the investigation of first-century Judean and Galilean society. Yet now, with wide-ranging surveys of settlement patterns and increased interest in social and economic history, additional insights may be gained into the social experience of the vast majority of the Judean and Galilean population. In tracing the changes in the size and placement of rural settlements in relation to the cities, and in concentrating on the changing technology of such prosaic installations as workshops, olive presses, and dye vats—not as illustrations of a timeless New Testament age, but as evidence of changing economic structures—archaeology may provide important insights into the material reality that lay behind Qumran-style messianic expectations and the yearning for change and liberation that characterized earliest Christianity.

That yearning, however, could exact a fearful price. Among the most poignant of the archaeological finds uncovered in one of the vast ancient cemeteries that surround Jerusalem, archaeologists excavated a tomb containing an ossuary with the fragmentary remains of a man named Yehohanan. Hundreds of similar family tombs have been discovered dating from the first century B.C. and the first century A.D., typified by the use of ossuaries, in which the bones of the deceased were gathered up, placed in stone boxes, and labeled with the name of the deceased, apparently in expectation of resurrection in the World to Come. But the bones in this ossuary told a grim story. An iron spike, driven through Yehohanan's ankle bone, was still deeply embedded in a fragment of olive wood—evidence of the grisly method of crucifixion that was meted out to those who, by their criminal or political activities, challenged (or were accused of challenging) the economic and political status quo.

In sandy mounds by the Mediterranean shore, the sprawling ruins of Caesarea, seat of the Roman administration of Judea, have yielded some of the most telling archaeological evidence for understanding the rise of early Christianity. In the 1960s, an Italian expedition uncovered a fragmentary Latin inscription that gained headlines all over the world. Apparently recording a building commissioned by "Pontius Pilatus, Prefect of Judea," it was the first and is still the only archaeological remnant of the fabled Roman governor. But as the excavations of Caesarea have continued, they have offered evidence far more important than relics of identifiable personalities. In charting the construction of the impressive port city, with its harbor facilities, warehouses, and temples, the archaeologists of the American Joint Expedition to Maritime Caesarea and the Haifa University Underwater Expedition have uncovered the docks, wharves, warehouses, and public administrative buildings that facilitated and encouraged an ever-greater Judean economic link to Rome.

In fact, some of the most ambitious archaeological undertakings under way today in Israel are further documenting the extent to which Roman civilization, with its dominating culture and enormous imperial power, swept over and utterly transformed the province of Palaestina ("the Land of the Philistine"), as Judea, Samaria, and Galilee were renamed after the rebellion of A.D. 66–74 was crushed. The progressive assimilation of Palaestina into the Roman world system is amply documented in the new excavations at Caesarea, and at the impressive Roman-period cities and commercial centers of Banias (Caesarea-Philippi), Beth Shean (Scythopolis), and

> **DISTANT ECHOES OF THAT FIRST-CENTURY RAGE AGAINST A CORRUPT ARISTOCRACY CAN BE PERCEIVED EVEN IN THE MUCH LATER RABBINIC LITERATURE**

Beth Guvrin (Eleutheropolis).

Archaeological research has neither proved nor disproved the historical existence of Jesus, John the Baptist, or the Apostles. Yet it has provided information on a wide range of early Roman period sites in Judea and Galilee and has documented their changing material culture. This evidence has now become the raw material for a far-reaching historical reassessment of first-century Judean and Galilean life. Archaeology's power lies in its ability to provide material explanations for the twists and turns of history-the economic, social, and cultural transformations that have given rise to history's great achievements and great tragedies. In the coming years New Testament archaeology will continue to deepen our understanding of Christianity in its first-century context-as part of a wider Judean movement of protest against economic dislocation and political and cultural tyranny.

EARLY CHURCH AT AQABA

THE WORLD'S OLDEST CONSTRUCTED CHURCH
WAS UNEARTHED AT A RED SEA PORT

by MARK ROSE

The remains of the oldest known structure designed and built as a church have been found at the Jordanian Red Sea port of Aqaba. Pottery, such as Tunisian red-slipped tableware, from the building's foundations dates the church to the late third or beginning of the fourth century, according to its excavator, North Carolina State University archaeologist S. Thomas Parker. That the building was a church is indicated by its eastward orientation, overall plan (a basilica with a central nave flanked by side aisles), and artifacts, such as glass oil lamp fragments.

In an adjacent cemetery, 24 human skeletons, most interred in simple mud-brick tombs, have been excavated. Pottery and coins indicate that the cemetery, like the church, was in use in the fourth century, and one tomb

A Church Pew with a View

A second church has been found beneath the waters of the partially submerged settlement of Aperlae on the southern coast of Turkey, adding credence to the idea that the city was a popular pit-stop for Christian pilgrims traveling to the Holy Land from the fourth to seventh century A.D.

This latest discovery has brought the total number of churches identified at Aperlae to five, an unusually high number, considering the pop-ulation of the settlement most likely never exceeded 1,000 people.

"During the first several centuries of the Christian era, churches were a sign of regional importance, much like domed sports stadiums are today," said Robert Hohlfelder, an underwater

archaeologist and history professor at the University of Colorado, who, along with Lindley Vann of the University of Maryland, has led surveys of the site since 1996. "It looks like this city invested considerable capital in these prestige symbols. Another reason for so many churches is that Aperlae may have been a way station for pil-grims traveling to and from the Holy Land."

The location of the two submerged churches, which were originally built on the shores of the city and later fell victim to earthquake-related shoreline subsidence, emphasized the religious importance of water and gave seafarers a place to pray for safe journeys, says Hohlfelder.

by KRISTIN M. ROMEY

Gustave Doré

Jesus' Sermon on the Mount, was held on the Mount of Olives, overlooking Jerusalem. Today's Mount of Olives boasts trees that are to almost two thousand years old.

yielded a fragmentary bronze cross, suggest-ing the deceased was a Christian. A bishop of Aila, as ancient Aqaba was known, was present at the Council of Nicaea convened by Constantine in 325 to debate the nature of the holy trinity and other matters. Partic-ipation of Aila's bishop in the council sug-gests the city had a significant Christian community.

The church, about 85 feet by 53 feet, had mud-brick walls built on stone founda-tions with arched doorways. Both the nave and side aisles appear to have been vaulted. Traces of red and black paint are preserved on the white plaster of one wall of the nave, but no images are clearly discernible. Seven stone risers from a staircase suggest the building had a second story. East of the nave are the chancel area and a rectangular apse. Only part of the chancel has been exca-vated, but two phases of a stone foundation, apparently for the screen, have been revealed.

A few earlier churches are known, but these were originally built for other purposes, such as a house at Dura Europos in Syria that was converted into a church. Usually dated to ca. 230–240, it apparently went out of use when the city was captured by the Persians in 256. Mud-brick churches similar to the one at Aila are known from Egypt, but they are slightly later. Other early Christian churches, like that of the Holy Sepulcher in Jerusalem, originally erected ca. 325, have been in continuous use and rebuilt over the centuries, making their original architecture difficult to discern. The church at Aila was used for less than a century. Its latest coins date to 337–361, suggesting the church was a victim of an earthquake that, according to historical sources, devastated the region. The building was then abandoned and quickly filled with wind-blown sand, preserving its walls up to 15 feet in height.

THE ROOTS OF CHRISTIANITY

SCHOLARS CLOSE IN ON THE SOCIAL AND POLITICAL WORLD OF JESUS AND HIS FOLLOWERS

by NEIL ASHER SILBERMAN

The archaeology of the New Testament, like that of the Old Testament, has undergone a profound transformation. Modern tools and analytical techniques have replaced reverent curiosity, and the archaeology of early Christianity has become identified with the study of the economic and political world of the Roman Empire. In recent decades, spectacular discoveries and archaeological insights have deepened our understanding of the world of Jesus and his followers.

Villagers and Peasants

Regional surveys, fresh analysis of historical texts, and excavations at the sites of Nazareth, Capernaum, Magdala, and

Bethsaida suggest to some scholars that Roman imperial rule ushered in a period of profound dislocation and economic stress among the agrarian population. The 1986 discovery of a first-century fisherman's boat in the mud along the shore of the Sea of Galilee has provided a fascinating look at the carpentry skills and boat-building methods in the lakeside towns during the time of Jesus' ministry.

How Cosmopolitan Was Jesus?

Biblical scholars long thought the Aramaic-speaking villagers of Galilee were little affected by the fashions and ideologies of the Greco-Roman world. Yet excavations of the Romanized city of Sepphoris, less than four miles from Nazareth, indicate how close, and how visible, the public monuments and institutions of Roman civilization were to early Christians. Some scholars believe Jesus was a wandering adherent of the Cynic school of philosophy made famous by Diogenes in the fourth century B.C. Others suggest that while Greco-Roman influence was pervasive in Lower Galilee, its appeal was restricted to aristocratic circles. They argue that Jesus was a prophet of the traditional values of Israel against the seductions of imperial life.

Pontius Pilate and a Crucified Man

In 1960, an Italian expedition digging at the ancient port city of Caesarea Maritima, the civil capital of the Roman province of Judea, uncovered a fragmentary building inscription bearing the name of the Roman governor Pontius Pilatus, the first archaeological confirmation of this scriptural figure's presence in Judea. No less evocative was the discovery in 1968, in a northern suburb of Jerusalem, of the remains of a young man whose anklebones were pierced by an iron spike driven through them when he was crucified. The finds confirmed the historicity of the notorious governor as well as the brutality of his rule.

Lifestyles of the Rich and Famous

Excavations around the Temple Mount in Jerusalem have uncovered the monumental entrances to Herod's temple, while exploration throughout the modern Jewish Quarter has revealed a neighborhood of luxurious villas described in the writings of the first-century Jewish historian Flavius Josephus as Jerusalem's "Upper City." An inscribed stone weight found in 1972 in one of the houses links it with the high priestly family of Bar Kathros, long remembered in Rabbinic literature for its wealth and power. To the south of the city, an elaborate family tomb excavated in 1990 was found to contain an ossuary, a ceremonial urn for bones, bearing the name of Joseph Caiaphas, the high priest who, according to the gospels, presided over Jesus' trial. Herod's palace-fortress of Masada, though more famous for the bloody resistance of its rebel defenders against the Romans, is perhaps the most spectacular archaeological monument highlighting the opulent lifestyle enjoyed by Judea's secular and religious leaders.

Early Religious Texts

Beyond specific finds illustrating places, lifeways, and people otherwise known only from the gospels, the most important archae-

Sacred Stone

A rock venerated by early Christians as the place where the Virgin Mary rested on her way to Bethlehem has been found, according to Rina Avner of the Israel Antiquities Authority. The Church of the Kathisma ("seat" in Greek) had been built in the fifth century to enshrine the stone, according to Byzantine records, but by the twelfth century it had been destroyed and its exact location forgotten.

Five years ago, roadbuilders found the ruins of an octagonal church, at 173 by 143 feet the largest of its kind in the Holy Land. Excavations revealed that an earlier church, dating to the fifth century, had been destroyed and rebuilt at least once before its final destruction in the eighth or ninth century.

Suspecting that the ruins were those of the Kathisma, Avner reasoned that since it was octagonal the rock had to be at its center. Its tip was exposed during initial excavations, but work was halted in 1993 and resumed only last year after bulldozers working on a housing project accidentally damaged the church's foundations. New excavations showed that the rock was about six feet across, protruded a few inches above the floor, and was set off by a low wall.

by ANDREW L. SLAYMAN

Jack Hazut, JHM Photography

St. Peter in Gallicantu, with structures that date to 37 B.C., is built near the place of the rooster crowing, identified in Mark 14:53.

ological discoveries have been large collections of religious texts from the first and second centuries A.D. The Dead Sea Scrolls, the first of which were discovered in 1948, do not mention any scriptural personalities by name, but they offer vivid glimpses of the intense messianic expectation and apocalyptic fervor that gripped Judea in the first century B.C. and first century A.D. They were presumably hidden in caves to prevent their destruction at the time of the Judean revolt against Rome in A.D. 66–73. Also important are the second-century codices discovered at the village of Nag Hammadi in Upper Egypt in 1945, which included previously unknown gospels and religious writings held sacred by early Christian groups. Like the Dead Sea Scrolls, they were hidden in caves, in their case to escape detection by officials of the established church in Egypt who were bent on destroying "heretical" literature.

Paul's Ministry

While much of New Testament archaeology has centered in Israel, scholarly interest is now focusing on the social landscape of the Roman provinces of Syria, Galatia, Asia, Macedonia, and Achaia, where Paul reportedly founded the first Gentile Christian communities. Wide-ranging surveys and analysis of early Roman settlement patterns point to the same kinds of agrarian disruptions and economic transformation known from Judea and the Galilee in the first century. In ongoing surveys of the provinces in which Christianity first took root, archaeologists have discovered how former scattered farming villages were being consolidated into huge plantations. The rural populations were either being transformed into serflike tenant farmers or forced to find work in the expanding towns. This vast restructuring of the ancient economy, which was impoverishing masses of people throughout the Roman world, may have encouraged many to seek the new sources of spiritual guidance and new forms of community that earliest Christianity offered.

The archaeological search for the roots of Christianity continues throughout the Mediterranean, concentrating on the social and economic changes of the period. In addition to ongoing surveys in Greece, Turkey, and Israel, new explorations in the rural areas of Jordan and southern Syria promise to provide new insights on the character of earliest Christianity. Of course, excavations and surveys can only provide the material background. Assessing the impact of Jesus, Paul, and the early Apostles on the hearts and minds of their contemporaries lies well beyond the grasp of even the most advanced archaeological techniques.

GALILEE IN THE TIME OF CHRIST

ARCHAEOLOGY DISCOVERS THAT GALILEE WAS OVERWHELMINGLY JEWISH AND ENJOYED ROMAN COMFORTS, A FAR DIFFERENT PLACE THAN BIBLICAL SCHOLARS' RURAL AND BACKWARD TOWN

by ERIC M. MEYERS

While not devoid of geographic detail, the Gospels lack the description of Galilee that is available in Josephus, Talmudic literature, and pagan writers such as Strabo and Pliny. Jesus moved freely about in Galilee, though he probably didn't visit its urban centers. If New Testament references are accurate, he might very well have journeyed to the northern edges of Upper Galilee, which bordered the Hellenized, gentile cities of Acco-Ptolemais, Sidon, and Tyre. Part of the reason for Jesus' visits to gentile cities was to preach to Jewish residents there, "the lost sheep of the house of Israel." Tyre, Gerasa, and Scythopolis had significant Jewish populations, as did many other gentile cities.

Why are two Jewish cities, Sepphoris and Tiberias, which played so central a role in the cultural and economic life of Galilee, omitted from the New Testament? It is reasonable to assume that Jesus' Galilean ministry could hardly have avoided these cities, which represent the changing demography of Galilee at the end of the Second Temple period (first century), a transition from a village-centered, agrarian population to an urban-centered one, including residents with close ties to the central government. Villages, farms, and hamlets were now called upon to provide food for growing city populations and cash crops soon replaced subsistence farming. There were no towns and villages in all of Galilee that were more than 15 miles from either Sepphoris or Tiberias. While some of the smaller communities kept their distance from the gentile cities, literally and figuratively, it seems less likely that they would have avoided these two Herodian cities, which called upon their populations for food, sundry goods and supplies, and labor.

The archaeology and history of Sepphoris suggest that in the time of Jesus the city was overwhelmingly Jewish in population, traditional in orientation toward language and common religious practice, urban in character (but not a city of the magnitude of the gentile cities), connected to the other towns and villages of Galilee by trade and the new requirements of an expanding population base, somewhat aristocratic because of its priestly component, retainer class, and pro-Roman posture, and perhaps an uncongenial but not unfamiliar place for Jesus as he went about Galilee preaching his new gospel. Jesus' avoidance of Sepphoris (as well as Tiberias), if we interpret the silence of the New Testament somewhat narrowly, could well have been to avoid a clash with Antipas, the authorities, or upper-class citizens who might have been uncomfortable with his message.

Galilee in the time of Jesus was first and foremost Jewish in population and in its political and administrative form. Its growing urbanism was somewhat modest compared to that of gentile centers like Scythopolis, south of the Sea of Galilee, where a Jewish minority flourished and where apparently a gentile administration tolerated the Herodian client king, Antipas, rather well.

I have argued elsewhere that we not consider the Hellenization of language and architecture so much as an invasion of indigenous

> **IT IS HARD TO UNDERSTAND WHY SO MANY SCHOLARS HAVE ASSOCIATED THE RURAL LANDSCAPE OF GALILEE WITH ALL ITS TOWNS AND VILLAGES AS BEING DEVOID OF JEWISH LEARNING**

Ship Ahoist

After 2,000 years in the mud and another 14 in a lab, the first-century B.C.–first-century A.D. fishing boat found in the Sea of Galilee has reached its final destination in an Israeli museum. The boat was exposed in 1986 when a severe drought caused the shoreline of the Sea of Galilee to recede. The badly water-logged 27-foot-long wooden hull was excavated from the lake bed in eight days, reinforced with fiberglass frames, and encased in polyurethane foam. It was then floated up the coast to a specially designed conservation pool at the Yigal Allon Museum at Ginosar, where it was submerged in a hot polyethylene glycol bath until 1995 to preserve its waterlogged timbers. After extensive cleaning, the boat was hoisted by crane into its new exhibition hall at the museum, where it will remain on permanent display.

by KRISTIN M. ROMEY

culture from the outside, but rather as a force that gave both Jews and gentiles a new means of expressing local culture in alternative and often exciting ways. The appearance of some forms of Greco-Roman culture in a Jewish context need not signify compromise or traumatic change. In Jesus' Galilee, incipient urbanism and rural village culture lived in harmony. City and town were economically linked, as we know from ceramic finds. The Jewish towns and four large villages of Upper Galilee, and the two Herodian cities of Lower Galilee were in regular contact.

That Galilee in Jesus' time was overwhelmingly Jewish should come as no great surprise. It is thus hard to understand why so many scholars have associated the rural landscape of Galilee with all its towns and villages as being devoid of Jewish learning, as well as lacking in the everyday accoutrements of a Greco-Roman life-style. Archaeology has told us otherwise for a long time. As the present generation gets more accustomed to reading archaeological reports, perhaps the simplest artifact will

speak to historical questions with the same authority and clarity as the acknowledged sayings of Jesus.

Jack Hazut, IHM Photography

Zippori, spared from destruction by the Romans during the A.D. 70 revolt, was Galilee's capitol and became the Jewish center of religious worship and study in A.D. 200.

Megiddo, overlooking the Jezreel Valley, was an important Canaanite city-state, as well as the supposed location of Armageddon in *Revelations*. Archaeologists are reexamining the biblical assertion that Solomon rebuilt it.

An imposing ancient mound containing the remains of thirty superimposed cities, Megiddo's stormy history covers over six thousand years, from the Neolithic period in the seventh millennium B.C. to the Persian period in the fifth century B.C.

Herod the Great rebuilt a ruined Phoenician port into the impressive harbor city of Caesarea, seat of the the Roman Procurators in the first century A.D. An aqueduct, hippodrome, amphitheater, and other imposing structures have been uncovered by excavations.

A strategic Mediterranean port for nearly 5,000 years, Ashkelon retained its importance from the time of the Canaanites, Philistines, and Phoenicians to the Crusader era in the Middle Ages.

Early remains found near the city gate at Tel Beersheva, the biblical Beer-Sheba, were initially dated to the tenth century B.C. and connected with the building program of King Solomon. Today the association is disputed by some archaeologists.

The stronghold of Masada was constructed by Herod the Great in the first century B.C. as a place of refuge for his family and followers and a strategic fortress overlooking the Dead Sea. During the Jewish Revolt against Rome (A.D. 66–73), Masada became an outpost of the rebels.

According to the first-century A.D. Jewish historian Josephus Flavius, Masada was the final pocket of resistance to the Romans. According to his account, the 960 rebels occupying the mountaintop fortress committed suicide rather than surrender to the besieging Roman forces.

Capernaum, a site mentioned prominently in the Gospels, is located on the north shore of the Sea of Galilee. First-century A.D. remains have been found beneath the reconstructed remains of this fourth-century A.D. synagogue.

A major city north of the Sea of Galilee, Hazor controlled an important trade route between Canaan and the north. Known as "head of all those kingdoms" in the Bible, the Canaanite city shows signs of decline and destruction around 1250 B.C., associated by some archaeologists with the settlement of the Israelites in Canaan.

Bar'am, a large two-story synagogue built in the early fifth century A.D., is the best preserved example of Galilean synagogue architecture in the Byzantine period.

Excavations at Khirbet Qumran, on the northwest shore of the Dead Sea, revealed a unique communal settlement associated by most scholars with the Dead Sea Scrolls, found in nearby caves.

Excavations at Jericho in the 1950s revealed a Neolithic (8500 B.C.) wall and tower, but no remains of fortifications destroyed by the invading Israelites, as described in the Bible, were discovered.

Located in the Sharon Plain, Aphek was an important royal Canaanite city. Known as Antipatris in the Roman period, it was the site of Paul's imprisonment on the way to Caesarea, according to the Book of Acts.

An impressive synagogue was built in the ancient town of Hammat, just to the south of Tiberias, in A.D. 341. Its elaborate mosaic floor features Greek inscriptions and a depiction of the zodiac and seasons of the year in typical Roman style.

Jack Hazut, JHM Photography

The massive platform on the Temple Mount in Jerusalem was constructed by Herod the Great in the late first century B.C as a foundation for the Jewish Temple. The Dome of the Rock, an important Muslim shrine, was built there in the late seventh century A.D.

Jack Hazut, JHM Photography

Jerusalem's Kidron Valley, at the foot of the Mount of Olives, is the site of monumental tombs from the time of the biblical Kingdom of Judah.

Richard T. Nowitz

The Church of the Nativity in Bethlehem has been venerated as the site of Jesus' birth since the time of its construction during the reign of the Emperor Constantine in the fourth century A.D. No first-century remains, however, have been found at the site.

Haldun Aydıngün

Built by the Byzantine Emperor Justinian in the sixth century, on-going restoration in Hagia Sophia's dome is being carried out on scaffolding that rises more than 180 feet from its marble floor.

A major Canaanite city during the Early Bronze Age (3150–2200 B.C.) and an important desert fortress of the Kingdom of Judah (ca. 900–600 B.C.), Tel Arad's urban plan was designed for defense. Many wells like this provided a water supply for the upper fortress.

THE WORLD OF PAUL

REGIONAL SURVEYS IN GREECE AND ASIA MINOR POINT TO THE IMPACT OF ROMAN RULE ON THE SPREAD OF CHRISTIANITY

by Neil Asher Silberman

Paul's epistles, written in the mid-first century A.D., bristle with complex, passionate arguments that offer insights into the heart and mind of a remarkable person and his times. For centuries, theologians and biblical scholars relied on scripture and church tradition to assess Paul's career and missionary achievements. Now archaeology is offering intriguing data about the lands where Paul preached and organized his churches and about the broader social context behind the spread of Christianity.

Some evidence is drawn from large-scale excavations of temples, forums, and private houses in the cities of the Roman provinces of Galatia, Macedonia, Achaia, and Asia. Other clues come from salvage excavations beneath the bustling streets of modern Mediterranean cities. Perhaps the most important sources of new information are regional survey projects in Italy, Greece, Turkey, Syria, Israel, and Jordan, which are documenting the changing settlement patterns and economic life of the rich along with the peasants, plebeians, and slaves of the empire.

In the past few decades, the archaeology of the New Testament world has achieved some striking successes, particularly in the reconstruction of the social world of first-century Galilee. Finds including inscriptions naming Pontius Pilate and the high priest Joseph Caiaphas have provided tangible evidence for the historical existence of scriptural characters. Other recent discoveries, such as a first-century fisherman's boat from the Sea of Galilee and the simple houses of the Galilean village of Bethsaida mentioned in the gospels, have yielded raw material for an increasingly detailed reconstruction of daily life. Now scholars are going beyond using archaeology as a means of "biblical illustration," identifying the particular villages and cities Jesus and the apostles visited, the types of pottery they used, the boats in which they traveled, and the robes and sandals they wore. Today's challenge is to reconstruct the wider social and economic climate of the first century, which allowed Christianity to gain a foothold in many cities of the Roman Empire.

Richard Horsley, a biblical scholar at the University of Massachusetts, and I have spent the past two years assessing recent archaeological discoveries to see how they may help explain the growth of the Jesus movement as it was carried by the early

apostles from Jerusalem to Damascus, to Antioch, to Asia Minor, to Greece, and finally to Rome. We began with Galilee and Judea but widened our search to include evidence from surveys and excavations in Turkey, Greece, and Italy. The evidence suggests to us that the world of Paul and the earliest Christians was affected by far-reaching economic dislocation, cultural conflict, and political change as formerly autonomous regions—from Spain to the Euphrates and from Britain to Upper Egypt—were linked by a centralized administration and increasingly regulated channels of trade.

Reassessment of Augustan art, architecture, and literature by classical scholars such as Paul Zanker of the University of Munich and Karl Galinsky of the University of Texas at Austin show how Roman authorities promoted universal allegiance to the empire. Paul and the early apostles traveled through this world of imperial power, yet they gave voice to an alternative vision, one in which scattered, self-supporting communities looked forward to the imminent end of earthly status, privilege, and violence in a new kind of "kingdom" ruled by God.

Churches and shrines throughout the eastern half of the Mediterranean commemorate various events of Paul's career as recorded in the book of Acts and his epistles. From the church erected in the Syrian village of Kaukab to commemorate his conversion on the road to Damascus (Acts 9:3–8), to the statue on a rocky islet off the northwest coast of Malta designating the site where he was stranded after a shipwreck (Acts 28:1–10), visitors and pilgrims can follow the scripturally attested path of his journeys. From a strictly archaeological standpoint, however, it is impossible to determine whether Paul was actually present at any of these sites.

In the late nineteenth century a wave of inquisitive explorers, versed in classical history and the New Testament, began identifying and documenting archaeological remains of Christianity's origins. Chief among them was Oxford University's William M. Ramsay, who traveled throughout the rugged hill country of south-central Turkey from the 1880s up to the eve of World War I. He discovered hundreds of Roman-era inscriptions and architectural remains at some of the most important cities visited by Paul, places like Pisidian Antioch, Iconium, Lystra, and Derbe (Acts 13–14), whose precise locations had long been forgotten. Ramsay's aim, like that of the archaeologists then digging up Old Testament sites in Ottoman Palestine, was to demonstrate that New Testament narratives (particularly Acts, with its detailed itineraries and geographical information) were reliable historical sources. He contended, for instance, that Paul and Barnabas' missionary travels through southern Galatia (Acts 13–14) closely followed the Roman highway known as the Via Sebaste.

In the following decades, Austrian, French, and American scholars began excavating some of the larger cities where, according to scripture, Paul had established early Christian communities. Although the excavators often focused more on the harvest of classical art and architecture for western universities and museums than on the clarification of early Christian history, their work at Philippi, Thessalonika, Corinth, and Ephesus provided details about daily life in those cities during the first century.

Austrian excavators concentrated on uncovering the splendor of Ephesus, the city of the Great Temple of Artemis, where Paul and his colleagues spent two or three years preaching and healing (Acts 19:1–41), while a French expedition to Philippi discovered the elaborate religious and administrative structures on the Via Egnatia, where Paul's European mission began (Acts 16:12–40). Great efforts were made to link archaeological finds with passages in Acts and Paul's letters. In Corinth, excavated and studied almost continuously since 1896 by the American School of Classical Studies at Athens, a judicial podium, or *bema*, was identified by Jerome Murphy-O'Connor of the École Biblique et Archéologique in Jerusalem as the possible site of Paul's trial before the Roman proconsul Iunius Gallio (Acts 18:12–17). A fragmentary inscription of uncertain date reading "Synagogue of the Hebrews" was used by other New Testament scholars to identify the location of a synagogue where Paul reportedly preached (Acts 18:4). The stadium near Corinth where the Isthmian Games were held every two years was offered as the inspiration for Paul's reference to "a race in which all runners compete, but only one receives the prize" (1 Corinthians 9:24). The votive clay arms, legs, breasts, and genitals uncovered at the local temple to Asclepius, the god of healing, were said to have inspired a passage in 1 Corinthians where Paul used vivid imagery about the various parts of the human body, stressing that "God arranged the organs of the body, each one of them, as he chose" (12:18).

Some archaeological finds did not require such a lively imagination to link them to scripture. Fragments of a Latin inscription at Delphi naming Iunius Gallio, the proconsul of Achaia mentioned in Acts, established the precise date for his term of office (and presumably for Paul's presence in Corinth) as A.D. 51–52. No less striking was the discovery at Corinth of a first-century dedicatory inscription mentioning a man named Erastus who had served as *aedile*, or municipal market inspector, thought to be the same person addressed by Paul as "Erastus the oikomenos [city treasurer]" in Romans 16:23.

These discoveries helped bring Roman urban history and Pauline studies together. Paul's movement came to be viewed as essentially urban, his followers as members of a restless generation of upwardly mobile professionals and tradespeople who had abandoned or lost their traditional family connections and ethnic identities. In *The First Urban Christians* (1983), New Testament scholar Wayne Meeks surveyed epigraphic, textual, and archaeological evidence, concluding that "it was in the cities of the Roman Empire that Christianity, though born in the village culture of Palestine, had its greatest successes until well after the time of Constantine."

Today, archaeologists are redefining the relationship between country and city, calling into question the understanding of Paul's mission and churches as a purely urban phenomenon. Surveys throughout the territories of the Roman Empire have shown that imperial rule brought about profound changes in agricultural methods, settlement patterns, and interregional economic links. Although specific changes were tied to local conditions, native crops, or specialized products, a general pattern of economic reorganization is evident throughout the lands conquered by Augustus and his successors. Formerly autonomous regions were drawn into an increasingly uniform economy. Literary sources tell of widespread confiscation and redistribution of land to Roman veterans and officials, the growing burden of taxation and debt on formerly independent peasant farmers, and the occasionally crippling levies of tribute imposed on conquered lands.

Evidence gathered from surveys throughout the Mediterranean indicates dramatic shifts in rural settlement patterns from many dispersed farmsteads to far fewer plantation-like estates, the settlement and cultivation of previously neglected areas, and the sudden shrinkage or expansion of regional market towns or provincial capitals-all brought on by the region's incorporation into the Roman Empire. The cost in terms of displaced peasants, villagers, and townspeople is only now being recognized.

Recent surveys of rural archaeological remains in Galilee by Mordechai Aviam of the Israel Antiquities Authority point to the impact of economic conditions on the beginnings of the Jesus movement. Horsley's review of the disintegration of traditional village life under the Roman client-king Herod Antipas (4 B.C.–A.D. 39), and ongoing excavations at the Galilean administrative center of Sepphoris by the Hebrew University,

Duke University, the University of Southern Florida, and Tel Aviv University, show, through the discovery of elaborate urban monuments and public buildings, the extent to which the former frontier region of Galilee was coming under imperial control. Surveys of the highlands have revealed a first-century landscape of small, hilltop villages strikingly similar to Israelite settlements of the Iron Age (ca. 1200–600 B.C.). Literary sources, primarily Josephus Flavius, reveal that the villagers' flexible system of mixed agriculture, orchard crops, and herding came under increasing pressure from Herodian taxation and repeated Roman military campaigns.

Conscription of peasants to serve Herod Antipas may have contributed to the breakdown of traditional economic patterns. His new, Roman-style capital of Tiberias was populated, according to Josephus, by a "promiscuous rabble, no small contingent being Galilean, with such as were drafted... and brought forcibly to the new foundation." Such demographic shifts and new levels of taxation would have had far-reaching effects on the rural population from Nazareth to the Sea of Galilee.

The abundant archaeological evidence—in architecture, pottery forms, city planning, and artistic styles—for the spread of Greco-Roman culture throughout Galilee has been characterized by Eric M. Meyers of Duke University as a "force that gave both Jews and gentiles a new means of expressing local culture in alternative and often exciting ways." Yet this cultural milieu was part of a wider social system that served the interests of the rich over those of the poor. We tend to assume that the teachings of Jesus were purely religious, yet we must remember that those he rebuked, "who are gorgeously appareled and live in luxury" (Luke 7:25), are those whose homes, monuments, places of entertainment, and tombs are the most conspicuous in the archaeological record. That is why archaeology is so significant in understanding the rise of early Christianity and its spread across the Mediterranean. Was the organization by Paul of self-supporting assemblies, or *ekklesiai*, an extension or transformation of a Galilean movement of protest in which the sacrifice of Jesus and the coming Kingdom of God were seen as events meant "to deliver us from the present evil age" (Galatians 1:4)? Centuries of faithful Christians have interpreted that phrase in a purely spiritual way, yet Paul may have intended it to be taken literally as well.

Recent studies of first-century Galatia by Stephen Mitchell of the University

IMPERIAL RULE BROUGHT ABOUT PROFOUND CHANGES IN AGRICULTURAL METHODS, SETTLEMENT PATTERNS, AND INTERREGIONAL ECONOMIC LINKS

College of Swansea have highlighted the far-reaching economic changes brought about by Roman rule in one of Paul's early mission fields (Acts 13–14 and the Letter to the Galatians). After the annexation of the province by Augustus in 25 B.C., new, higher taxes were imposed. Vast grain-growing estates owned by Roman and Romanized local aristocrats were created. Roman colonies were established at the southern cities of Pisidian Antioch, Iconium, and Lystra (all of which Paul visited). The result was social dislocation in which old traditions were altered and family networks shattered. Such developments did not affect Galatia alone. The Macedonian cities of Philippi and Thessalonika, through which Paul later traveled, were in a region scarred from decades of warfare (Philippi was the scene of two major battles after the assassination of Julius Caesar). Colonized by Roman veterans, its urban communities were transformed into centers of administration and trade.

The prosperity visible in the monuments of the Romanized cities of Greece and Asia Minor was not shared by all who lived under Roman rule. Augustan ideology, symbolized by grandiose temples and shrines to the deified emperor, cynically assured people that Rome's expanding programs for trade, development, and modernization, entrusted to the Roman aristocracy, provincial officials, and local nobles, would benefit rich and poor alike. Paul warned that a new age was dawning in the midst of this imperial triumph, that "sudden destruction will come upon them as travail comes upon a woman with child, and there will be no escape" (1 Thessalonians 5:3). There were, of course, satirists who deflated imperial pretensions, yet early Christianity offered a more practical way to resist this new world order by rejecting the basic principles of power and status upon which it was built.

Recent work in central Greece by the Boeotia Survey Project of the universities of Bradford and Cambridge and in Corinthia, the region around Corinth, by the joint American-Greek-British Nemea Valley Archaeological Project reveal a pattern of rural depopulation, expanding and shrinking cities, and changing trade routes and administrative and religious centers, all of which enabled Roman authorities to incorporate these regions into the empire.

Paul's choice of Corinth as headquarters of his Achaian mission makes sense in this context, for it was the political, economic, and cultural center from which Greece was controlled. The Greek city of Corinth had been destroyed by the Romans in 146 B.C., but Julius Caesar established a colony for veterans and freedmen there in 44 B.C. This "New Corinth" quickly became the provincial capital and the greatest metropolis in Roman Greece—a full six times larger than any other city of the province. It became a centerpoint for the worship of the deified emperor as well as a meeting place of people, goods, and ideas from around the Mediterranean. Any modern reading of Paul's two letters to the Corinthians must take this historical context into account and see the actions of the members of his community as responses to this imperial reality. At Corinth, the current topographical survey project of David Gilman Romano of the University of Pennsylvania has defined the colonial plan of the city in 44 B.C., documenting successive Roman land development efforts as well as the major Roman highways between cities and harbors in Corinthia.

Susan Alcock of the University of Michigan demonstrated, in *Graecia Capta: The Landscapes of Roman Greece* (1993), just how dynamic and challenging the imperial period was for the people of Achaia—among whom Paul founded his most important early community. She shows how the process of imperial incorporation was inscribed on the landscape not only in public monuments and major highways, but also in the redistribution of farms and the placement of shrines marking new boundaries, both territorial and cultural, between struggling ancient communities and newly established Roman cities. Corinth and Nikopolis in northwestern Greece (31 B.C.), Dium in Macedonia (27 B.C.), and Patrai in the northwestern Peloponnese (14 B.C.) became new centers of power that quickly eclipsed native Greek communities, leading to their decline and abandonment.

No longer can we view Paul's world as a static backdrop of columns, aqueducts, and elegant Romanized cities. It must be regarded, as Alcock wrote, not as a "cultural haven, an imaginary world, or a museum locked in spiritual twilight," but rather as a "society in the process of change, adapting and assimilating itself to a new position within an imperial system—just as countless other subordinate societies have been forced to do throughout the centuries."

It is in this specific historical milieu of urbanism and economic change that the roots of Christianity lay. As University at Buffalo (SUNY) archaeologist Stephen L. Dyson recently noted, the rise of Christianity can "only be understood as part of wider, complex cultural and social developments within the Roman Empire." This lesson has already been taken to heart by New Testament scholars such as John Dominic Crossan in his writings on the "historical" Jesus, Neil Elliott in his study of the political context of the Pauline mission, and Elizabeth Schüssler Fiorenza in her research on gender roles in earliest Christianity. The movement that began 2,000 years ago in Galilee and spread across the Roman Empire through the efforts of Paul and the other apostles can be seen as a unique event in Western religious history and as a tangible historical process. Their wide-ranging quest for the Kingdom of God may well have been both a spiritual journey and an evolving social response to the changes wrought by Roman rule.

JEWS AND CHRISTIANS IN A ROMAN WORLD

NEW EVIDENCE STRONGLY SUGGESTS THAT BOTH IN
ROMAN PALESTINE AND THROUGHOUT THE
DIASPORA, JUDAISM, CHRISTAINITY, AND PAGANISM
THRIVED SIDE BY SIDE

by Eric M. Meyers *and* L. Michael White

More than a century ago, archaeologists began to rediscover the ancient world of the Mediterranean: the world of Homer and the Bible. Much of the early fieldwork in the classical world arose from a romantic quest to bring ancient literature to life. One thinks instinctively of Schliemann at Troy, a shovel in one hand and a copy of Homer in the other. In the Holy Land, the first biblical archaeologists were theologians and ministers who sought to identify and explore cities of the biblical world and to authenticate biblical stories and traditions: thus they arrived with preconceived ideas drawn from biblical texts and other literary sources. Because many were Old Testament scholars, New Testament archaeology in the Holy Land took a back seat. Outside the Holy Land, it remained for years in the shadow of classical archeology.

Since World War II, and especially since the discovery of the Dead Sea scrolls in 1947, archaeology has been more attentive to the world of the New Testament. But the new archaeology knowledge has only slowly begun to have an impact because New Testament scholars have been slow to take archaeology seriously. Some scholars think archaeology is of peripheral concern to early Christian studies, concluding debatably that the "earthly" dimension of early Christianity is irrelevant. New Testament archaeology is also given low priority in Jewish studies, which traditionally have placed far greater emphasis on sacred texts. Many believe New Testament archaeology to be of limited value in the study of ancient Palestine, erroneously assuming that the archeological time frame is restricted to only two generations, from the time of Jesus to the destruction of Jerusalem in the year 70. In fact, one cannot understand the development of either. Judaism or Christianity without looking at the historical context over centuries, beginning with the introduction of Greek culture into the ancient Near East.

The Homeland

Scholarly understanding of Judaism and Christianity in the Roman province of Palestine during the early Common Era (abbreviated C.E. and chronologically the same as A.D.) has long been burdened by some dubious suppositions. One is the belief that after the First Jewish Revolt against Rome in 66–70 C.E., the new Jewish-Christian community fled the Holy Land. Certainly there was significant emigration to other Mediterranean lands, but in light of archeological evidence from the first two or three centuries C.E., a growing number of scholars have found the idea of wholesale Jewish-Christian migration untenable.

Actually, the first followers of Jesus were basically indistinguishable from their fellow Jews. Although they believed Jesus was the Messiah and professed a radical love ethic that had few parallels in Judaism—for example, love for one's enemies—the first Jewish-Christians observed most of the Jewish laws and revered the Temple in Jerusalem. They apparently got along well with their fellow Jews, contrary to the impression created in the Gospels and other New Testament writings, where the Pharisees, the "mainstream" religious party of ancient Judaism, are presented in a negative light. The new Christians, in fact, were at odds mostly with the Sadducees, who were much more rigid in their religious outlook than the Pharisees, and far fewer in number. When the Apostles were persecuted by the Sadducean high priest, it was the Pharisee Rabbi Gamaliel who intervened to save them (Acts 5:17–42); when Paul was called before the

Sanhedrin (the High Council) in Jerusalem, he obtained his release by appealing to the Pharisees (Acts 22:30–23:10); and according to the Jewish historian Josephus, when Jesus' brother James was put to death by order of the Sadduccean high priest in 62 C.E., the Pharisees appealed to the king to depose the high priest. Jesus' natural constituency was the Pharisees, whose doctrine of love for one's fellow humans must surely have been the foundation for Jesus' ethical teaching.

The belief that all or most of the Jewish-Christians left Palestine after the First Revolt stems partly from the lack of clear material traces of the Christian community in the Holy Land from about 70 to 270 C.E. Early Christianity, however, vigorously sought to win converts both among gentiles and in the many Jewish communities throughout the Mediterranean. It is exceedingly hard to imagine these efforts bypassing the large Jewish community in Palestine.

Moreover, Jews from Jerusalem and the surrounding area fled in large numbers to Galilee after the revolt was crushed. Would the first Jewish-Christians have ignored Galilee, where Jesus spent his childhood and where he conducted his ministry? Later generations of Christians certainly did not, as evidenced by the numerous churches they built in Galilee. The presence of important Christian centers of worship makes it difficult to imagine a great Christian "repopulation" of Palestine between the third and fifth centuries. Rather, it seems there was a large community of Jewish-Christians in Palestine from the first century onward, a community later augmented by pilgrims in the age of Constantine.

Jerusalem is central in the study of early Christianity. It is there that the new religion received its most compelling moments of inspiration in the death and burial of Jesus; and it is from there that its followers took their message to the other cities and towns of the land. As long as the Temple stood, the first Christians continued to worship there and in private household meetings. With the destruction of the Temple, however, both Jews and Christians had to establish new patterns of worship. Thus the local synagogue, which was both a meeting place and a center of worship, became the focus of spiritual life for Jew and Jewish-Christian after 70 C.E.

Recent synagogue excavations have revealed that Jewish life enjoyed remarkable vitality in Palestine during the Roman period, and in some localities into the Byzantine period and beyond. In the pre-Constantinian era, the synagogue was quite possibly where Jewish-Christians worshiped as well. Although the archaeological record shows very little definitive evidence of Christianity until the end of the third century, the textual record is quite clear. In a reference that may go back to 100 or 120 C.E., the Jerusalem Talmud implies that Christians are a sect of *minim*, or heretics. Irenaeus, the first Christian theologian to systematize doctrine, speaks of Ebionites, who read only the Gospel of Matthew, reject Paul, and follow the Torah and the Jewish way of life. Epiphanius, another early Christian writer, speaks of Nazarenes, or Elkasaites, as Christians who insist on the validity of the Torah and laws of purity.

Whether one looks at early Christianity

or rabbinic Judaism in Roman Palestine, it is clear that this was a period of great cultural and religious pluralism. One finds this pluralism in the Lower Galilee, at Sepphoris, and at the great site of Capernaum on the northwestern shore of the Sea of Galilee. The octagonal Church of St. Peter of Capernaum is built over what some excavators believe is a Jewish-Christian "house-church" dating back to about the third century. The excavators have also found evidence of a first-century house below this church edifice that may have been Peter's residence. It is clear that by the fourth century, Christians venerated the site by erecting churches there. Next to these Christian structures are Jewish buildings, including a reconstructed synagogue. Archaeologists once thought the synagogue was from the first century C.E., the very building in which Jesus would have walked. Today there is universal agreement that it is a later structure, dating to the fourth or fifth century, that survived for hundreds of years into the early medieval period. Excavators have recently claimed finding another synagogue, from the first century, beneath this fourth-or-fifth-century synagogue. If they are right, then in Capernaum a Jewish synagogue and a Jewish-Christian church existed side by side from the end of the first century on. The grander structures above both the early synagogue and the house of Peter in Capernaum suggest that Jewish and Christian communities lived in harmony until the seventh century. The continuous Christian presence for six centuries also casts serious doubts on the idea that the early Christians fled Palestine after 70 C.E. Evidence like that found in

Capernaum is plentiful in the Beth Shean Valley and in the Golden Heights, although the evidence there begins later, toward the end of the Roman period and into the Byzantine period.

In the middle of the fourth century, pluralism began to suffer as the Roman period in Palestine came to an end and the Byzantine period began. The transition from Roman to Byzantine culture as revealed by the archaeological and textual records was dramatic and coincides with either the so-called Gallus Revolt against Roman occupation in 352 or the great earthquake of 363. In the case of the revolt, the Byzantine emperor might have taken the opportunity to place the unruly province under his direct rule. In the case of the earthquake, the damage to Roman buildings would have presented the opportunity for a Byzantine architectural and cultural style to emerge as cities were rebuilt.

In either case, the revolt and the aftermath of the earthquake mark the beginning of a difficult period for Jews, in which they had little choice but to adjust to Christian rule. The Palestine of the Roman period, when Jewish sages spoke in Greek and when Rabbi Judah the Prince reputedly numbered the Roman emperor among his friends, became a land undergoing thorough and vigorous Christianization after the conversion of Constantine. Money poured into Palestine, and much of it went into building churches.

Nevertheless, archaeological evidence prompts us to exercise caution. Pockets of Judaism and Christianity remained in close contact during the Byzantine period. They may well have continued the harmonious relations established during the period of pluralism, even as Christianity became the dominant religion.

The Diaspora

Archaeology has also enriched our understanding of the New Testament world outside Palestine. It is significant to both Jewish and Christian history that the bulk of the New Testament is set outside the Jewish homeland. Jews and Christians alike called their communities outside Palestine the Diaspora, or "dispersion."

While the religious heritage of the New Testament may be Hebrew, its language is Greek. Its cultural heritage is not that of the ancient Near East but that of Greece and Rome. The world of the New Testament was fluid and pluralistic, with an extensive transportation network crisscrossing the Mediterranean. Christians and Jews traveled the highways and seaways, carrying their religion with them. This mobility is vividly reflected in the extensive journeys of Paul.

The New Testament record of Paul's travels provided early investigators with both an itinerary for their archaeological work as well as a "case" to be proved. From the 1880s to the 1920s, for example, the eminent Sir William Ramsey sought to corroborate the account given in the Acts of the Apostles of Paul's activities on his way to Rome, in Ephesus, Athens, Corinth, and Philippi. Shaping Ramsey's approach were attractive images of Paul, such as the one in chapter 17 of Acts, where he is depicted preaching to the philosophers on the Areopagus, or Mars Hill, below the entrance to the Acropolis. The story in Acts, and later Christian legends attributed to Paul's followers, are the only evidence we have for this. Paul left no footprints on the Areopagus for archaeologists to follow. It is also interesting that Paul, in his own letters, never once mentioned his activities or this episode in Athens. Still, this remains a popular tourist spot, and the legacy of early archaeologists like Ramsey lives on.

All over the eastern Mediterranean, tourists play out variations on this theme with local guides. (Though Paul was a tireless traveler, if he had visited every one of these places, he might have died of old age before he got to Rome.) Often the difficulties arise when local legends, which seem to grow like stratigraphic layers, become attached to a site. A prime example of this occurs at Paul's *bema* at Corinth.

Excavations at Corinth have revealed a fifth-century Christian church erected over what appears to be a *bema*, or speaking

> JEWS FROM JERUSALEM AND THE SURROUNDING AREA FLED IN LARGE NUMBERS TO GALILEE AFTER THE REVOLT WAS CRUSHED

platform. The obvious assumption was that this was the site of Paul's defense before the Roman governor Gallio in Acts 18:12 ("But when Gallio was proconsul of Achaia, the Jews made a united attack upon Paul and brought him before their tribunal"). Indeed, the story is given further credence by the discovery of an inscription from Delphi that bears the name of Gallio as well as his title. This inscription has been very important in dating Paul's stay in Corinth to around the years 51 and 52 C.E. But it is most difficult to place Paul's trial on this particular bema, since the South Stoa of Corinth, where the bema is found, was expanded and rebuilt during the next two centuries. Other evidence found at Corinth does little to clear matters up. A pavement bearing the name of Erastus, the city treasurer named in Roman 16:23, identifies him as an *aedile*, a minor administrative official, not as treasurer ("Erastus, the city treasurer, and our brother Quartus greet you"). Is this a tangible record of a follower of Paul at Corinth? One cannot be sure. As at the Areopagus, the best advice may be *caveat* pilgrim.

Similar problems arise in trying to place Paul or John in Ephesus, since Byzantine and medieval accounts have been overlayed on the biblical stories. Current excavation at Ephesus have revealed an elaborate Roman city of the second to sixth centuries C.E., but evidence of the first-century city remains sparse. Extensive excavations at Philippi, in Macedonia, have uncovered a second-century forum and main roadway, but most of the remains come from churches and basilicas dating from the fourth to the s eventh centuries. Once again, the remains of Paul's day are difficult to identify.

In some cases, the connection of a site with Paul is demonstrably wrong. For example, Christian pilgrimage and devotion in Philippi helped to equate a Hellenistic pagan crypt with Paul's "prison," as described in chapter 16 or Acts. In the late fifth century, a basilica was built around this site. In short, the work of archaeologists should not be used to prove such New Testament stories. Instead, archaeological work should be used more as a "backdrop" for the discussion of Paul's letters to Christian congregations living in these cities of the Roman world. The focus of archaeology

Gustave Doré

St. Paul at Ephesus, one of his many stops as the spread of Christianity began.

should be placing the Christians and Jews in a cultural context.

More recent archaeological perspectives shed light on the development of Jewish and Christian institutions of the New Testament world. Originally, "church" (the Greek *ekklesia*) and "synagogue" (the Greek *synagoge*) were synonymous terms for assembly or congregation. Especially in the earliest days of the Diaspora, Christian groups, including gentile converts, were considered to be following a form of Jewish practice. Only in the second century would the terms "church" and "synagogue" begin to become specific to Christians and Jews. In fact, distinct architectural differences between them did not begin until the fourth century. In other words, if we were following Paul through Ephesus or Corinth, we would not be able to distinguish Christian or Jewish meeting places from the exteriors of the buildings.

Most of the congregations founded by Paul met in the houses of individual members. Significantly, Diaspora Jewish groups would have met in houses, too; but over time, more formal synagogue buildings appeared. If anything, house-synagogues were in use earlier in the Diaspora than in Palestine (as early as the first century B.C.E.). Of the six early Diaspora synagogues known from excavations—at Delos, Priene, Ostia,

ARCHAEOLOGICAL WORK SHOULD BE USED MORE AS A "BACKDROP" FOR THE DISCUSSION OF PAUL'S LETTERS TO CHRISTIAN CONGREGATIONS

Dura-Europos, Stobi, and Sardis—five were originally houses that were renovated and adapted to special religious use. The earliest of these, from Delos, dates to the very beginning of the Common Era, or even slightly earlier.

There is evidence that Jews and Christians worshiped as neighbors in the Diaspora, as in Roman Palestine. One of the most impressive discoveries in this regard comes from Dura-Europos, a Roman garrison on the Euphrates River in what is now Iraq, dating to before 256 C.E. On one street was a house that had been renovated, in three stages, into a sanctuary of Mithras, a Persian god whose cult spread throughout the Roman empire from the second half of the first century C.E. onward. Farther down the same street, another house had been converted, in two stages, into a synagogue. Its assembly hall contained one of the earliest datable Torah niches, and on its walls were elaborate frescoes depicting stories from the Hebrew Scriptures. Farther down the same street was a house that was renovated to become a Christian church, with a small assembly hall and a room set aside for baptism. The baptistery room in particular has attracted considerable attention, since it contains some of the earliest clearly datable Christian art, including representations of

Surprise Findings from Early Synagogues

The synagogue provides a rare opportunity to study the Jewish people—and Jewish-Christians—as they forged a new religious way in Roman Palestine after the fall of Jerusalem. Even within a given region, we find a great variety of architectural forms and artistic motifs adorning the walls and halls of ancient synagogues. This great divergence of synagogue types suggests great variety within Talmudic Judaism, even though the members of different congregations belonged to a common culture.

Such diversity resulted in part from the catastrophe of 70 C.E., after which many sectarian groups were forced to fend for themselves in a new and often alien environment. Some groups settled in towns, others in urban centers; their choices reflected their understanding of how hospitable a setting their beliefs would find in either the sophisticated cities or the agrarian towns.

Synagogue excavations also attest the primacy of Scripture in Jewish worship and provide a clearer view of the place held by the bema, *or raised prayer platform, and the Ark of the Law. The Ark is the fixed repository for the biblical scrolls, which were stored in central place in the synagogue by the third century C.E. Until recently, the dominant view was that the Ark remained portable throughout most of antiquity.*

Some synagogue mosaics even suggest that Jewish art played an integral part in the composition of new poetry recited in the synagogue. In late Roman synagogue mosaics, themes based on the zodiac begin to appear. These mosaics are followed in the textual record by poems that name the actual constellations of the zodiac. The setting for reciting such poems, or piyyutim, *was undoubtedly the synagogue, where the intelligentsia would have gathered and included the poems in their worship.*

Finally, survey and excavation of numerous synagogue sites in the Golan Heights have revealed an astonishingly lively and vigorous Jewish community in Palestine in late Roman, Byzantine, and early Islamic times. The supposed eclipse of Jewish life at the hands of early Christendom—especially after the convention of Constantine and, later, the establishment of Christianity as the state religion in 383 C.E.— needs to be reexamined. In fact, one of the surprises of recent synagogue studies is the generally high level of Jewish culture in Palestine at the end of the Roman period (third and fourth centuries C.E.) and the continued though sporadic flourishing of synagogue sites in the Byzantine period (from the middle of the third century to 614 C.E., the year of the Persian conquest of Palestine.) All the evidence points to a picture of a Judaism in Palestine that was very much alive until the dawn of the medieval period.

by ERIC M. MEYERS *and* L.MICHAEL WHITE

Jesus in scenes from the Gospels.

More evidence of religious pluralism in the Diaspora can be seen in Rome. Excavations beneath several basilicas, such as those of St. Clement and SS. John and Paul, reveal earlier buildings-houses or apartment complexes-that were being renovated for religious use as early as the first century. The house-church of St. Clement, for example, is generally identified with the first-century levels below St. Clement's Basilica. Interestingly, the second-century house adjacent to

Palestine's Sophisticated Cities

In recent decades, a number of important cities besides Jerusalem have undergone major excavation, yielding evidence of a sophisticated life-style in Palestine. These were Roman cities, built for the administrative infrastructure of imperial rule, but they also became conduits through which Greco-Roman culture was introduced into Palestine.

These cities dominated Palestine, except for the Upper Galilee and Golan regions in the North, but the level of sophistication dropped steeply when one moved away from these urban cores. In the surrounding areas, the older agrarian life-style was still very much dominant, and it was town more than city that ultimately encompassed most of Jewish, and Jewish-Christian, life in Palestine.

Nonetheless, there were some Hellenized centers of Jewish life, mostly along the major roadways, the Lower Galilee, the Rift Valley, and the coastal plain. The primary language here was Greek, and the surrounding Jewish population used Greek for trade and day-to-day discourse. In time, Greek eclipsed Hebrew as the common language, and many of Israel's most important sages buried their loved ones, or were themselves buried, in containers or sarcophagi that bore Greek epigraphs or Greco-Roman decorations. In striking contrast, virtually no Greek is found in the Upper Galilee or the Golan.

Such tombs are exceptionally instructive. For example, the Jewish catacombs of the sages in Beth Shearim, excavated in the late 1920s, attest the high level of Greek spoken by the sages. They attest as well to the fact that the sages were comfortable with a style of decoration in their tombs that was thought by contemporary scholars to be incompatible with Jewish sensibilities and law, and with the proscription against representational and figural art contained in the Second Commandment. With the discovery in 1987 of the extraordinary Dionysos mosaic at Sepphoris, the heartland of the Jewish sages, an exciting new perspective was provided on the Hellenization of Roman Palestine.

It is not yet clear who commissioned the colorful mosaic stone carpet, found near both the Roman theater and Jewish buildings and homes, but the ramifications of the discovery are most significant. The mosaic dates to about 200 C.E., the time of Rabbi Judah the Prince, who was both a leader in the compilation of the Mishnah (Jewish traditional doctrine) and reputedly a close friend of the Roman emperor Caracalla. The central panel of the carpet shows Herakles/Dionysos in a drinking contest. The 15 panels that surround this scene depict the life and times of Dionysos, god of wine, the afterlife, revelry, fertility, and theater. What is so amazing is that they are all labeled in Greek, either to clarify the contents for those who didn't know Greek mythology—a gap in knowledge probably not uncommon in these eastern provinces—or to jog the memory of those who ate in the hall in which the stone carpet was located.

The implication of this discovery are many, but the three most important may be summarized as follows: the extent of Hellenization in Palestine by the third century C.E. is greater than was previously believed; Jews were more accepting of great pagan centers than was previously believed, and had more access to them; Jewish familiarity with Hellenistic culture in urban centers such as Sepphoris was a positive force afflicting Jewish creativity. It hardly seems coincidental that the Mishnah was codified and published at Sepphoris during the very same period when a highly visible Hellenistic culture and presence flourished in Palestine.

by ERIC M. MEYERS and L. MICHAEL WHITE

the house-church of St. Clement was used as a Mithraic cult sanctuary. Seven such Mithraic halls are known from Rome, and another 14 from the nearby port of Ostia. In addition, inscriptions from Jewish catacombs suggest at least 11 synagogues existed in Rome during imperial times.

The complex society that sustained such pluralism is now the focus of much research. A new group of biblical archaeologists, using what they refer to as a "social history" approach, are attempting to bring biblical texts and archaeological evidence into a more cohesive historical framework. The basis of their work is the use of archaeological evidence not merely as proof or illustration but as a key to the historical and social context of religion. In the Hellenized Roman cities of Palestine, such as Sepphorism, and in major urban centers of the Diaspora, such as Corinth, the activities of Jews and Christians must be seen as part of a complex culture and viewed over several centuries of development.

For example, textual evidence shows the existence of a Jewish community at Sardis in Roman Lydia (western Turkey) since the time of Julius Caesar; however, the first significant archaeological evidence of its activities comes hundreds of years later with the renovation of a public hall, part of the bath-gymnasium complex, to serve as a synagogue. Thus we know that Jews and Christians were both in Sardis for a long time, but apparently with no distinctions by which we can recognize their daily activities. The synagogue was in use from the third century to the sixth century, and its size and opulence attest to the vitality of Jewish life in Sardis. The synagogue was renovated by Jews at least twice after its initial adaptation, and these renovations were extensive and costly. Moreover, its inscriptions give evidence of the social standing and connections of the Jewish community; a total of 12 known donors to the renovations are titled "citizen" or "city councilor," and in some cases both. Other notables, including several Roman bureaucrats, are also named in the roster of donors. Here the archaeological record yields a picture of a Jewish community, over several centuries, that was politically favored and socially "at home" in the civic life of Sardis. To understand the life of the Jews of Sardis, however, one must place them not only in the context of their city but also ask how their local conditions compare to other Jewish groups from the Diaspora.

This same social history approach may be applied to Christian groups as well. At stake are a number of traditional assumptions about Judaism and Christianity in relation to their social and religious environment. It would seem that Jews and Christians were able to live in much closer harmony both with one another and with their pagan neighbors than has often been assumed. To an outsider, both church and synagogue might have resembled foreign social clubs or household cults.

The mobility within the Diaspora produced cultural as well as theological diversity, even within the Jewish and Christian traditions. We should not assume that the Diaspora synagogue communities conformed to Talmudic Judaism. A good case in point in seen in recent archaeological evidence, especially from inscriptions, for active participation and even leadership by women in Diaspora synagogues—something also seen in the

Israel's Oldest Synagogue

Remains of the oldest known synagogue in Israel, dating to between 75 and 50 B.C., have been found a mile southwest of Jericho near the ruins of a winter palace built by the Hasmonean monarchy that ruled Israel shortly before the Roman conquest. The find gives scholars a clearer idea of the appearance and function of early synagogues, says Ehud Netzer of the Hebrew University of Jerusalem's Institute of Archaeology. Netzer identified the building as a synagogue because its design and proximity to a water source matched literary accounts of early temples.

The synagogue was housed in a stone and mud-brick building that included a ritual bathing area, a small courtyard flanked by seven or eight rooms, and a rectangular main hall measuring 53 by 37 feet. A colonnade, on a platform nearly two feet above the nave, surrounded the hall. The platform provided seating for nearly 70 people; a congregation member is believed to have read from the Torah in the cen-

ter of the hall. In the northeastern corner, Netzer found a niche with an upper compartment (now mostly destroyed) that may have held Torah scrolls. A lower compartment, mostly intact, possibly functioned as a genizah, where old or unused scrolls were stored. Adjacent to the west side of the main hall was a room that functioned as a triclinium, or banqueting hall, for ceremonial meals and a triangular space most likely used as a kitchen. The triclinium was added to the synagogue hall some years later. Diners reclined on benches against three walls of the chamber while eating. The walls and some of the floors were covered with white plaster.

The synagogue and nearby winter palace were destroyed by an earthquake in 31 B.C. Herod, the Roman client king of Judea, built another palace atop these ruins in the latter part of the first century B.C. The synagogue does not appear to have been rebuilt.

by SPENCER P. M. HARRINGTON

---

homeland. This could eventually shed light on the significant role of women in Paul's churches. To date, however, the main information comes from the New Testament writings, which give evidence of women as house— church patrons, as in Romans 16:2-5.

There are numerous ways in which Jews and Christians of the Diaspora were influenced by their cultural environment. Especially noteworthy are conventions of letter writing drawn from the analysis of papyri, which can enhance our understanding of the

letters of Paul. Likewise, conventions of building or donation inscriptions offer a means of understanding many synagogue inscriptions, such as those at Sardis. Still more common are Jewish and Christian burial inscriptions. Both in burial inscriptions and in funerary art one finds that the earliest Jews and Christians, when one can distinguish them at all, regularly used motifs and language common in the larger pagan environment. Thus there is wide array of new and old archaeological data available for students of Judaeo-Christian antiquity. Whether it comes from East or West, whether it is inscribed with letters or decorated with figural art, it constitutes the most significant body of evidence for reconstructing the cultural context in which Jews and early Christians lived.

Of all the human sciences, archaeology is best equipped to deal with such complex matters. When strongly tied to the literary and historical disciplines, it becomes the most reliable tool for reconstructing the ancient societies in which Judaism and Christianity, orphaned from Jerusalem, found new homes.

MISSION TO ISRAEL

HOW JESUS RESPONDED TO THE
NEW ROMAN WORLD ORDER

Highlights from a paper delivered at the symposium,
"Jews and Christians in a Roman World,"
held at the University of Pennsylvania in March, 1999

by RICHARD HORSLEY

In order to deal with the historical Jesus, we need to recognize the transformative impact of Roman conquest and the new world order the Roman Empire imposed on subject people, and how those such as the Judeans and Galileans responded to their transformed life.

Generally speaking, the impact went from West to East and from city, where the rulers lived, to country, where the subject people lived. In the case of Judea and Galilee, the people were living out of the Israelite tradition, the central contents of which included stories of resistance and rebellion against foreign rulers and an ideal social order of free, independent existence for Israel in its village communities. Not surprisingly, given that tradition, the Jews proved to be the most intransigent people the Romans subjected, repeatedly resisting and rebelling against Roman imperial rule despite being conquered and punitively reconquered. Jesus belongs precisely in that tradition.

Beside his huge fortresses and the massive reconstruction of the Temple in Jerusalem, Herod sponsored the building of temples and indeed whole cities in honor of his patron, the Roman emperor Augustus. These projects, of course, were built on the backs of the Judean and Galilean peasants. The peasant producers were already paying both tithes to the Temple and priesthood and tribute to the Romans when the latter imposed Herod as king of the Jews. So Herod's demands for taxes came on top of the previous two layers of tithes and tribute. The people then saw a steady transformation of their land and capital city of Jerusalem as Herod installed a Greek administration and Roman institutions and customs that were in violation of their own sacred traditions and the Torah.

As for the scribal rabbinic elite, so also for the ordinary people, resistance under Herod's iron-fisted rule was futile and suicidal. But the minute Herod died, revolt erupted in every major district of the land, and the Romans mounted a massive expedition to reconquer Galilee and Judea. Thus,

THE MINUTE HEROD DIED, REVOLT ERUPTED IN EVERY MAJOR DISTRICT OF THE LAND

Jesus' parents' generation and his own generation as children in villages such as Nazareth suffered the slaughter or enslavement of family members, burning of their houses and goods, and the general trauma of war.

Herod Antipas, whom the Romans imposed as Tetrarch after his father's death in 4 B.C., immediately rebuilt the old fortress at Sepphoris as his capital city which he made into "the ornament of all Galilee." The new city was built in lavish Roman fashion befitting a Roman client ruler who had been raised and educated at the imperial court in Rome. In an ancient agrarian society such as Judea and Galilee, virtually the only economic base from which revenues could be drawn was agriculture. Antipas, however, had less than a quarter of the taxable village revenue base of his father Herod. How could he raise the revenues on a sustained basis year after year, decade after decade? By setting a relatively high rate of taxes on the produce of the peasants and by ruthlessly efficient tax collection, which was made easier because the cities which took the produce were in such immediate proximity to the villages from which the produce was taken at harvest time.

The impact on the Galilean peasants and their village communities of the sustained demand for high taxes from Antipas, on top of the tribute paid to Rome and whatever tithes and offerings sent to the Temple and priesthood in Jerusalem, is not difficult to deduce. Hunger. Debilitating malnutrition. And debt. Spiraling debt. If they could not feed their families after paying taxes to Antipas as well as tribute to Caesar and tithes to the Temple, they had to borrow. But villagers quickly exhausted each others' minimal margin of surplus, and had to seek loans from those who held the key to the storage silos, i.e. Antipas' officers, who had collected the crops as taxes in the first place. And the going interest rate, as we know from one of Jesus' parables, was 25% for grain and 100% for oil. Two or three bad harvests and you were sunk so deeply in debt that you either had to send a daughter or son to the creditor's household as a debt slave, or become a sharecropper on your own land. It is precisely when peasants are faced with heavy debts and potential loss of their land that they will join movements and even revolts. We can add to this picture the closely related disintegration of village communities. As peasant families exhausted each others' extra little reserves of grain or oil and sank into chronic hunger, debt, acute tensions arose between them. They were resentful of each other and at each others' throats to pay back even those little neighborly loans to feed their starving children. The Judeans and the Samaritans, unable effectively to fight back against the Roman order that oppressed them, turned

JESUS' BASIC MESSAGE, IS DIRECTED TO THE POOR, HUNGRY, AND INDEBTED

their hatred and violence against each other, which supplies the background of Jesus' parable of the Good Samaritan. So also Galilean peasants within village communities turned against each other in local conflicts and others, ashamed at the prospect of losing their family inheritance and proud membership in their Israelite village community, simply became debilitated and paralyzed.

What was Jesus' creative response? His basic message, his proclamation of the presence of the Kingdom of God is directed to the poor, hungry, and indebted. To people who may have assumed they were cursed by God because of their poverty and sickness he declared, "Blessed are the poor, for yours is the kingdom of God, Blessed are those who hunger, for they shall be filled." In its more original form, following the Lukan length but the Matthean wording: "Father: May thy kingdom come, give us today, day by day our subsistence bread. Forgive us our debts as we herewith forgive our debtors. And lead us not to the test." What is the kingdom of God about: subsistence food and freedom from debilitating indebtedness to the creditors, who were probably Antipas' officers, the wealthy and powerful based in Sepphoris and Tiberias. One of the most fundamental features of the Mosaic covenant tradition was the provision that every seventh year debts would be canceled. The kingdom for which Jesus is teaching the people to pray will involve the cancellation of debts, just as was supposed to be done following the Mosaic covenant. Note in the prayer the people, in anticipation that God is about to act on their behalf to cancel their debts, promise that they "herewith forgive" their debtors. Keep that in mind when we come to "love your enemies."

Besides preaching the kingdom of God, Jesus also manifested its presence in healings and exorcisms. The healings that were included in the gospels are probably the most typical cases for the various sicknesses and malaise that the people were suffering under the new Roman order: hemorrhaging or near death, perhaps from malnutrition (Mark 5:21–43), and paralysis, blindness, and deafness. Jesus also heals the self-blame by which people contribute to their own further debilitation. When faced with the paralyzed man, Jesus does not first say "you are healed, take up your bed and walk." He says first "your sins are forgiven," which in effect means the same thing as "you are healed." If the people feel that they are forgiven, then they are no longer blaming themselves and have energy to heal themselves. In the healings and forgiveness, Jesus thus gives the people a new lease on life.

The fundamental social forms of Israel were family and village community. Early Israel, when the ideal had been established, did not have a Temple and a monarchy. The ideal from early Israelite times was that Israel was a free, independent peasantry living in village communities, each of which ran its own internal affairs according to Mosaic covenant. It is the disintegration of these

local village communities under the impact of the new Roman order that Jesus addresses in much of his teaching, some of which is straight out of the Mosaic covenant tradition that dates back to early Israel. Listen to the social context indicated in the content of those sayings: "If someone strikes you on one cheek, turn the other." "If someone asks to borrow from you, give...." "Love your enemies, do good, and lend." Jesus is addressing cases of local social and economic interaction among villagers, not their stance toward the Romans. Jesus is addressing people who are mutually in debt to each other and for that reason and others have become resentful, edgy, spiteful, and "enemies" to one another. He is saying to them, in traditional, covenental teaching such as that found in the covenant codes of Exodus, Leviticus, and Deuteronomy, get your act together here in the village community. Quit quarreling with one another, and instead help each other out in your mutual need. Lend to each other whatever you have and do not ask it back. Jesus was renewing the traditional Mosaic covenental principle of mutuality, mutual aid in times of distress as a response to the desperate situation they had been placed in the new Roman order.

Insofar as the families and the village communities in which Israel was constituted were disintegrating, Israel as a people was disintegrating. This is not simply something we discern from our historical distance of two millennia. This is the way it appeared to many Israelites at the time, both Judeans and Galileans, the many who led or joined the Dead Sea community at Qumran, the popular messianic movements in 4 B.C. and again in A.D. 67–68, the popular prophetic movements in the A.D. 50s and 60s. All of these, popular or scribal, were movements with programs for the renewal of Israel. If we quit reading certain of Jesus' sayings with Christian supercessionist eyes, it becomes clear that this is what Jesus was up to as well. In both Mark and Q (the non-Markan speeches of Jesus used by both Matthew and Luke), Jesus commissions envoys for a mission to Israel. These speeches include instructions for the missionaries, but are not admonitions of individual discipleship as often read by pious modern Christians. The instructions have two key parts: they are to stay with individual households eating whatever the family can afford. And they are to work in villages, both preaching the kingdom and healing people. In modern-day terms, these are movement organizers, attempting to catalyze local "chapters" of the movement in the individual village communities around Galilee and beyond, from a headquarters in Capernaum.

Another saying of Jesus that indicates clearly he was spearheading a renewal of Israel is that passage mistranslated in terms of the Twelve sitting on twelve thrones "judging the tribes of Israel." That is an utter mistranslation. In the Psalms, for example, God does not "judge" the poor and the orphans and the widow; God "defends" or "delivers" them. Similarly, in Luke 22:28–30 and Matthew 19: 28, Jesus declares that the Twelve, appointed as the symbolic representatives of Israel, are to be "delivering" of "establishing justice for" the twelve tribes of Israel.

SEARCHING FOR PAUL

THE IMPACT OF ROME ON
THE EASTERN MEDITERRANEAN

Highlights from a paper delivered at the symposium,
"Jews and Christians in a Roman World,"
held at the University of Pennsylvania in March, 1999

by Susan E. Alcock

This paper is about searching, in various ways, the world of Paul, the world of the eastern Mediterranean around the turn of the millennium. Our first search employs an archaeological technique known as regional surface survey, which involves teams of people walking across the present-day landscape, staring at their feet or to put it a bit more formally, literally surveying for any traces of past cultural activity. Contrary to popular opinion, there is actually quite a bit to find out there on the ground. This material is all counted up, recorded, mapped and, if more information can be gained, collected for further study. The basic object of the whole enterprise is to reconstruct past human activity in a particular region, where people lived and where they farmed their fields, where they worshiped their gods and buried their dead. When we map our results, we generate period-by-period views of the same region. What must be remembered is that mapped here, however indirectly and however crudely, are the patterns of people's lives. Remember that and any change in our regional "snap-shots" from one period to the next takes on a great deal of significance.

To archaeologists of the end of the twentieth century, one of the great appeals of regional survey is that it allows us to approach what the late Eric Wolf called "the people without history." People dwelling and farming in these countrysides are not the ones that make the history books; they show up occasionally in minor arts, but are rarely recorded or heard from in any formal sense. But these silent populations are the majority of those people who would ultimately listen (or not listen) to the disciples of the disciple Paul.

So, what changes in human landscapes do we see around the "time of Paul" (or in survey terms, the centuries around the turn of the millennium)? Here, writing about the Roman province of Achaia (Greece) where the most intensive survey work has been done. To make a long story short, that epoch witnesses one of the most radical alterations ever observed in Greek settlement patterns, a depopulation of the countryside. You could describe it most simply as an "emptying out."

How do we interpret this? Surveyors' first impulse was to assume the obvious, and the worst—that everyone died when the Romans showed up. And there is some good contemporary lamenting literature to back it up. Other takers? Very likely there was a change in land owning patterns, with the rich getting richer. In survey terms we can monitor this by observing the appearance of fancy tombs and rich villas in the Greek landscape. Such things stand out as markers of the big estates that probably pushed some of the "little people" out of the countryside. Pushed them out—and pushed them on. I think we have to look at our survey patterns and think about people on the move, on the move to cities.

We can monitor one other major development over this time period. In the second century A.D., the traveler Pausanias tromped all over Greece, and on his way sometimes refers to sanctuaries and shrines as "in ruins." Archaeological work, both survey and excavation, does suggest that this same early imperial period was again a watershed time for change. Let me give you just one survey example: a little rural shrine found in the Nemea Valley in the northwestern Peloponnese was used well into the Hellenistic period, then snuffs out at about the same time horizon as the loss of rural settlement. Without getting carried away, there does appear to be some correlation between human and divine abandonment of the Greek countryside; we see disruption in both spheres.

Now let's follow those people I've argued were displaced from the countryside and let's turn our attention to the cities of the eastern Mediterranean. Major centers such as Ephesus or Athens have long been explored through architectural study of often impressive standing remains or through long-term excavation. Less recognized perhaps is that this world of cities was also a world of change and of flux, also adapting to the new global framework established by Rome. Or trying to adapt, for some cities do die at this time blown out of the water by Roman foundations. In Greece, for example, we get the new city Nikopolis (literally "Victory City," near the site of Actium) and colonies at Patras and at Corinth. These had a negative impact on nearby pre-existing cities. Land and natural resources were reassigned; population and even cult statues left their home towns and moved to new and Roman-backed cities. So some cities fail, or turn into villages, and this all adds to the number of people on the move.

If you look at the eastern cities as measured by size and wealth (relying on archaeological work, numismatics, textual sources), you find that there are a few very large, dominant centers and lots of much much smaller cities (and you don't find much in between). In other words, the Roman east saw the rise of super cities very influential, busy, cosmopolitan, and populous places, places sucking in those people on the move. Included among these few super cities are places familiar from the Pauline itinerary: Corinth, Athens, Ephesus, and ultimately the super-city to end all super-cities, the black hole of Rome itself.

If you put together the results of our first two searches into the countryside, into the cities you see two common elements emerging. First, that the eastern Mediterranean world of Paul was a world in a state of great transformation, even dislocation, from previous patterns of life, with people on the move, on the hop. And second, that the presence and interventions of Rome are everywhere implicit in these changes. As my students like to ask, so what? Well, it is a very big "so what" going on here. These developments can be linked directly to conditions of Paul's mission and reception. In part, there is the fact that he could travel easily and reach wide audiences in super-sized cities. But more than that, the disruption we see, this interference in eastern landscapes and communities, would have shaken people out of traditional social frameworks and would have contributed to the creation of an audience arguably more responsive to new messages and new ways of thinking about their altered world.

I would argue that the dislocation we've been observing the movement, change in

> MANY FACTORS HAVE BEEN ADVANCED TO EXPLAIN CHRISTIANITY'S EXPANSION ACROSS THE EASTERN EMPIRE

settlement patterns, loss of cult places, urban variation all this didn't just "soften up" people so they might consider new ideas. These changes would actively have worked to undercut and displace long-standing memories and long-standing identities; not the least of which was the powerful heritage of pagan Hellenism. Many factors have been advanced to explain Christianity's expansion across the eastern Empire: but we might now need to add another: and that is a failure, or a breakdown, in shared social memory. Simon Swain, author of *Hellenism and Empire*, has remarked: "We should at least note in the Greek world the likely appeal of a very different set of priorities and paradigms to those who had no secure or direct interest in the Greek past and who were excluded from its benefits." And he identifies Christianity as one form of these new "priorities and paradigms" made possible by the slackening hold of one particular version of the Greek past upon a new and as we've seen very different present.

This rejection of the classical heritage shouldn't be overstated. Christianity and its institutions were built firmly on a classical base, and there were many individuals such as Bishop Synesius of Cyrene who, in the late fourth century A.D., was still boasting how his family tree went back to Sparta. But there seems no denying that new forms of social memory evolved, invested in new monuments (such as churches or martyria) or in new ways of dividing up the world (such as the distribution of bishoprics). Even when old and venerated pagan buildings were adopted and "converted," it was no simple matter of continuity. The most famous case is probably the Parthenon, turned to the worship of the Virgin in the fourth or fifth century A.D., and later becoming a mosque. According to some authors nothing really changes here, Athena equals the Virgin, and so on. That's not so: the building was much reworked (given an apse for starters), its external decorations often took a beating (a literal beating!) unless the images could be interpreted in appropriate ways. The most famous example of this is the metope at the Parthenon's northwestern corner, which was read in Christian terms as the Annunciation, and thus spared. The Parthenon now was not the same building as its classical incarnation; it conjured up different associations and meanings; it integrated its community in a different way from its pagan predecessor. All of this involved a reconfiguration of social memory, of what identified these people, gave them a sense of their past, and defined their aspirations. This reconfiguration, and these new "priorities and paradigms" can be traced back, at least in part, to the radical social transformation of the east around the time of Paul.

SAVING A FABLED SANCTUARY

CONSERVATORS STRUGGLE TO RESTORE JUSTINIAN'S GREAT CHURCH IN ISTANBUL

by Şengül Aydingün *and* Mark Rose

From the top of the scaffolding in the immense dome, rising 185 feet above the marble floor, one sees the golden mosaics up close, and the beautiful nineteenth-century calligraphy spelling out a passage from the Koran, beginning: "The inherent light illuminates earth and sky." This is Hagia Sophia, for over nine centuries the principal church of the Byzantine Empire, and for nearly five centuries the principal Ottoman mosque. Gazing down to the floor and then up, the eye catches walls veneered with colored marble, massive monolithic columns of green and purple stone, and then the mosaics: angels, the Archangel Gabriel, and the infant Jesus on the lap of the Virgin Mary in the apse. Above all is the golden dome, which a sixth-century poet described as "formed of gilded tesserae set together, from which pour golden rays in an abundant stream striking men's eyes with irresistible force."

Hagia Sophia's mosaics were also admired by Sultan Abdülmecid in the nineteenth century. He gazed for a long time at the mosaics of Jesus and Mary, then commented, "They are all very beautiful, but for the time it is not appropriate to leave them visible. Clean them and cover them over again carefully, so that they may survive until they are revealed to view in the future." Gaspare and Giuseppe Fossati, the sultan's Swiss architects, completed the necessary structural repairs to the building, and by 1849 Hagia Sophia's exquisite mosaics were covered by fresh plaster painted with Gaspare's hybrid Ottoman-Byzantine motifs.

The sultan's order was in keeping with the sensibilities of his times, but times change. In 1934, Mustafa Kemal Atatürk, founder of the modern Turkish republic, signed an order making a museum of Hagia Sophia, which had served as a mosque for nearly five centuries. It was Atatürk's belief that the mosaics should be revealed, and the work was entrusted to Thomas Whittemore and the Byzantine Institute of America, which he directed. In a letter to his former teacher, Henri Matisse, Whittemore wrote, "My Dear Master, the fourth year of my work uncovering and cleaning the mosaics in Hagia Sophia in Istanbul is now over. Peerless examples of Byzantine art have been preserved in this great church for a thousand years."

TRAPPED IN THE HIPPODROME, SOME 30,000 OF THE REBELS WERE SLAUGHTERED

Today, conservators on the scaffolding are busily examining the tesserae, the small cubes making up the mosaic, each one cut from a layer of glass on which leaves of gold or silver were placed, covered by a thin piece of clear glass, then fused together in a kiln. They are checking each of the millions of tesserae, cleaning and consolidating them. This, the most recent of many efforts to restore and preserve Hagia Sophia, began in 1992. According to Seracettin Sahin, director of the Hagia Sophia Museum, the scaffolding will be moved to the dome's southeast quarter, and by the end of 2004, work there will be completed.

Honoring not a Saint Sophia, but Christ as the Holy Wisdom (Hagia Sophia) of God, this is the third church to be built here. The first was completed by Constantius, son of Constantine the Great, in 360. Burned down in 404, it was replaced by a church opened by Theodosius II in 415. There's no evidence to suggest the first two churches were anything more than conventional Roman basilicas: long rectangular naves with side aisles and pitched roofs built on wooden trusses.

The opportunity for something exceptional to be built at the site came in 532, when the Blues and the Greens, rival chariot-racing factions, united in a general rebellion against the emperor Justinian. Once enough loyal troops had been assembled, Justinian sent them against the mob.

Trapped in the hippodrome, some 30,000 of the rebels were slaughtered, but Theodosius' church had been destroyed by fire on the first day of the uprising.

Justinian had to reassert his authority, not just as emperor—the slaughter had done that—but as a ruler with the stamp of divine authority. On February 23, 532, scarcely a month after the end of the revolt, Justinian began work on the third church, Hagia Sophia. The heavenly inspiration and approval of the emperor and his work is clear in the words of the historian Procopius, who witnessed its construction firsthand:

> The emperor, thinking not of cost of any kind, pressed on the work, and collected together workmen from every land. Anthemius of Tralles, the most skilled in the builder's art, not only of his own but of all former times, carried forward the king's zealous intentions, organized the labors of the workmen, and prepared models of the future construction. Associated with him was another architect named Isidorus, a Milesian by birth, a man of intelligence, and worthy to carry out the plans of the emperor Justinian. It is indeed a proof of the esteem with which God regarded the emperor, that he furnished him with men who would be so useful in effecting his designs, and we are compelled to admire the wisdom of the emperor, in being able to choose the most suitable of mankind to execute the noblest of his works....

Anthemius and Isidorus' design for the new church was revolutionary. It would be roofed with a great central dome supported by arches springing from four massive pillars. Additional pillars would carry half or semidomes on the east and west, forming a vast open area 245 feet by 230 feet. The building's scale would be unprecedented and its interior decoration lavish and costly. In an incredibly short time, less than six years, the building was finished. Procopius described it in terms of astonishment:

> [The Church] is distinguished by indescribable beauty, excelling both in its size, and in the harmony of its measures, having no part excessive and none deficient; being more magnificent than ordinary buildings, and much more elegant than those which are not of so just a proportion. The church is singularly full of light and sunshine; you would declare that the place is not lighted by the sun from without, but that the rays are produced within itself.... A spherical-shaped dome...makes it exceedingly beautiful; from the lightness of the building, it does not appear to rest upon a solid foundation, but to cover the place beneath as though it were suspended from heaven by the fabled golden chain. All these parts surprisingly joined to one another in the air, suspended one from another, and resting only on that which is next to them, form the work into one admirably harmonious whole, which spectators do not dwell upon for long in the mass, as each individual part attracts the eye to itself...

Justinian's pride in Hagia Sophia and his central role in its building were canonized in legend. One later account claims that on December 27, 537, the day Hagia Sophia was consecrated, Justinian exclaimed, "Glory to God who has thought me worthy to finish this work. Solomon I have outdone you." The divine inspiration of the church was suggested in another story. During construction, the emperor was said to have dreamed that he saw an old man in green robes holding a silver plaque with the plan of a temple engraved on it, and "the old man turned to Justinian and said, 'The time has come and I have brought it. This is Hagia Sophia, whose plan has been waiting so long on the Plaque of Destiny.' 'What is Hagia Sophia, old man?' Justinian asked. 'Hagia Sophia is the house of God whose name has been etched since the beginning of time.'"

Divinely orchestrated or not, for the next thousand years, Hagia Sophia would be the world's largest church. As late as 1950, its dome had been surpassed by only three others. It is "one of the greatest architectural achievements of all time," says historian Rowland Mainstone, "and no other has been so influential."

Fourteen centuries after Hagia Sophia was built, Mainstone headed a UNESCO mission inspecting the condition of the church and its mosaics. In the 1993 report he authored, Mainstone noted that the Fossatis' nineteenth-century painted plaster decoration was badly discolored by moisture in most of the vaults and in places had fallen altogether. Water came in through the poorly maintained lead roofing and windows, water condensed from the air on the cooler walls in early summer, and there was rising damp from the foundation level. The mosaics were once much more extensive, said Mainstone, noting that depictions of the Baptism and Pentecost in side galleries recorded in early descriptions were now gone. "But the loss of so much of the figural mosaic cannot be blamed on Muslim religious zeal," he concluded, "but must be attributed chiefly to loosening of the plaster setting beds as a result of water seepage, earthquakes, and long-term structural movements." Too long neglected, Hagia Sophia was overdue for an overhaul. Mainstone's report called for repair of the roof and windows, conservation of the mosaics, and cleaning of the marble facings on the walls.

Because of Hagia Sophia's long and complex history, no conservation or restoration project is simple. There were difficulties during its construction from the start. Procopius records the main eastern arch nearly collapsing in one instance, and columns in the clerestories so overloaded with weight that they began shedding flakes of stone. Then, on May 7, 558, the central part of the eastern main arch collapsed, taking with it part of the dome and semidome on that side. Hagia Sophia was simply built too quickly. The slow-drying lime mortar used in the massive pillars did not have time to fully set before the immense weight of the dome was placed on them. The dome's low curvature sent pressure not straight down the pillars but outward, deforming the pillars and tilting back four massive buttresses on the sides of the church. A series of earthquakes hit Hagia Sophia from 542 to 557, opening cracks that masons were repairing when the arch gave way. Justinian entrusted the repair of the church to Isidorus the Younger (nephew of the deceased elder), who erected a loftier dome with a higher curve that reduced the lateral stresses caused by the shallower original dome. The repairs took two-thirds the time of original construction, but finally, on December 24, 563, Hagia Sophia was reconsecrated.

Despite the improvements made by Isidorus the Younger, earthquakes in the ninth and tenth centuries brought down the western arch and one-third of the dome in 989. The emperor Basil II's Armenian architect, Trdat, made major repairs, and Hagia Sophia was reopened in 996. Following major earthquakes in 1343 and 1344, the eastern main arch gave way in 1346, along with the eastern semidome and part of the main dome on that side. Reconstruction was completed nine years later, but by then the Byzantine Empire was in terminal decline.

The last Christian liturgy was performed in the church the evening of May 28, 1453. The city fell the next morning to the army of the Ottoman ruler Mehmet II, who ordered the immediate conversion of Hagia Sophia into a mosque. A mihrab (a niche indicating the direction toward Mecca) and mimber (pulpit) were installed and a wooden minaret was added to the southwest corner of the structure (later rebuilt in brick by Mehmet's successor). In the late sixteenth century, Sinan, the great Ottoman architect, made repairs to the fabric of the building and added the three stone minarets. The last renovations before the Fossatis' were in the first decades of the nineteenth century. And the mosaics? They remained uncovered for some time following the conquest of Constantinople, despite the conversion of the church into a mosque. Only gradually, in 1603, during the reign of Ahmet III, and in the reign of Mahmud I (1730-1754) were they plastered over.

The Fossati brothers' restoration of the interior of Hagia Sophia in 1847 through 1849 was a marvel in terms of speed. Though their methods and work—covering over the mosaics with plaster and concocted painted designs—would never be condoned today, their efforts did preserve the mosaics. Their extensive use of iron reinforcements and pins to consolidate areas of mosaic that had pulled away from the dome was successful, the hand-forged iron being resistant to rust. Less careful was the work from 1894 to about 1909, when Hagia Sophia was administered by the General Directorate of Pious Foundations, which oversaw mosques.

A SERIES OF EARTHQUAKES HIT HAGIA SOPHIA FROM 542 TO 55

More successful was the work uncovering and restoring the mosaics begun by the Byzantine Institute in 1931, just eight years after the establishment of the Turkish republic.

In 1985, Hagia Sophia was added to UNESCO's World Heritage list as part of the Historic Areas of Istanbul (the part of the city within the Byzantine fortification walls built by the emperor Theodosius). The international effort to restore dome mosaics began in 1992. Funding has come primarily from the Turkish government, with outside contributions from UNESCO and the World Monuments Fund amounting to about $700,000. The northeast quarter of the dome was treated first, followed by the northwest quarter, which was completed in December 2002. Now the scaffolding is in the southwest quarter.

Revza Ozil of Turkey's Central Laboratory for Restoration and Conservation in Istanbul was a key figure through much of the conservation work on the dome. Ozil estimates that about 53 percent of the original mosaics (from the sixth century or the rebuildings of the tenth and fourteenth centuries) are still present. Some 15 percent of the surface is covered by the mid-nineteenth-century Fossati restoration and another 29 percent from the restoration work of the Pious Foundation at the beginning of the twentieth century. In both of these cases the repaired areas are a plaster surface painted to resemble the Byzantine mosaics.

Problems in the dome range from individual pieces of mosaic being loose or missing to whole areas where the mortar bearing the mosaic has separated from its masonry support. The various rebuildings and earlier restorations have left a legacy of problems, such as numerous metal nails and clamps at the juncture of sixth- and fourteenth-century mosaics, and extensive painting over original mosaic. "The area by the windows near the base of the dome is worst," says Ozil. "The glass was broken sometimes, so wind and rain got in. Humidity and salts have affected arches, so the area to around ten feet above the windows is all very deteriorated."

Much of the restoration work is small scale, the patient cleaning of old varnish applied by the Fossatis or the reattachment of outer glass layers on the gold and silver compound tesserae. In places, mortar is injected behind the mosaic where it has separated from its brick support or is cracking or beginning to disintegrate. While priority is given to the Byzantine mosaics, the Fossati restoration is also treated, and is removed only if there is a compelling reason to do so. After 150 years, it has become part of the building's history, explains Ozil.

The Ottoman calligraphy in the center of the dome, executed in the mid-nineteenth century by Mustafa Izzet Effendi, was also in need of treatment. Powdery areas of the gilding had to be consolidated and badly flaking paint needed to be reaffixed to the surface. And what is beneath the calligraphy? The original sixth-century cross mosaic was later replaced by one of Christ Pantokrator (the ruler of all), as often appears in Byzantine churches. But Ozil is doubtful that any mosaic remains here. "In the center of the dome, in the calligraphy area, in the northeast quarter there were a lot of problems, many iron nails in the mortar," she recalls. "They were rusted and had affected the mortar around them, so we took away maybe 200 nails, and we looked inside and we found sixth-century mortar, but no tesserae."

Restoration of the dome mosaics is only one step in preserving Hagia Sophia. The northern and southern walls below the dome need to be conserved. Mosaics of saints on the bottom of the eastern arch that the Fossatis covered are now partially exposed, not through any restoration effort but simply because humidity and penetration by salts is causing the Fossati plaster to flake off. New plaster in the upper galleries is flaking off. "All these things should be cleaned and consolidated," says Ozil. "These recent plasters should be taken down, and if no mosaic exists beneath them, proper plastering should be done." And, she notes, all of the mosaics exposed and cleaned by the Byzantine Institute in the 1930s through the 1950s need to be reexamined, from the Virgin Mary in the apse to the mosaic at the entrance showing Justinian presenting a model of Hagia Sophia to the infant Jesus.

On the north side of Hagia Sophia, Metin Ahunbay of Istanbul Technical University's Faculty of Architecture is supervising work on the exterior, where cement plastering is being stripped away, revealing the brickwork and greenstone from the original structure and later additions. Half a dozen architecture students are kept busy recording the walls, while workmen make needed repairs and repoint the masonry with a lime-based mortar that matches the original. The work is time consuming, says Ahunbay. It took one year to record the area currently being treated, and it will be three years in all to finish the project. And beyond Hagia Sophia itself, there are Byzantine structures that were part of the church, such as its baptistry and adjacent tombs of Ottoman sultans that require attention.

And the work at Hagia Sophia must be placed in the larger context of restoration in Istanbul. Zeynep Ahunbay, an architecture professor at Istanbul University and long involved in efforts at Hagia Sophia, directs the work at Zeyrek Mosque with Robert Ousterhout of the University of Illinois. The converted twelfth-century Church of the Pantokrator, Zeyrek is much smaller than Hagia Sophia but shares many of the same difficulties. Funding is problematic. Simply put, there are too many worthy projects and too little money. Zeyrek has been fortunate, receiving support from the city of Istanbul, UNESCO, the World Monuments Fund, the University of Illinois, and private donors. Even so, the funds have amounted to only a fraction of the $3 million that Ahunbay estimates it would take to complete the job. How funds are administered can create problems. If they are granted for projects before the necessary background studies are completed, it may mean determining what conservation treatments are required as you go along rather than studying the situation first. Regulations may mandate selection of a contractor who bids the lowest but may lack the necessary expertise or simply doesn't care about the work. Ahunbay also points out that restoration in Istanbul is not limited to its Byzantine and early Ottoman structures. Near the Süleymaniye Mosque and in the area around Zeyrek, for example, are neighborhoods of traditional nineteenth-century wooden houses, most of which have been demolished or burned down elsewhere in the city. There's much historic preservation work in Istanbul that ought to be done, as in any major city, but there are few full-time positions for restorers.

What are the prospects for Hagia Sophia as it approaches its first century as a museum open to all? The current work is encouraging, but it is far from comprehensive. Future restoration, no less essential than that of the dome, will have to face competing claims for funding, and priorities may shift with political and bureaucratic changes. In 1993, Mainstone and UNESCO supported a Turkish suggestion that a single entity responsible for Hagia Sophia be established, noting that the head of such an organization "should be able to command considerable authority." But that has not happened. "There should be a special team only for the conservation of Hagia Sophia," says Ozil. "It needs continuous maintenance from a team, a small nucleus of two or three people, dealing with the maintenance of the building, the mosaics, the marble slabs that I know are ready to fall. The lead sheathing on the roof should be examined regularly, every week or fifteen days." Such steps would help ensure that Hagia Sophia continues to receive the attention it deserves.

William Emerson, dean of MIT's School of Architecture, and Robert Van Nice, who spent many years studying and documenting Hagia Sophia, wrote in the conclusion of their 1951 articles about it in *Archaeology* that "this unique architectural achievement of the sixth century may well, with careful and continuous maintenance, stand for another fourteen hundred years." Half a century later, those words still apply, both as a caution that the preservation of this monument must be an ongoing effort and as an optimistic prediction that, if it is cared for, it will not fall.

PART IV:

THE HOLY LAND TODAY

A FIGHT OVER SACRED TURF

EVEN TODAY, THE CULTURAL CHASM BETWEEN JEWS, MUSLIMS, AND CHRISTIANS OBSCURES WHO IS TRULY IN CONTROL OF JERUSALEM'S HOLIEST SHRINE

by SANDRA SCHAM

Anewly opened Israeli museum in the shadow of the hilltop known to Jews as the Temple Mount, and to Muslims as the Haram al-Sharif (Noble Sanctuary), aptly symbolizes the histori-cal relationship between Israelis and Palestinians over that site. The museum is designed to give tourists the experience of being on the Mount during the time of Herod—the glory days of the Jewish Temple. The exhibits show the Israeli concept of the Temple Mount-Haram al-Sharif site, devoid of the Dome of the Rock and Al-Aqsa Mosque, both built by the Umayyad Muslims in the seventh century A.D. Only the newest of many such reconstructions in Jerusalem, they would hardly be noteworthy were it not for the fact that the museum was constructed within the walls of an Umayyad palace. The age-old impulse to build on, and to some extent obscure, the remains of a past culture is still very much at work in this region.

In a way, the joint U.S.-Israeli proposal put forward at Camp David last year that the hill could be "horizontally divided" between Israelis and Palestinians, with Palestinians controlling what is above the surface and

Israelis what is below, makes historical sense given the nature of the site. It was, however, a major factor in the disintegration of the peace talks, according to negotiators on both sides. One Palestinian spokesman and his colleagues were "stunned" by this scheme since, as they put it, no Israeli government had ever brought up such a thing before. In discussing the failure of the Camp David negotiations before an Israeli audience in Jerusalem several months ago, former U.S. Ambassador to Israel Martin Indyk confirmed this. He told his incredulous listeners that the breakdown occurred because Israelis had not realized that Yasser Arafat could not negotiate anything short of absolute Muslim sovereignty over the Haram al-Sharif, and Palestinians had not realized that Israelis were deeply attached to the site.

Indyk's comments and the spirit in which they were received only highlights how little the Israelis and Palestinians comprehend each other's beliefs and ideas regarding this place. Almost as soon as the Israeli flag was hoisted over the site in 1967, at the conclusion of the Six-Day War, Israelis lowered it on the orders of General Moshe Dayan, and invested the Muslim Waqf (religious trust) with the authority to manage the Temple Mount-Haram al-Sharif in order to "keep the peace." In the 30 or so years that have elapsed since then, the Waqf has remained relatively independent of Israeli control.

Because of this informal understanding between Israel and the Waqf, Muslims have assumed that Israelis don't care very much about the place and their current interest is just another excuse to cheat Palestinians out

of what is rightfully theirs. After all, the Haram al-Sharif, revered as the site of Mohammed's ascension to heaven, is one of the three holiest places in Islam (the other two being Mecca and Medina); Muslims would never simply "give" control of it to the followers of another religion. Nevertheless, the Temple Mount is Judaism's holiest site-so holy that many religious Jews will not set foot on the hill, lest they inadvertently tread on sacred and forbidden ground. Equally important, it is a site of great national significance. In the eyes of many Israelis, the "return to Zion" that Jews living in Israel believe they have effected was completed by the capture of the Temple Mount.

The cultural chasm that exists between Jews and Muslims over the site is not simply played out on the political level. Social conversations with Israelis and Palestinians on this subject demonstrate it as well. Among friends, a liberal academic, who is not religious, recently reiterated what is a commonplace sentiment in Israel-that the Temple Mount is "far more important to Jews than to Muslims." Noting that the site is mentioned in the Jewish Bible hundreds of times, he stated that he, himself, was "willing to fight and die for" Israel's sovereignty over the embattled property.

Palestinians, on the other hand, while insisting on the primacy of their claims, will often downplay the extent to which they need the site for political as well as religious reasons. They need it for the prestige it would lend their fledgling state. They need it because it establishes a vital connection between the Palestinian Muslims and their co-religionists elsewhere in the Middle East. Most of all, they need it for the same reason

A rally in Jerusalem is watched over by an Israeli soldier wielding a rifle.

question what they believed to be a well-intentioned effort to confront and solve the most difficult issues in Israeli-Palestinian relations as part of a comprehensive settlement. What he meant was that any change in the status quo of Israeli secular sovereignty-Muslim sacred sovereignty that didn't hand the site over completely to Muslims would be perceived as a loss throughout the Arab world. In his estimation, it would have been better to have not discussed it during the negotiations at all.

Against this backdrop of historical conflict, with hidden and not-so-hidden agendas, an archaeological drama has been unfolding. It incorporates many of the issues involved in the current battle over the Temple Mount-Haram al-Sharif. The seemingly mundane construction of an exit and stairway at the site, initiated by the Waqf, has become a reminder of the battle for control there. Some archaeologists and other prominent Israelis, including well-known Jerusalem archaeologists Gaby Barkai and Eilat Mazar, as well as author Amos Oz and former Jerusalem mayor Teddy Kollek, have styled themselves as the Committee to Prevent the Destruction of Antiquities on the Temple Mount (CPDATM), and vowed to stop this building program.

Begun in 1999 and now almost complete, this construction project possibly represents the most substantial alteration that the area has undergone in some time. It includes a new path to the Al-Aqsa Mosque, a recently renovated prayer hall in the area known as "Solomon's Stables" (now the Al-Marwani Mosque), a staircase leading from the top of the Haram platform to the

that Israelis do—because it represents an important link with their past and their history in the land, and also because it represents a religious and historical affirmation of their right to be there.

A week before the current intifada, a Palestinian archaeologist told a mixed dinner group of Palestinian and Israeli friends that former prime minister Ehud Barak was "stupid" for bringing up the question of Jerusalem and the Temple Mount-Haram al-Sharif at Camp David. The Israelis present were somewhat shocked to hear him

Al-Marwani Mosque beneath it, and possibly a renovation of certain underground portions of the existing Al-Aqsa Mosque. "Solomon's Stables," like many such sites in the Holy Land, has nothing to do with its namesake. Primarily an Umayyad (seventh and eighth centuries A.D.) building, this pillared "hall" was reconstructed from earlier, possibly Herodian, remains. It was used as a stable by the Crusaders, subsequently destroyed by an earthquake and rebuilt again. The gates to this space have been blocked since the Mamluk period (thirteenth–sixteenth centuries A.D.). Access from the platform was via a long narrow tunnel which, in the event of an emergency crowd control situation (unfortunately, not an unusual occurrence there), was very dangerous.

Because the Waqf has a certain amount of independence from the Israeli bureaucracy, it has found it necessary only to deal "unofficially" with the Israeli police over security matters. The police gave permission, for safety reasons, for the construction of a new entrance and exit. Israeli protesters, however, are less concerned with the construction than with the earth removed to make way for it. Many Israelis believe that major portions of Herod's Temple and perhaps even the Temple of Solomon are beneath the surface of the Haram, and are irate over what they see as unnecessary destruction of important archaeological strata.

EVIDENCE RELATING TO WHAT WAS ON TOP OF THE HILL FOR PERIODS BEFORE THE UMAYYAD IS SCANT

There is every reason to suppose that there are archaeological remains beneath the surface of the Haram, but evidence relating to what was on top of the hill for periods before the Umayyad is scant, although substantial archaeological work done in its vicinity has revealed evidence of Bronze and Iron Age occupations. Various earlier structures, in addition to the Kotel or Western ("Wailing") Wall, which is believed to be a retaining wall for Herod's Temple, surround the Haram.

"It is an archaeological site but, before that, it's a holy site," says Yussuf Natsheh, archaeologist for the Al-Qaf Admininstration, the Waqf's managerial arm. Its purpose "is to fulfill the spiritual needs of Muslims and prayer... The conclusion was reached that this was not a safe place... We removed the earth after doing an investigation, after doing some documentation." Notwithstanding this, CPDATM member Barkai characterizes the work as an "archaeological tragedy... I say it not because I am Jewish but because I think it should be important to any civilized person in the world—and to Muslims."

Natsheh and Barkai do not disagree on the site's basic nature. Both recognize that it is still in use as a place of prayer by one of the religions that revere it, but they part company in what they consider to be archaeologically significant. Natsheh justifiably sees his mission as supporting and

Jerusalem's Temple Mount Flap

Construction of an emergency exit at a mosque within Jerusalem's Temple Mount has sparked a fierce controversy between archaeologists, the Israel Antiquities Authority, and the government.

Israeli police originally urged the Waqf, the Muslim religious trust that oversees public works in the religious complex, to construct the exit in the Marwani Mosque last fall. The mosque is located inside the superstructure that supports the southeast corner of the Temple Mount, an enormous stone platform built by Herod the Great (73–4 B.C.) and known by Arabs as the al-Haram al-Sharif, or Noble Sanctuary. Islam's third holiest shrine, the al-Aqsa mosque, is located atop the Temple Mount. Somewhere beneath the mosque lie the remains of the Jewish Second Temple, destroyed by the Romans in A.D. 70. Part of the western wall of the Second Temple is incorporated into the platform, and is the most sacred place of worship for Jews.

Israeli archaeologists were angered at the Waqf's use of bulldozers to reopen a twelfth-century Crusader entrance for use as an emergency exit for the mosque, charging that archaeological material possibly dating to the First Temple Period (ca. 960–586 B.C.) was being destroyed. A group of archaeology students examined Temple Mount fill dumped by the Waqf in the nearby Kidron Valley and recovered ceramic material dating to this period and later.

Gustave Doré

An artist's rendering of the ruined Temple of Jerusalem.

Agents from the Israel Antiquities Authority, which had originally announced there was no material of "serious archaeological value" at the construction site, raided the home of the leader of the student group, Zachi Zweig. Claiming that they found artifacts from various sites in the Judean foothills as well as a metal detector, which is illegal to use on archaeological sites, the authority filed charges against Zweig for stealing antiquities and causing damage to archaeological sites. "They are trying to invent a case about me that I did some robbery excavation in some cave," Zweig told ARCHAEOLOGY. *"This is a joke."*

Right-wing opposition leader and Mayor of Jerusalem Ehud Olmert has asserted that allowing the Waqf to excavate without the supervision of state archaeologists undermines Israel's legal and moral claim to the Temple Mount. Meanwhile, the Israeli High Court of Justice recently rejected a petition to halt all construction by the Waqf on the complex, arguing that the matter was political and should be left to the government.

In 1996, the opening of an ancient tunnel beneath the Temple Mount sparked fierce Palestinian protest. Ensuing gun battles in the West Bank and Gaza Strip killed 54 Palestinians and 14 Israeli soldiers.

Israel captured Arab East Jerusalem, including the Old City, from Jordan during the 1967 Middle East war. After the city's capture, control of the Temple Mount was ceded to the Waqf.

Waqf head Adnan Husseini stated that the Israeli government had no right to demand a halt to construction at the complex. "We never asked for permission from the occupation," he said.

by KRISTIN M. ROMEY

maintaining the values of the buildings visible in the Haram—almost all of them Early Islamic. As he explains it, "Archaeology is very important but the feelings of the people, human beings, the needs of the people should be taken into consideration when we discuss heritage and archaeology. The main thing is to preserve this area for Muslims and not to cause harm to other civilizations." In contrast, Barkai and his fellow committee members, while appreciative of the site's present architecture, are also fully convinced that some of those "other civilizations" are of equal, if not greater, importance.

The Haram is visited annually by hundreds of thousands during the brief period that marks the Muslim holiday of Ramadan, as well as tens of thousands every Friday. Thus, it is difficult to dispute the Waqf's right to make some accommodations for these numbers of pilgrims—neither the CPDATM nor the Israeli Antiquities Authority (IAA) have tried to. According to Jon Seligman, IAA's Jerusalem District Archaeologist, the real question for the Authority "was not 'if' but 'how.'" Both Barkai and Seligman agree that the work could have been done with proper archaeological supervision but that, in their estimation, it was not. Neither takes issue with Natsheh's abilities to do so—rather, they both claim he wasn't present at the time that the work was done. Natsheh maintains that the questions raised are not archaeological ones. "They [the protesters] have their own motivations," he says, "but archaeology is the least one... Nothing was destroyed, no buildings, no walls, no capitals." Seligman argues that this is beside the point. "This is the very

first time in which work has been done under the levels of the platform. In a case like that this really demands that you have to do it properly."

The new construction was undertaken primarily in the southeastern corner of the Haram but Barkai cites rumors, dismissed by Natsheh and Seligman, that further destructive projects are being carried out on and below the platform. Barkai also asserts that important strata "saturated with archaeological material" were removed and dumped in the nearby Kidron Valley and the village of Azzaria. Tests conducted at the dump sites by his students, says Barkai, found significant amounts of sherds representing "all periods." Natsheh's survey of the area excavated before construction indicated that "all of this earth was filled during the Ayubbid period [beginning in A.D. 1187]," and that any sherds from earlier periods there were in stratigraphically disturbed contexts and cannot, with certainty, even be considered from the Temple Mount-Haram al-Sharif itself. The IAA's tests report the majority of material at the dump sites was from the seventh to eleventh centuries A.D., with insignificant percentages from earlier periods.

The two Israelis also disagree about the separation of archaeology from politics in discussing what happened at the site. While Barkai firmly maintains that the debate must focus on archaeology, Seligman says, "The truth is it's both. I think it's not honest to the subject to separate them—the reason it's so potent is because of the politics."

These "potent politics" may be the reason why a number of Israeli archaeologists whom one might expect to take an interest in the affair have declined to do so and others have even taken a view in opposition to Barkai's and, to some extent, Seligman's. Meir Ben-Dov, who is recognized primarily for his Jerusalem excavations, has publicly supported the claims of the Al-Qaf Adm inistration that construction in the Haram was properly carried out. He has also argued that the original Temple Mount was some 16 feet higher than the present day platform, suggesting that the remains from prior occupations of the site—of greatest interest to Israelis—have already disappeared or been displaced.

The Temple Mount-Haram al-Sharif is registered with UNESCO as a World Heritage site, but why the work was done without UNESCO involvement is closely linked to the politics of the region. "There is a problem with the UNESCO registration of Jerusalem. It was done without consulting Israel," says Seligman, referring to the registration of the site as "a separate entity" nominated by Jordan in 1982. The fact that the site appears on the list "without the consent of the sovereign power," to quote Seligman, and the fact that certain past dealings between UNESCO and Israel have been less than cordial, means that their intervention would not be a prospect Israel would enthusiastically embrace.

Natsheh has no problem with UNESCO observing their work and states that a such visit, while welcomed by the Waqf, was postponed three times by Israeli authorities. Consulting the IAA, however, was out of the question. "The Al-Qaf Administration, which is responsible for Muslim affairs and the holy places, never

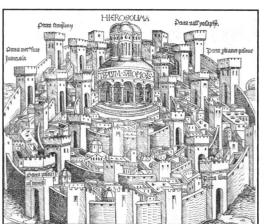

This 1493 woodcut illustration of the city of Jerusalem, titled in the Latin, by the German cartographer Hartmann Schedel (1440–1514).

Hartmann Schedel

admits the Israeli occupation," says Natsheh. "We never applied for the permission from the Israeli authorities and we are not going to apply." Interestingly, he was somewhat less candid when asked if the site should be under the sovereignty of the Palestinian Authority. It is possible that the Waqf, not entirely anxious to be enfolded in the arms of a new and poverty-stricken nation-state, may prefer an autonomous position for management of the Haram.

Reflecting Israeli concerns about the site, Barkai charges that, "what goes on, on the Temple Mount, is outrageous... it's being constantly damaged," while Seligman states angrily, "Here we have a situation where, at one of the most important of World Heritage Sites, work has been done in a really charlatan manner, causing real vandalism and UNESCO has said nothing—zero." CPDATM has managed to persuade prime minister Ariel Sharon to appoint a panel of scholars and politicians to look into the matter, but the panel has yet to convene. The

construction work has been almost completed, and the only course of action left to
them is to seek to prevent similar occur-
rences. "We really have to make sure that
this can't happen again," Seligman says.
"There have to be some sort of safeguards."
On the other side of the controversy, Natsheh voices the anxieties of fellow Muslims,
"This area is a holy area for Muslims. It was
made holy by God. This can't be changed...
We have fears, worries that all of these
attempts will lead to the destruction of the
Dome of the Rock. We are very nervous
and worried about what is going on around
us."

It is difficult to envision that Israeli participation in the Waqf's prospective decisions
on maintenance or construction in the
Haram could take place without a significant change in the archaeological management of the site, a change that would have to
be preceded by a political agreement that is
now more elusive than ever. Although no
one would suggest that the current conflict
in the Middle East is about the Temple
Mount-Haram al-Sharif any more than it is
about any other single issue, the site remains
a powerful symbol of the past, the present,
and possibly the future of Israeli and Palestinian relations.

HOPE AMID THE CARNAGE

AS CONFLICT RAGES IN THE MIDDLE EAST, A HANDFUL OF PALESTINIANS AND ISRAELIS HAVE JOINED FORCES TO PROTECT ENDANGERED SITES

by SANDRA SCHAM

We met in a small, empty hotel in the Arab town of Beit Hanina in the suburbs of Jerusalem. Two of us had come from Ramallah in the West Bank representing the Palestinian Association for Cultural Exchange (PACE). Three of us had come from Jerusalem, associated with Israel's University of Haifa. We were to continue our work developing an Israeli-Palestinian archaeological program for schools and colleges and a program for community involvement in the development of archaeological sites in the region. The singularity of our group had more to do with the dearth of Israelis and Palestinians willing to work together these days than to anything else.

We gathered in March 2002, at a time that seemed to

mark the pinnacle of carnage in the current Israeli-Palestinian conflict—more than 100 people had been killed in the week just passed. Our discussions were warm and amicable; we were, after all, both friends and colleagues. Adel Yahyeh, an archaeologist working out of Ramallah, was our project coordinator and director of PACE. His associate, Jamal Jafra, founder and general manager of Arab Commercial Television, was PACE's projects manager. Adel and I had worked together for almost four years. In the days when it was possible to visit each other we had dined together fairly often, and our children (both girls of the same age) had played together. His acquaintance with our project leaders from the University of Haifa, archaeologists Rachel Hachlili and Ann Killebrew, extended back one or two years.

For six hours we talked, ate, and drank coffee. We spoke about families, trips, and current events, but mostly we talked about our collaborative archaeological project. Two years ago, Ann, Adel, and I had helped organize a workshop in Ramallah on the presentation of the past in the Holy Land. At the time, we heard that funds for a project such as ours might be available from the U.S. State Department under the Wye River Accords-the prelude to the disastrous

GIBEON IS NEAR THE VILLAGE OF AL-JIB AND IS KNOWN FROM THE BIBLE AS THE SITE OF THE BATTLE THAT ESTABLISHED THE MONARCHY OF KING DAVID

Middle East peace talks at Camp David in the summer of 2000. Ann had been trying for years to do something on the Arab and Jewish heritage of the Israeli site of Acre (ancient Akko), and Adel had been seeking money to preserve West Bank biblical sites. Eventually, the State Department provided the bulk of our support (about $400,000) and we were now trying to raise matching funds from our administrative budgets and other sources.

Originally, we had planned to have Israelis work with Palestinians at two small sites in the West Bank and one large site in Israel. Now the only way that Israelis could visit the West Bank was in uniform—and Palestinians were forbidden to cross the border into Israel. We discussed courses the University of Haifa would soon be providing to Jewish and Arab students covering the multicultural heritage of Israel. Our Palestinian partners showed us photos of the work they had done with local Palestinians, cleaning up and repairing the sites of Gibeon and Bethel in the West Bank. Adel had insisted at the outset that he start his community projects immediately because the sites were in trouble and the local people were desperate for employment. Gibeon is near the village of Al-Jib and is known from the Bible as the site of the battle that established the monarchy of King David, where Joshua made the sun stand still, and where the prophet Elisha made bitter water drinkable. The ancient cistern in Gibeon is mentioned many times in the Bible. The city was destroyed by the Babylonians but was revived in the Roman–Byzantine period, and the village near the site today dates primarily from Ottoman times. Bethel is where Abraham built an altar, where King Jeroboam established an important sanctuary to rival that in Jerusalem, and where a large Byzantine monastery was restored by Crusaders and later turned into a mosque. It has long been considered synonymous with the Arab town of Beitin, which is close to the archaeological site.

Adel and Jamal told us that because they had provided employment to local residents to help restore and protect the sites, "looting had almost stopped." We talked about visiting the sites despite the ban on Israeli travel to the West Bank; after all, two of us, Ann and I, had American passports. These sites are totally undeveloped for presentation to the public, but we had seen their potential. Both of them are revered by Jews, Christians, and Muslims as places mentioned prominently in the Bible. We returned to West Jerusalem that night, fairly satisfied with the way things were going. Two hours later, a suicide bomber at the Café Moment, five blocks from where I live and across the street from Prime Minister Ariel Sharon's residence, killed 14 people. Three hours later helicopter gunships from Israel were on their way to destroy Yasser Arafat's compound in Gaza and targets in the West Bank. The real war had begun.

The current Intifada was just underway when we wrote our funding requests. As our plans progressed incrementally, the Israeli-Palestinian conflict progressed exponentially—not exactly thwarting us at every turn but certainly making the work more difficult. Initially our plans were to meet regularly throughout the first year of the project and to start with the educational phase. Community work would follow. When it became apparent that the West Bank sites might disappear, considering the rate at which they were being destroyed by looters, we all agreed that preservation work should begin there immediately. The Intifada had resulted in massive Palestinian unemployment, according to Adel and Jamal, and the economic base of the region was rapidly eroding. Israeli military authorities had control over many West Bank historical sites but, not surprisingly, had done little to protect them.

We agreed that Acre was the best site in Israel for starting a multicultural education program. Israel's cultural heterogeneity is often forgotten in the preoccupation with the Israeli-Palestinian struggle, and Acre represents aspects of all of the cultures and religions within Israel-Arabs, Jews, Europeans, Christians, and Muslims. This site is considerably larger than Bethel or Gibeon and is in the center of a living city. In 2001, it became one of Israel's designated UNESCO World Heritage Sites.

Although Acre's archaeological and preservation needs are less critical than those of Bethel and Gibeon, such activities may potentially be a source of greater anxiety for the people living there. Acre is a mixed

WAC vs. the Wall

The World Archaeological Congress (WAC) has condemned the destruction of heritage sites in Palestine by Israeli forces. "Of particular concern," notes the scholarly organization's January 2004 press release, "is the destruction of heritage sites by the wall being constructed by the Israeli government." Israel justifies the wall as a necessary security barrier.

In the fall of 2003, bulldozers preparing ground for a section of the wall running through Abu Dis, East Jerusalem, damaged remains of a 1,500-year-old Byzantine monastery. Construction was halted, and Israel Antiquities Authority (IAA) archaeologists conducted an excavation, recovering a mosaic and other artifacts. An IAA official quoted in the press blamed the army for proceeding without a go-ahead from IAA.

Currently threatened by construction of the barrier is the West Bank site of Gibeon. Mentioned several times in the Bible, Gibeon is the focus of an Israeli-American-Palestinian initiative to protect heritage in the area. (The project is funded by a $400,000 U.S. State Department grant.) Unless plans for it are altered, the wall will certainly damage the site. Jobs created by restoring and protecting Gibeon are important to the nearby village of Al-Jib, says Palestinian archaeologist Adel Yahyeh. He is afraid that if the wall separates the village from the site, Al-Jib will become little more than a refugee camp. According to Yahyeh, the IAA is aware of the threat and sympathetic but may not have jurisdiction.

WAC has called upon Israel to abide by UNESCO conventions intended to protect cultural heritage. "It's a no-brainer to assume that a large-scale regional project in this part of the world will destroy a lot of sites," says Catholic University's Sandra Scham, a key player in the joint initiative and a contributing editor to ARCHAEOLOGY.

by MARK ROSE

community with a higher population of Arabs than Jews. Its modern residents have generally seen the historical nature of the buildings they inhabit as a limitation rather than a source of pride and are concerned that development plans for the site might uproot them. Community education would be the first priority of the project there. This summer, Jewish and Arab archaeological heritage students at the University of Haifa will be presenting workshops, taking oral histories, researching the history and archaeology of Acre, and promoting tourism.

The last time we visited Acre we were with a group of University of Haifa students, which included Jews, Arabs, and Jewish and Christian Russians. Seeing it through these diverse eyes, we realized that the city was a site that catered to many historical interests. It was an important Canaanite, Phoenician, Hellenistic, and Roman port in antiquity. Byzantine Acre was the seat of a bishopric in the archdiocese of Tyre and had a large Samaritan community. In 636, Arabs gained control of the city. At the beginning of the twelfth century, Acre was a Crusader naval base until it became the Crusader capital in 1191 and served as the port of disembarkation for both pilgrims and immigrants to Palestine. During this time Jews continued to live in the city and their thriving community was visited by a number of famous Jewish scholars. In 1291 the town was conquered and destroyed by the Mamluks. It regained its importance as a port only after the Ottoman conquest in 1516.

We hope that our work will become a model for other regions where heritage wars and real wars threaten coexistence. Peace in the Middle East now seems more elusive than when our project began and we're discouraged—but not entirely so. The University of Haifa's participation will continue as long as it is possible for the partners to work together—in spite of a wave of suicide bombings by Palestinians that in Haifa alone has killed dozens of Arab and Jewish Israelis. "It's a matter of archaeologists taking social responsibility," Ann Killebrew says. "It's important for us to recognize that heritage is more about people than it is about places."

As I write this, two of our Haifa project leaders have been called up by the Army to serve in the West Bank, the center of Ramallah is in ruins, its residents under curfew, and everyone, whether Israeli or Palestinian, seems to know someone who has been killed. Meanwhile, Adel and his colleagues are virtual prisoners in their own homes. "Even though we can't move at this stage," he told me by phone, "I think that what we are doing is important—and we will resume work as soon as we can."

THE GOSPEL'S HOLIEST SANCTUM

AT JERUSALEM'S CHURCH OF THE HOLY SEPULCHRE, TWO MILLENIA OF DIVERGENT TRADITIONS COLLIDE

by Elizabeth J. Himelfarb

*I*t *was preparation day (that is, the day before the Sabbath). So as evening approached, Joseph of Arimathea, a prominent member of the council, who was himself waiting for the kingdom of God, went boldly to Pilate and asked for Jesus' body. Pilate was surprised to hear that he was already dead. Summoning the centurion, he asked him if Jesus had already died. When he learned from the centurion that it was already so, he gave the body to Joseph. So Joseph bought some linen cloth, took down the body, wrapped it in the linen, and placed it in a tomb cut out of rock. Then he rolled a stone against the entrance of the tomb. Mary Magdalene and Mary the mother of Joses saw where he was laid.*

When the Sabbath was over, Mary Magdalene, Mary the mother of James, and Salome bought spices so that they might go to anoint Jesus' body. Very early on the first day of the week, just after sunrise, they were on their way to the tomb and they asked each other, "Who will roll the stone away from the entrance of the tomb?"

But when they looked up, they saw that the stone, which was very large, had been rolled away.

Mark 15:42–16:4

Three hundred years after Jesus was crucified, the emperor Constantine, freshly converted to Christianity, identified a rock-cut tomb in the heart of Jerusalem as Christ's burial place. He had torn down a pagan temple to Venus and in its place planned to erect a monumental domed Church of the Holy Sepulchre, soon to become Jerusalem's most sacred place of Christian pilgrimage.

Constantine's church was demolished by a Muslim ruler in 1009 and rebuilt by Byzantine emperors from 1012 to 1041. The Crusaders added further chapels and a belfry in the following century, only to see the church fall again into Muslim hands in 1187. Instead of destroying the church, however, the new regime merely limited access to it, sealing off one of two Crusader-era doors. Unwilling to empower any one Christian sect, a later ruler entrusted the only key to two Muslim families, whose

SINCE THE FIFTH CENTURY, VARIOUS CHRISTIAN SECTS HAVE SHARED SPACE IN THE CHURCH, BUT NOT WITHOUT CONTENTION

descendants safeguard it to this day, opening the door each morning and closing it again each night.

I recently spent a week in Jerusalem trying to make sense of this place that has drawn religious pilgrims for more than 1,000 years. It was July: mosquitoes seemed to outnumber people and it was too hot to eat until the sun set. Every day, I navigated the twisting streets of the Arab Market or souk to reach the church. Stray cats with small, flat faces and pointy ears brushed by, and old women hawked lapfuls of figs and apricots. Vendors mingled with backpackers, shoppers, and groups of pilgrims. The souk is a maze, and trying to follow a map to the church sheer folly.

I had envisioned an arresting cathedral with an imposing facade. Instead, I found the only entrance to the church off a modest, enclosed stone court. From outside, the asymmetrical sanctuary reminded me of a monastery, its humble, drab stone adorned only by crosses carved by pilgrims on columns flanking the tall entrance door with a pointed arch. I joined a jostling mob pushing through, and the cool, dark interior brought relief from the sun. Light filtered through high windows casting hazy rays, and the smell of incense was strong. Just within the door, I noted the long, low Stone of Unction, a pink slab drizzled with rose

C. Middleton

A copper engraving, a perspective view of the Church of the Holy Sepulchre at Jerusalem, by C. Middleton in 1773.

water and worn to a sheen by the caresses of pilgrims. On this stone, today overhung with silver lamps capped with jewel-colored glass, believers say Jesus was anointed after being taken off the cross. Devotees place plastic bags, presumably containing objects they wish to have blessed, upon it. To the right, a stairway led to four Stations of the Cross, points on Jesus' journey from trial to tomb. Beneath the airy rotunda lies the edicule, the little house Constantine built to enclose the rock-cut tomb, renovated for the last time in the nineteenth century.

Two millennia and countless phases of construction have left the church a bewildering, sprawling, and disorienting place. Photographs fail to capture the Escheresque quality of the architecture, inaccessible balconies, arches, and stairways appearing in unexpected places. Chapels jut in every direction. A labyrinthine complex of smaller rooms appears interconnected by impractical doors and passageways.

Since the fifth century, various Christian sects have shared space in the church, but not without contention. Territorial holdings shifted many times when high government

taxes forced different groups to sell their holdings to one another. Infighting came to a head in 1852 when the Ottomans, then in control of Jerusalem, issued what is known as the Status Quo agreement. The agreement defined the territorial rights of the competing communities—Greek-Orthodox, Armenian, Latin, Syrian-Jacobite, Coptic, and Ethiopian—within the edifice and set down the order of mass, paths of procession, and timetable of liturgies. Provisions of the agreement continue to govern daily life at the church.

Vying for territory remains an issue here—holdings are far from equal. Recently, the sects proved unable to agree on where to put a second door for use in event of emergency; whoever owned the segment containing the door would have gained special access to the church. So despite the urgings of Israeli police, no new door is to be installed. An American Franciscan friar who sits on a subcommittee responsible for the administration of the Status Quo compares the situation to "sharing a kitchen."

Cleaning something is owning it, explained a friar I met at a late-night mass. While disputes over the right to clean an area go unresolved, sections of the church wallow in disrepair. One patch of floor wasn't washed for years because it was a disputed area not accounted for by the Status Quo. Beneath the sparkling rotunda, rebuilt in 1997 after decades of debate between the sects, the edicule is shrouded in scaffolding, as it has been since a 1927 earthquake; church factions have been unable to agree on a design for its reconstruction.

Monks patrolled the immaculate main

chapel and crumbling side chapels, swinging incense burners with jingling bells, trailing smoke. "My heart is beating faster," I heard a woman say as she neared the front of the line outside the edicule. You have to duck to enter the enclosure, whose inner sanctum contains a marble slab that covers the actual tomb and a small altar adorned with flowers, candles, and icons.

Signs are lacking, and trying to determine from my guidebook just what belongs to which sect was proving futile. No divisions are marked; concentrations of monks clad in the particular garb of one sect or another—Franciscans in sack cloth, Greek Orthodox in black caps—are the only hint at territorial ownership. So on my second visit, I brought along Jon Seligman and Gideon Avni of the Israeli Antiquities Authority, who spent several months excavating a related church here in 1997. Difficulties of access to the complex, they told me, have discouraged comprehensive research. Because closed-off areas belonging to different sects abut, it is no simple matter for an archaeologist to search for spatial relationships that might enhance understanding of the church's complex phases of construction. One must first find the monk with the key to a room to be surveyed, then hope the monk's in a good enough mood to hand it over, then coordinate with the key-keepers of adjoining rooms.

We walked through the rotunda, and Seligman stopped abruptly. "Do you hear that?" he asked. Avni nodded. I couldn't imagine what noise they'd isolated amid the midday din of rewinding film, clanging church bells, bellowing tour guides, and

Jerusalem juxtaposes modern amenities and turmoil over the foundations and traditions of the ancient world.

Jack Hazut, JHM Photography

prayer. Avni cocked an ear. "The Greeks are hammering," he announced.

"Yes," Avni confirmed. "And the Copts are sanding."

We followed the sounds up the narrow stairs—clogged with two-way traffic—past the Stations of the Cross to a nook out of view of the masses. We hopped over a railing to investigate. Sure enough, minor repairs were underway. The Antiquities Authority is sometimes viewed with suspicion in this city, where Christians, Muslims, and Jews are happy with their own versions of the past. So the agency keeps on the lookout for any sign of construction at the myriad archaeological sites.

It was this watchfulness that alerted Seligman and Avni to what would turn out to be the most exciting recent excavation on these premises, that of an unknown church within the Coptic holdings. We walked there and found a small, dank room guarded by a smiling deacon who shadowed us with great interest. I asked him if he liked his work. "Yes," he said with a laugh, "but it's so noisy, like a supermarket. Supermarkets are for shopping, not for praying."

Seligman and Avni explained that the space had filled with rubble in the Crusader period, by which time it was out of use. In a 1997 bid to expand its holdings, the Coptic sect decided that the room should be cleared and began removing rubble at night. Seligman was chagrined that a proper archaeological investigation had not been conducted and wanted to get one underway as soon as possible. "It was half done by the time we got there," he said. "We saw trucks going out with dirt and went to the Coptic archbishop to explain our position."

The remains of a medieval apse were eventually discovered once the rubble was removed. With additional excavation, small patches of a floor paved with mosaics and marble were unearthed along the apse contour. A few sherds of pottery and glass beneath the floors of the church revealed that it was built in the ninth century. It was most likely destroyed in 1009 along with the rest of the church complex, which it seems to have adjoined even in the Byzantine period. For beneath the medieval church—newly dedicated as the church of St. James the Less after the first

bishop of Jerusalem—lie sherds dating to Constantine's time. With great excitement, Seligman and Avni showed me a small area of fourth-century wall. They wondered whether the space—rebuilt in the ninth century, destroyed in 1009, and filled in soon after—might have been the baptistry of Constantine's church.

I wanted to meet the Coptic archbishop, so my guides led me through a private inner courtyard to his cloister in the northern part of the church complex. We were taken to what looked like a throne room with an extravagant seat of honor on one wall and dozens of modest chairs lining the other walls. After several long minutes, the archbishop arrived dressed in black. He didn't take the throne, instead, the four of us sat side by side along one wall. A tight cowl covered his head, but his puffy gray beard poked out. He offered us tea. We declined, but it appeared nonetheless, along with juice and cake. The archbishop urged us to eat.

"There will be a time—not in this generation—when the three religions, Christianity, Judaism, and Islam, will be one," he said, navigating the ideological divide separating his Arab Christian constituents and these representatives of the Israeli state. "The differences are so small," he said, an astounding comment from a man who lives among Christian sects struggling to bridge their own differences.

WINE WAS SPOONED FROM THE CHALICE INTO THE MOUTHS OF THE FAITHFUL

I returned by moonlight to witness the closing of the church. A small and ardent crowd of nuns and a few tourists crowded around the gate as two policemen stood by. With two resonant bangs, the sun-blanched wooden doors swung shut. Omar Nusseibeh, a layman in a pink shirt, the latest in the Arab lineage to control the sole key, climbed a ladder and closed a latch high on the door. "Crash, bam," an American friend said, trying to capture the moment. "The house of God is now closed." Omar let me examine the key. It was a heavy iron instrument about ten inches long, one that might have unlocked a medieval implement of torture. It was shaped like an arrow, the head tipped with an open circle.

Returning the next afternoon, I found one of the church's two tiny Ethiopian chapels, usually closed, packed wall to wall with worshipers, the women draped in filmy white wraps. I stood on tiptoe to see into the ground-floor sanctuary, not wanting to interrupt the prayers. The room was dark and vaulted, lit by tall, thin tapers with leaping flames. Worshipers sang a wailing, undulating hymn.

There, I met Sarah, an Ethiopian woman in Western dress with intelligent, deep-set eyes. The chanting intensified, and Sarah told me to watch closely. Priests, some clad in black robes and others in white, gathered in a circle holding candles. The faithful surged forward, and only then did I notice still more women and children at prayer on the periphery, crouched or standing, wrapped in white. The priests appeared and disappeared from a narrow half-circle cut from the back wall. They entered with a chalice and a tray of glasses filled with a clear liquid symbolic of Jesus' last meal. Wine was spooned from the chalice into the mouths of the faithful, who then swallowed the clear liquid. Babies were held up to receive their share of both.

As the service ended, Sarah squeezed my hand and whispered, "I want to invite you to share our meal." She led me upstairs, through the second, more highly trafficked Ethiopian chapel and onto a quiet, white-washed section of roof, where the monks and nuns lived in small rooms. Simplicity rules atop the Church of the Holy Sepulchre, shaded by a cluster of trees, where the only adornment is a cross painted in two rough strokes on a door. The women had prepared food in the monastery kitchen, savory plates of *injera* (spongy flat bread) and a spicy brown sauce called wat, salad, potatoes, and carrots. Everyone dug in, eating expertly with fingers, scooping up food with the bread.

Seduced by the gentle chatter, my mind drifted to the noisy shuffling of the tour groups below, of the pilgrims who linger, memorizing each stone with their fingers, and of the monks who lovingly tend this place in the name of one sect or another.

My thoughts turned to a Franciscan mass I'd watched at the church one midnight. The only light came from hand-held candles, and the rotunda, empty of tourists, filled with the sound of Gregorian chanting. From another part of the church, strains of prayer sung in Greek wafted in. The overlapping voices hung for a moment in the air.

OPERATION SCROLL

THE ARCHAEOLOGICAL LANDSCAPE OF THE HOLY LAND BECAME A POLITICAL BATTLEFIELD IN THE FALL OF 1993, AS SCHOLARS HUNTED FOR ANCIENT DOCUMENTS DURING THE ISRAELI OCCUPATION

by Neil Asher Silberman

As Israeli and Palestinian diplomats edged toward a delicate agreement on coexistence in the fall of 1993, the archaeology landscape of the Holy Land became a political battlefield. On November 14, a month before Israeli forces were have to begun a staged withdrawal from the Gaza Strip and the Jericho region, the Israel Antiquities Authority (IAA) launched an ambitious survey and excavation projected dubbed "Operation Scroll." At the very moment when Israeli and Palestinian negotiators were working out the details of the Israel-Palestine Liberation Organization understanding signed in Washington in September, 20 teams of Israeli archaeologists began searching for, and removing, ancient coins, pottery, manuscript fragments, and other archaeological finds from the caves and ravines of a 60-mile stretch of the lower Jordan Valley and the western shore of the Dead Sea. Though the precise size of the proposed autonomous Palestinian enclave around Jericho had not yet been determined, the timing and scale of Operation Scroll, carried out in the same general area, led many Palestinians and outside observers to condemn the IAA for making a crude, eleventh-hour grab for what they thought was rightfully Palestinian antiquities.

The urgency of Operation Scroll was certainly hard to fathom: though this was the area where the Dead Sea Scrolls and other ancient documents had been discovered, the last major manuscript find in this region took place in the early 1960s (the result of illegal digging by local bedouin who thoroughly scoured the area for marketable antiquities). The IAA explained the operation as an attempt to prevent looting in the area. Yet in recent years, other areas on the West Bank and in Israel have been far more seriously ravaged by antiquities thieves. An intensive archaeological effort *there* might have been more understandable. Though the IAA spokeswoman denied that Operation Scroll had any political implications, its timing, at least, was awkward. "The French did the same thing before they left Algeria," charged Nazmi Jubeh, a technical advisor to the Palestinian delegation to the Washington peace talks.

There were, of course, some significant differences. The most important artifacts in the Operation Scroll dispute were not artworks or treasure, but ancient Hebrew and Aramaic documents whose emotional importance to the Israeli people was considerably greater than any attachment felt by the Palestinian people to them. Expeditions to the caves of the Dead Sea region in the 1950s and the 1960s had uncovered—in addition to the vast collection of ancient Jewish religious writings known as the Dead Sea Scrolls—letters, deeds, and hastily gathered belongings of ancient Jewish rebels, religious visionaries, and frightened refugees, who sought asylum in this remote and desolate region during the two great Jewish revolts against Rome in the late first and early second century A.D. Since the 1950s, these finds have captured the popular imagination of modern Israel. The reaction to the Dead Sea Scrolls and the so-called Bar-Kokhba letters on the Jordanian side of the border was never quite so enthusiastic. In fact, in 1957, the Jordanian director of antiquities, Abdul Karim Gharaybeh, ordered the removal of one of the newly found Bar Kokhba letters from display in the Palestine Archaeological Museum in Jerusalem because "it served as open propaganda for the Zionists."

AS THINGS TURNED OUT, OPERATION SCROLL REAPED A MEAGER HARVEST

New Texts from Qumran

Three ostraca, one inscribed with 16 lines of Hebrew text from the first century A.D., *have been found in Qumran, Israel. This is the first textual material discovered at the site since the Dead Sea Scrolls were found there in 1947. The sherds were spotted on the east side of the Qumran plateau by volunteer excavators led by James F. Strange of the University of South Florida.*

One ostracon, broken into two pieces, mentions several commodities and is believed to be a list of food and supplies. The text opens, "In the second year," probably referring to the second year of the First Jewish Revolt, or A.D. *68. The next line reads, "In Jericho," most likely indicating where the ostracon was made. The text, which has not yet been deciphered completely, is significant because it refers to the life of the whole com-munity, not the life-style of the elite class, well known from the Dead Sea Scrolls. A Jewish refugee settlement on the northwest shore of the Dead Sea eight and one-half miles south of Jericho, Qumran was destroyed by the Romans during the First Revolt. According to Strange, the pottery pieces were probably thrown out in haste or were part of the debris left after the Roman looting of the site.*

One of the other ostraca found nearby has parts of four lines of text. The last ostracon shows traces of ink. The ostraca are being examined by Esther Eshel of Hebrew University in Jerusalem, who has studied and published several of the Dead Sea Scrolls.

by SUSAN STANLEY

Yet in late 1993, with the prospect of independence looming, many Palestinians saw a necessary link between archaeological finds and territorial sovereignty. The unilateral action of the IAA was seen as the illegal plunder of cultural resources from lands that Palestinians hoped would become the nucleus of a state. Even some prominent Israelis believed that there should have been consultation with Palestinian authorities before Operation Scroll was sent out into the field. Knesset member Anat Moar of the leftist Meretz party put it succinctly: "We have to find a balance between our deep feelings regarding our own history and respect for international law."

The international law referred to is contained in the ponderous 1954 Hague Convention, some of whose provisions deal with the proper treatment of cultural property in occupied territory. According to the Convention, an occupying power must preserve and protect all antiquities, sites, and cultural treasures for the benefit of the inhabitants, restrict excavation to necessary rescue digs or salvage work, and remove no cultural property from the occupied territory. These guidelines were established to prevent wholesale looting of art treasures such as had been carried out with ruthless efficiency by Nazi forces during World War II. Unfortunately, the situation envisioned by the authors of the Convention—hobnail-booted occupiers pulling down Old Masters from drawing room walls and pilfering statues from museum cases—bears little relation to the far more complex conflict between Israelis and Palestinians.

Vegetarian Essenes?

Twenty-eight spartan dwellings on the edge of the Ein Gedi oasis in southern Israel may have been the home of a community of Essenes, the Jewish sect thought by some to have collected the Dead Sea Scrolls. While no inscriptions have been found positively linking the site to the group, its proximity to the village of Ein Gedi a mile away is grounds for assuming that its inhabitants belonged to the same community, says Yitzhar Hirschfeld of Hebrew University, the site's excavator. Descriptions of the Essenes by ancient authors such as Pliny the Elder "fit the character of the site," he says. Another clue is the presence of a mikveh, or Jewish ritual bath.

The Essenes are thought to have flourished between the second century B.C. and the destruction of the temple in Jerusalem by the Romans in A.D. 70. Ancient sources describe them as a tightly knit group of men, possibly celibate, who practiced communal ownership of property. "The people who lived here worked the fields of the oasis," says Hirschfeld, who suspects that the site was a permanent, rather than seasonal, settlement. The dwellings were built for one person only and measure six by nine feet. They appear to have been occupied twice, in the first and early second centuries A.D., and between the fourth and six centuries. Three larger buildings possibly had a communal use; one, likely a kitchen, had three stoves and a thick layer of ash on the floor.

While the site yielded a fairly rich collection of pottery vessels, glass sherds, and seven coins from the early Roman and Byzantine eras, it is most remarkable for its lack of animal bones. "Although we worked carefully, sifting everything, we didn't find any," says Hirschfeld, adding that the settlers might have been vegetarian. Although Josephus noted that the dietary restrictions of the Essenes were stringent, the nearby village appears not to have been bound by vegetarianism. "We've found 4,000 animal bones in the village of Ein Gedi," he notes. Judaism has historically advocated vegetarianism only occasionally for ascetic reasons or during periods of mourning.

by Spencer P. M. Harrington

The territorial situation is legally tangled. Rightly or wrongly, the Israeli government has always bridled at the blanket description of the West Bank as "occupied territory" since it has never legally recognized the area's annexation by the Hashemite Kingdom of Jordan in 1948. To make the situation even thornier, the areas of the West Bank to be evacuated by Israel would not be returned to Jordan, but would be handed over for administration to the PLO. The real issue—and the issue that the Hague Convention was utterly unequipped to deal with—was not the physical possession of relics but the equitable apportionment between two peoples laying claim to them.

Are the Israelis justified in mounting an effort to retrieve documents and artifacts of direct and demonstrable relevance to their culture and tradition—even if those artifacts lay in disputed territory? Do Palestinians, on the other hand, have a right to claim owner-ship of ancient Jewish artifacts in their part of the country, even if those artifacts are of relatively little significance to them? And if the antiquities of the country are to be partitioned by cultural association, do the Palestinians thereby have a right to custodi-anship of Muslim holy sites within Israel?

As things turned out, Operation Scroll reaped a meager harvest, proving how thor-oughly the local bedouin had searched the area 30 years before. The most noteworthy discoveries were some fragments of Aramaic papyri (probably deeds or other legal docu-ments, hidden by Jewish rebels at the time of the second-century A.D. Bar Kokhba Rebel-lion); a warrior's grave (first proudly attributed to the Maccabean period and then quietly redated to the Bronze Age); and various installations, coins, and ancient textiles. These finds hardly seemed worth the massive effort—or all the controversy and bad publicity they gained for the IAA.

As of this writing, the Israeli withdrawal from the area around Jericho, which was scheduled to begin on December 13, has not yet been implemented. The archaeological dispute over Operation Scroll was clearly just a minor skirmish in the larger Arab-Israeli conflict, yet it highlighted the need for international organizations to address the problems of disputed cultural heritage in the changing circumstances of a post-colonial, post-Cold War world. As new nation states spring up in the ruins of the Soviet Empire and across Africa and Asia, the disputes over archaeological resources are likely to become more frequent. Conflicting claims about cultural property may well arise in

places like Bosnia, Armenia, Kurdistan, the Ukraine, and other locales of ethnic, cul-tural, and political strife. Unfortunately, there is no easy solution to the politicization of archaeology. As long as ethnic groups and nation-states continue to find prestige and modern validation in the past, archaeology will continue to be a dependable source of patriotic symbols. And, as in the case of Operation Scroll and the Palestinian protests against it, ancient pottery, stonework, metal, and manuscripts will continue to be the stage props of international politics.

LEGACY OF THE CRUSADES

THE RUINS OF CASTLES ON HILLSIDES THROUGH-OUT THE MIDDLE EAST ARE MUTE REMINDERS OF A BLOODY CHAPTER IN MEDIEVAL HISTORY

by SANDRA SCHAM

A story is told in Kerak, a small city in Jordan domi-nated by a well-preserved crusader castle, about the fortress' most notorious denizen, Reynauld of Chatillon. According to this tale, the Hajj route to Mecca during Reynauld's time, the late twelfth century A.D., passed beneath his castle walls. Attracted by the richness of one caravan, Reynauld swooped down on the unfortunate pilgrims, capturing all and relieving them of their worldly goods. At the end of his foray, he found, to his immense glee, that one of his hostages was the sister of the legendary Islamic leader Saladin. Reynauld's fellow crusaders were appalled by his brazen violation of a rather tenuous truce.

Baldwin IV, king of Jerusalem, sent a message forthwith, demanding that Reynauld release his distinguished prisoner. Reynauld's answer reflects his customary bravado: "You are king of Jerusalem," he wrote, "but I am king in Kerak."

Kerak, though, never had a king, a fact well known to both Reynauld and the local guides who repeat this story. Nevertheless, although it was within the boundaries of the crusader kingdom of Jerusalem, Kerak was also far enough away from the center of power to enable its ruler to do pretty much as he pleased—that is, summarily executing prisoners, whether they were men, women, or children, in the most brutal manner imaginable. Reynauld eventually got his just desserts, and has the dubious distinction of being the only important crusader to have been personally executed by Saladin.

The castle of Kerak is built on a spur to take advantage of the natural defense accorded by this topography. The town of Kerak has grown all around the spur and it is usually a lively tourist destination. I visited the site, familiar to me from previous sojourns in Jordan, on a beautiful day this past summer 2003, when one would normally expect to see tour buses and guides hustling large groups through the castle gates. The streets were empty. Abdul Hamied, one of Kerak's more knowledgeable local guides, explained, "Tourism in Jordan is down by 70 percent—I worked only seven days this year." Jordan is feeling the effects of the prolonged Israeli–Palestinian struggle, despite the fact that it has been relatively free from conflict itself.

Reflecting on battles both past and present, and the physical legacy of these conflicts ever-present in the landscape, I asked Hamied what he learned about crusader history growing up in Kerak in the shadow of this looming medieval structure. "We were taught that they came from Pharaoh's Island [off the coast of the Sinai Peninsula] and built this line of castles here [from Aqaba to Turkey] to control the trading business," he replied. "When these crusaders came, they came as invaders-killing thousands. And they were not coming for religion or 'holy war.' It was an economic war that used religion."

Aziz Azayzeh, another guide at Kerak, agrees with this assessment. "As a Jordanian, I learned in school that the crusaders came and took our lands just because of greed and gave us nothing in return." Both men, however, true to their professions, say similar things about the crusader sites. Azayzeh continues, "Later, when I studied more about them, I think they did give us something—they were good architects. You know Saladin was smart. He asked the best architects and artists from the crusaders to stay and work." Hamied is more philosophical: "The crusaders—they came as invaders, the Romans came as invaders, in Hellenistic times also. The big powers everywhere—they look to their own interests, but they left something behind for us at these places."

Listening to these remarks, as I stood at the summit of Kerak, I recalled a conversation I had with a colleague before leaving the United States. Salman Elbedour, an American psychology professor who is also an Israeli Bedouin, told me that there is a "Crusader Complex" in the Middle East.

Consequently, it was no surprise to him that President Bush's rather bizarre juxtaposition of ideas, promising to rid the world of the perpetrators of violence in the name of religion, while at the same time labeling the American incursion in Afghanistan a "crusade," was perceived as a major affront by the Arab world. Elbedour and other Muslims, whose ancestors lived in the very heart of crusader territory, see the crusaders as the ultimate vicious usurpers. Archaeologist Adel Yahyeh, who lives in Ramallah on the West Bank, adds, "When we were children in Palestine, our nightmares were about monsters coming after us, wearing crosses on their chests. We even started to see Israeli soldiers that way—strange as it seems."

Crusader sites, like the crusader tradition, inspire a variety of emotions and thoughts. The castles are what most people think of when they envision the crusader period (1097–1291), and many Arabs, says Yahyeh, take a measure of pride in them, since it was the Arabs who liberated the castles from their Christian enemy. But there are other effects of the period to be considered, as well. "You go to Lebanon, Syria, Jordan today...you can see that many of the crusaders stayed and married, and that today we are a mixture of people," says Azayzeh. This casual statement actually reflects the focus of a great deal of new archaeological activity relating to crusader sites in the region. Although it was long believed that European culture did not penetrate rural areas in the Levant, excavations of villages and farmsteads with crusader architecture, sugar refining equipment (a fairly new industry in the medieval period), and a general increase in pig bones at rural sites now indicate otherwise.

Of course, Muslims are not the only ones to have suffered at the hands of the crusaders. Eastern Orthodox Christians and Jews have their own perspectives on this period. As Jörg Bremer, a German historian and journalist who is now living in Jerusalem, says, "Today, we talk of special [collective] memories of the Crusades." Jews see the Crusades, he continues, "as having started in Germany with killing of Jews." Then, there is "the tradition of the Eastern Church relating to the sack of Byzantium" (by crusaders in 1204–when it was an entirely Christian city). Finally, he speaks of the revival of crusader consciousness among Muslims who see "the state of Israel today as neo-crusader."

Bremer is a latter-day member of the Order of the Knights of St. John (the Hospitallers), as were his ancestors, and explains, "The Hospitallers were in the Holy Land long before the Crusades and were not called 'knights' until the real crusaders came." Hospitaller tradition, he says, avers that "we were the only European group that was allowed to stay [after the crusaders were defeated]." Bremer laments the fact that the Hospitallers, originally a peaceful group, were forced by the coming of the Templars to bear arms. The Templars were founded in 1119 for the purpose of defending Christian pilgrims in the Holy Land, while the Hospitallers, so-called because their principal mission was to care for the sick, did not become a military order until 1130, some 60 years after having been founded in Jerusalem.

The historical and cultural legacy of the Crusades is accompanied by a concrete, or

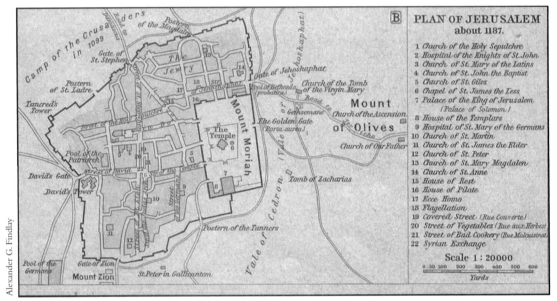

PLAN OF JERUSALEM
about 1187.

1 Church of the Holy Sepulchre
2 Hospital of the Knights of St. John
3 Church of St. Mary of the Latins
4 Church of St. John the Baptist
5 Church of St. Giles
6 Chapel of St. James the Less
7 Palace of the King of Jerusalem
  (Palace of Solomon)
8 House of the Templars
9 Hospital of St. Mary of the Germans
10 Church of St. Martin
11 Church of St. James the Elder
12 Church of St. Peter
13 Church of St. Mary Magdalen
14 Church of St. Anne
15 House of Rest
16 House of Pilate
17 Ecce Homo
18 Flagellation
19 Covered Street (Rue Couverte)
20 Street of Vegetables (Rue aux Herbes)
21 Street of Bad Cookery (Rue Malcuisinat)
22 Syrian Exchange

Scale 1 : 20000

Alexander G. Findlay

Map of Jerusalem in 1140 from a Classical Atlas of Ancient Geography by Alexander G. Findlay, written in 1849.

rather stone, legacy, dotting hillsides throughout the Middle East. Less obvious than the isolated castles like Kerak are the crusader remains in the cities, many of which were built upon in subsequent eras. Jerusalem and Akko (Acre), the two most important cities of medieval times, are replete with varied examples of crusader architecture. In Jerusalem, the centerpiece of the crusader kingdom, many sites were modified by the crusaders, but they built from the ground up as well. Not surprisingly, most of these activities centered on churches; the complete rebuilding of the Church of the Holy Sepulchre was a major project. The church was consecrated in 1149, a half-century after the crusaders first seized Jerusalem, and stands today largely in its crusader form.

Despite this fact, many members of

Eastern Orthodox denominations think of the Church of the Holy Sepulchre as Byzantine. "It was first built in the fourth century, and there are still Byzantine structures," explains Ardin Sisserian, an Eastern Orthodox gatekeeper and guide at the Church. The reason for his de-emphasis on crusader architecture here may have something to do with tensions between the Catholics, "whose ancestors came with the sword and the Cross," says Sisserian, and the other four faiths that have access to the Church—all Eastern Christian.

Bremer encountered similar tensions when he and other modern Hospitallers asked to pray at Jerusalem's twelfth-century Church of St. John the Baptist, patron saint of their order. Although the Greek Orthodox Church now owns the structure, it was once so important to the Hospitallers that they maintained guards there after the expulsion of other crusaders and the retaking of Jerusalem by Saladin in 1244. The Hospitallers were denied permission to pray there until 2001, when, Bremer says, they went to Greek Orthodox officials to open what he calls a "diplomatic channel," with the formal admission that "this part of our history is horrible" and that they wanted to go "on the record as recognizing special ties with the Eastern Church." As a result, Bremer says, they "could pray in the church for the first time in 800 years."

These days, most visitors to the Church of the Holy Sepulchre appear to be Israelis rather than Christian pilgrims—who, like many others, are leery of coming to what they perceive to be a war zone. Among the groups speaking Hebrew and touring the church on one Shabbat (Jewish Sabbath) afternoon were several people wearing yarmulkes, as well as seemingly secular Jews. A nonreligious member of a group of mixed religious and secular students, Hagai Dror, explained, "Christians today seem closer to Jews than Muslims do. We see these sites as European, and many of us who have a European background are interested in them." His friend, Gal Ariely, added, "The main reason we are here is because we live here. This is my city, and it's my duty to know about it." This last statement reflects the sense of ownership that many young Israelis feel about Jerusalem. Yossi is an ultra-orthodox

Founded in the Middle Ages to defend the city of Banias, this fortress changed hands many times during the twelfth and thirteenth centuries, staying largely in the control of the Muslims.

Jack Hazut, JHM Photography

Jewish resident of the Mt. Zion's Diaspora Yeshiva, which is housed in a building that was at one time a fourteenth-century crusader monastery. Yossi, who had a strictly religious education in Jerusalem, says that he knows nothing about crusaders except that "I live in a crusader house."

The city of Akko was the last major crusader foothold in Palestine—finally falling to the Muslim forces in 1291, after 100 years of renewed crusader rule. Akko's crusader remains can now be seen below the city's current street level in the northern part of today's walled Old Town. It's a fascinating labyrinth of underground structures unearthed by excavations that began in the late 1950s and continue today. There are barracks for the knights, a hall of the crusader palace, an underground sewage system with a number of public toilets, and portions of crusader streets and walls–all visible beneath the bustling Ottoman city above.

Akko's Ottoman structures, largely built on top of the crusader ruins, represent the Arab character of the city, past and present. The people who live in most of the houses in the Old City, however, were moved there from the Galilee after 1948 (the year of the establishment of the state of Israel), when Akko's older indigenous Arab population fled the city. Ron Be'eri, an archaeologist from the University of Haifa who works at Akko, says that the people who live there today "feel little connection with the city's history" and generally view the historical character of their own houses as an annoyance. Considered abandoned property owned by the State of Israel, these places are occupied mostly by Arab renters who are

not permitted, even if they have the funds, to buy them. They are also not permitted, because these are historic structures, to alter them in any way. Consequently, most of the Old City's residences are in great disrepair.

Nevertheless, Erica Gal of the Akko Development Corporation insists that Akko's locals take an interest in the heritage of their city. "Schools visit the subterranean [crusader] site all the time and, from the fifth grade, local students take a course called 'Akko, My Town' in which they learn all of the local history." She does suggest that visits by local people to Akko underground may be limited by the fact that they must buy tickets to gain access to it. Be'eri believes that "very few" of the Old City's residents have ever visited the crusader site, but this may reflect their hostility toward "heritage sites" in general, given their experience with them, rather than any residual resentment of crusaders.

Although the schools of Akko may take an interest in crusader sites as part of the local history, education in most of Israel, as distinct from Jordan, glosses over the crusader occupation. "We learn nothing about this period in school," says Salman Elbedour, who received an Israeli education. According to Israeli archaeologist Adrian Boas, the crusader period, which is his area of specialization, is not a favored subject for Israeli historians and archaeologists, although he points out that a recent crusader exhibit at the Israel Museum in Jerusalem drew large crowds. As to the historical antagonism, "If you asked the average Jew here about this," he says, "they wouldn't have a clue what you were talking about." Attitudes toward crusader sites in Israel are a reflection of cultural ties to, or antipathies toward, the Crusades as well as individually held beliefs. Boas, originally from Australia, says that his interest in the Crusades and crusader sites comes "from basically having grown up in an Anglo-Saxon country. As a child, I was always interested in the medieval period." Elbedour says that he has no interest in visiting crusader sites. Bremer, who has visited the sites, says that many of the castles look "so militant—like tank posts on top of a hill."

While Boas admires the "tactical advantages" of Kerak and other spur castles, he says that he is most impressed with Belvoir, a Hospitaller castle overlooking the Jordan River and the Damascus to Jerusalem Road. In this case, the strategical importance of Belvoir's location in the past is repeated in the present as today, it overlooks the boundaries between Israel and the West Bank, and Israel and Jordan. One of the earliest examples of the "concentric castle" or *castrum*, a building with one fortification wall entirely enclosing another, Belvoir remains one of the most remarkable buildings of this type.

On the coast south of Akko is probably one of the few crusader sites in the Middle East that is regularly visited by people who live there. Elbedour admits to having been to only one crusader site, Caesarea, but only "because it's on the [Mediterranean] Sea." Although the town witnessed few historical events in the past, some crusader buildings at Caesarea have an interesting modern history. One of them, the citadel, became a mosque after the defeat of the crusaders. With the founding of the state of Israel and subsequent displacement of the local population of Muslims, the mosque became a restaurant and bar, a state of affairs that was bound to offend those Muslims remaining in the region. The restaurant, called "The Castle," is now closed.

Caesarea, according to Pennsylvania State University archaeologist Ann Killebrew, was among those sites that the Israel Antiquities Authority decided early on to develop. Crusader remains and Roman ruins, although they do not precisely reflect the ethnic or religious character of the country today, were restored specifically to attract foreign tourists, she says. In the 1990s, Caesarea was further embellished as a result of the government's efforts to provide employment to workers from the nearby town of Or Akiva. As a result, says Killebrew, the site has been "completely uncovered, and has become unattractive to tourists."

Some writers who have recently looked at the legacy of the Crusades, such as Karen Armstrong (*Holy War*) and, to a lesser extent, Bernard Lewis (*What Went Wrong?*) believe they are the source of the troubles afflicting the Middle East today. Whether or not the Crusades were responsible for bringing West and East together or, conversely, the origin of the struggles now taking place in the region, it seems certain that a crusader legacy, lasting almost 1,000 years, is not a media fantasy. In few places in the world is ancient history given such immediacy as in the Middle East. The founding of the state of Israel in 1948 was partially predicated on the biblical history of the region during the Iron Age—a period some 3,000 years in the past. A trauma that is only 900 years old is relatively recent in a place where history is marked by millennia rather than centuries.

BIBLICAL ICONOCLAST

ISRAEL FINKELSTEIN TILTS WITH COLLEAGUES OVER THE HISTORY OF EARLY IRON AGE PALESTINE, STRESSING ARCHAEOLOGY OVER BIBLICAL REFERENCES

by HAIM WATZMAN

No one in the field of biblical archaeology likes the smell of battle better than Israel Finkelstein. When the director of Tel Aviv University's Sonia and Marco Nadler Institute of Archaeology gets up to speak at the institute's annual seminar on Early Iron Age Palestine, a ripple runs through the audience-the listeners know that within a few minutes they'll either be seething or cheering. This year, Finkelstein, 52, in white jacket and blue-and-yellow checked tie, saunters up to the stage with the usual impish grin that, together with his clipped beard and intense gaze, make him look like a natty young Elijah with a sense of humor.

His talk centers around Goliath. Deconstructing verses from Samuel that portray the giant warrior, Finkelstein maintains that the description is of a Greek mercenary in the Egyptian army of the seventh century B.C. rather than of a Philistine fighter from three centuries earlier. "The story of David and Goliath," he declares, "reflects the period in which it was written, not in which it supposedly took place."

That makes Goliath yet another literary creation that Finkelstein attributes to the reign of King Josiah (r. 639–609 B.C.), the time that Finkelstein believes the biblical account of Israel's origin and history was first drafted. According to that account, the Israelite nation is descended from Abraham, a tent-dwelling herdsman to whom God promised the land of Canaan. In an attempt to escape famine, his grandson Jacob and his family traveled to Egypt, where their descendants were enslaved. Moses led the Israelites back out of Egypt to Canaan, which they conquered under the leadership of Joshua.

Until relatively recently, archaeologists and historians attempted to match this story with the evidence provided by excavations and documents discovered in Egypt, Syria, and elsewhere in the Near East. Most, though not all, now believe that this biblical account is primarily mythical. There is little independent evidence to corroborate the stories of the patriarchs, the enslavement, the exodus, and the conquest, and what exists is ambiguous at best.

The archaeological record confirms that from 1200 to 1000 B.C.—corresponding to the period covered by the Bible's Book of Judges—a collection of small settlements appeared in the eastern part of the highlands of Palestine, in the area now called the West Bank or, by Israelis harking back to biblical history, Samaria and Judea. The population of these settlements displayed cultural elements that lead most scholars to identify them with the Israelites of the Bible (for example, an absence of pig bones, an animal not eaten by the Israelites). As the Israelite population grew in number and moved westward, according to the Bible, it developed into a loose confederation of 12 tribes that had neither the unity nor organization to ward off military threats, particularly from the Philistines, so they united first under Saul of the tribe of Benjamin, and then under David and his son Solomon, from the tribe of Judah.

Traditional chronology dates David and Solomon's united kingdom from ca. 1000 to 928 B.C. The Bible depicts it as a local empire that expanded beyond tribal borders, carried out extensive public works, and achieved great wealth. But the kingdom split after Solomon's death in 928 B.C., with his son and descendants of the Davidic line ruling Judah in the south with their capital in Jerusalem, and a series of usurpers ruling the northern tribes. The northern Kingdom of Israel was conquered by the Assyrians in 722 B.C., while the southern Kingdom of Judah survived until its conquest by the Babylonians in 586 B.C.

Archaeologists and historians long accepted this story of a glorious united kingdom, followed by a north-south split. Many still believe that it is fundamentally true, even if the Bible exaggerates the grandeur of David and Solomon's realm. But over the last three decades a growing number of scholars has begun to argue that archaeological finds previously taken as corroborations of the biblical story have, in fact, been misinterpreted.

Author and leading advocate of a new chronology for most of the major finds of Early Iron Age Palestine, Finkelstein maintains that major construction projects at northern sites such as Megiddo and Gezer, which other archaeologists and historians assign to the time of the united kingdom of David and Solomon, actually date to the period of King Ahab, a century later.

According to Finkelstein, the united kingdom of David and Solomon—and much of the history of the people of Israel presented in the Bible—represents the political and theological interests of the court of King Josiah, which reinstituted the exclusive worship of the god of the Israelites, centered on the Temple in Jerusalem, and aspired to see their king reign over both Judah and the territory of the former northern kingdom. The intellectual and spiritual atmosphere of this new religious movement led its leaders to create a coherent narrative of Israelite history as an instrument of god's will. Finkelstein has now presented this theory in *The Bible Unearthed: Archaeology's New Vision of Ancient Israel and the Origin of its Sacred Texts*, a book written with archaeological journalist Neil Asher Silberman.

Finkelstein is sometimes classified as a member of the "biblical minimalist" school. Minimalists believe that the tales in the Pentateuch, the first five books of the Old Testament, and the historical books of the Old Testament are fictions composed at a much later date than the events they claim to describe. In their view, the stories were meant to provide a mythical past for a Jewish people who achieved a national consciousness and unique theology only during the time of the Babylonian exile (586–538 B.C.) or perhaps even as late as the Hellenistic period (332–63 B.C.).

Among Israeli archaeologists, Finkelstein is considered a radical and a firebrand. To a large swath of the Israeli public, in particular those involved in the popular field of "Land of Israel Studies," Finkelstein is worse—they call him an anti-Zionist out to aid Israel's enemies. By challenging the truth of the Bible's version of history he is, they say, supporting the Palestinian claim that Jews are not really natives of their own land. Rabbi Yoel Ben-Nun, a leading figure in the West Bank settler community, said at a conference last year that the claims of Finkelstein and his like-minded colleagues are "really all an argument about Zionism."

Finkelstein rejects such charges: "I'm sick of people saying that we're putting weapons in the hands of Israel's enemies. We're strengthening Israeli society. The debate we're conducting testifies to the resilience of Israeli society."

In fact, Finkelstein disassociates himself from the minimalists, even if like them he rejects the "conservative" or "traditionalist" view that the stories of the period of the judges, the united kingdom of David and Solomon, and the early monarchy of Judah are fundamentally true and based on accounts compiled close to the time of the events they describe. He thinks that minor chiefs named David and Solomon founded the dynasty that later produced Josiah, but he is certain that their power never extended beyond the territory of Judah. He argues that demographic and material evidence produced by archaeological survey of the central highlands, the territory that was the cradle of the emerging Israelite nation, also show that Judah was a sparsely populated and economically backward chiefdom. Only when it absorbed refugees following Assyrian conquest and control of the north from 715 to 642 B.C. did Judah achieve the attributes of a state.

Finkelstein, who lives with his wife and two daughters in Tel Aviv, wasn't always such an iconoclast. Articles written in his younger days, when he began his career excavating at Beersheva, show him following the traditional pattern of trying to identify archaeological finds with peoples and events described in the Bible. As recently as the late 1980s, he asserted that the kingdom of David and Solomon was a full-blown, mature state that controlled a large territory extending from the Galilee in the north to the Negev in the south. At that time he believed, along with most of his colleagues, that excavations at important sites as far-flung as Beersheva and Arad in southern Israel and Hazor and Megiddo in the country's north had produced ample evidence of major building projects dated to the tenth century B.C., the period that both biblical and modern historical chronology identify with the united kingdom. But soon thereafter, during a 1992–1993 sabbatical at Harvard, he began a major rethinking of his work.

"I sat quietly at home and the picture began to clarify. And the picture was cyclical," he explains. Surveys and excavations showed a recurring Bronze Age pattern of a populous and prosperous northern highland region—the one that would later be the Kingdom of Israel—and a southern hill region, later Judah, that was largely pastoral, tribal, and lacking in influence. If geography and climate dictated such a pattern in the Bronze Age, would it not have done the same in the Early Iron Age, the period of Israelite settlement?

Megiddo is a key site in the debate over the historical veracity of the Bible. "It's one of the few places where text and archaeology cross," notes Baruch Halpern, a historian from Pennsylvania State University, who, along with Finkelstein and David Ussishkin of Tel Aviv University, is a co-director of excavations there. The Bible says that Solomon fortified Megiddo, and that King Josiah was killed here in an attempt to restore Judah's control over the northern territories that seceded after Solomon's death. "Everyone was basing their claims on the excavations at Megiddo," says Finkelstein. "I saw that if the chronology there didn't work, then the traditional view fell apart."

Halpern's expertise in textual study dovetailed with Finkelstein's growing interest in the use of the biblical record to interpret archaeological finds. Unlike the minimalists, who generally argue that the Bible was written so late as to be nearly useless as a historical record, Finkelstein was impressed by work done by his Tel Aviv colleague Nadav Na'aman and Harvard biblical scholar Frank M. Cross, who noted that many details of the Bible's stories from Genesis through Kings seemed to reflect the political, geographical, and social realities of the late monarchic period, in the decades before the Babylonian conquest of 586 B.C.

Finkelstein's dating of palaces and structures interpreted as stables, as well as a six-chambered city gate at Megiddo to the period of Ahab, a century after Solomon's supposed reign, is one of the foundations of his later chronology. While he is convinced he is right and gives no quarter in arguments with his colleagues, the evidence is complex and open to differing interpretations. Archaeological chronologies are based largely on the interpretation of potsherds and, more recently, on radiocarbon dating of wooden beams from the site. Both can be ambiguous and imprecise. "You can argue them five ways from Friday," asserts Halpern, who disputes Finkelstein's chronology.

Finkelstein is not one to present a balanced survey of scholarly opinion. *The Bible Unearthed* is a polemic, setting out the case for his chronology and the Josianic origin of the biblical text with great vigor and little acknowledgement of other points of view. That infuriates many of his colleagues. In a recent review of *The Bible Unearthed*, University of Arizona Bible scholar and historian William G. Dever, calls Finkelstein

AMONG ISRAELI ARCHAEOLOGISTS, FINKELSTEIN IS CONSIDERED A RADICAL AND A FIREBRAND

"idiosyncratic and doctrinaire." Furthermore, he charges, the book's "discussion of exceedingly complex matters is often simplistic and therefore misleading."

Finkelstein is nonplussed. "This is a question of how you write a book and how you do research," he says. "I don't sum up previous scholarship. I stir up an interesting argument and then the issues are clarified. I believe in the efficacy of stimulation and thinking to push scholarship forward."

Halpern is generous. "He's taken a position that in archaeology is extreme but in historical studies is not and which in textual studies is moderate. He's made a case for it. I disagree with it but there's nothing illegitimate about it. It's real scholarship and should be dealt with as such."

Halpern also credits Finkelstein with bringing the biblical text back into the debate, noting that over the last two or three decades reference to the Bible has gone out of fashion in archaeology, even among the conservatives. "That," Halpern says, "was because archaeology used to look at the Bible very simplistically. Now Finkelstein is looking at it through the lens of critical scholarship. You've got to give him a lot of credit for that."

In fact, Finkelstein's advocacy of a Josian origin for the Bible has given him something that his opponents on both sides lack—a narrative. It's a conceptual framework (some of his colleagues would say an obsession) that allows him to present a coherent account of the history of the kingdoms of Judah and Israel and of the composition of the Bible.

In fact, at the seminar, Finkelstein was practically the only speaker quoting the Bible. His talk on Goliath was laced with references to chapters and verses, whereas "mainstreamers" like Amihai Mazar of the Hebrew University had stripped their talks of biblical imagery and were referring staidly to Iron Ages IA and IB. Ironically, Finkelstein is doing just what he did when he was younger—and what so many archaeologists in this part of the world did until just a couple of decades ago. He's linking up archaeological finds to the Bible's story. He just tells that story differently than they did.

Finkelstein is certain that a large-scale radiocarbon survey of Iron Age sites currently underway will confirm his later dating of monuments. Preliminary results presented at the seminar point in this direction, although they are still far from conclusive.

Despite that, Finkelstein expects resolution. "Within five, six, or ten years the picture will have stabilized" and his chronology will have been confirmed, he proclaims with an infectious enthusiasm that is more reminiscent of his Hasidic forebears than of the halls of academe.

Will archaeology be free of controversy then? "No," he says, grinning. "Then we'll argue over the details."

FAKING BIBLICAL HISTORY

A LOOK INTO THE JAMES OSSUARY, AND HOW WISHFUL THINKING AND TECHNOLOGY FOOLED SOME SCHOLARS, AND MADE FOOLS OUT OF OTHERS

by NEIL ASHER SILBERMAN *and* YUVAL GOREN

Two centuries of intensive archaeological activity in the land of the Bible—surveying, digging, and frantic antiquities buying and selling—have yielded only a handful of artifacts that can be directly connected to specific biblical personalities. Yet since the beginning of the great search for archaeological proof of the scriptures, those personalities have loomed large in virtually every debate. Were the Patriarchs—Abraham, Isaac, and Jacob—genuine historical characters? Did David and Solomon really rule over a vast united kingdom? Was Jesus of Nazareth a real figure who lived much as he is described in the New Testament?

Archaeology has done a great deal to clarify the general social background and historical context in which the Bible was written, but scholars are still divided, often acrimoniously, about how much of the scriptural narrative is historically accurate. That is why the stakes were so high when two astounding discoveries recently surfaced in Jerusalem that, if authentic, would have offered convincing, perhaps even irrefutable archaeological evidence of the historical reliability of two important biblical events.

But the story that began with trumpet blasts of spiritual triumph was destined to end as an embarrassing farce. Indeed, the pious self-deception, shoddy scholarship, and commercial corruption that accompanied these relics' meteoric rise and fall as media sensations offer an instructive Sunday school lesson to anyone who would, at any cost, try to mobilize archaeology to prove the Bible "true."

The Greatest Discovery of the Century?

The story first exploded into the headlines on October 21, 2002, with the beginning of a skillfully orchestrated publicity campaign. At a Washington press conference jointly sponsored by the Discovery Channel and the Biblical Archaeology Society, Hershel Shanks, publisher and editor of the popular *Biblical Archaeology Review*, presented a large audience of reporters and TV crews with photographs and background supporting what he called "the first ever archaeological discovery to corroborate biblical references to Jesus." The discovery in question was a small chalk ossuary, or bone container, bearing the Aramaic inscription Yaakov bar Yoseph, Achui de Yeshua, "James, son of Joseph, brother of Jesus." According to Shanks, the ossuary belonged to an anonymous Tel Aviv antiquities collector who, having become aware of its significance, was now willing to

allow news of its discovery be made public.

Authenticated as dating from the first century A.D. by renowned Semitic epigrapher André Lemaire of the Sorbonne and by some laboratory tests carried out by scientists at the Geological Survey of Israel (GSI), the ossuary caused a worldwide sensation. No previous artifacts had ever been found that could be directly connected to the gospel figures Jesus, Joseph, or James— yet here was one that might have held the very bones of Jesus' brother. In the following days, excited reports about the "James Ossuary" appeared on NBC, CBS, ABC, PBS, and CNN and in *The New York Times*, the *Wall Street Journal*, the *Washington Post*, and *Time*. *Newsweek* suggested that "Biblical archaeologists may have found their holy grail."

The initial studies of the ossuary had indeed produced some dramatic conclusions. Lemaire reported that even though the ossuary seemed to be undecorated, its inscription was truly remarkable. He dated the distinctive forms of the inscribed letters to the period A.D. 20 to 70 and made a mathematical calculation about the possibility that this was in fact the container that had once held St. James' earthly remains. Relying on estimates of first-century Jerusalem's population (around 80,000) and the frequency of name combinations appearing on ossuaries from that period, Lemaire suggested that "it was very probable" that this was the burial box of James, who, according to the ancient Jewish historian Flavius Josephus, was executed by the order of the high priest Ananus in A.D. 62.

Shanks immediately understood the

potential significance of this find to his magazine's conservative Christian readers. In recent years, the literal reliability of the scriptural descriptions of Jesus' early life and ministry has been challenged by a significant number of biblical scholars. Shanks' publications *Biblical Archaeology Review* and *Bible Review* have covered the controversy in detail. And ever keeping his ear to the ground to learn of recent finds that might influence the course of the debate, Shanks solicited and received a manuscript from Lemaire describing his conclusions about the James Ossuary, to be published as a world exclusive in *Biblical Archaeology Review*.

A cautious lawyer by training, Shanks sought second and third opinions from other world-renowned experts in ancient Semitic epigraphy: Kyle McCarter of Johns Hopkins University and Joseph Fitzmyer of the Catholic University. Though McCarter detected two handwriting styles (and therefore two scribes) in the first and last parts of the inscription, both he and Fitzmyer agreed that the Aramaic letters were authentic and dated to the first century A.D.

Next, Shanks turned to hard science. Amnon Rosenfeld and Shimon Ilani of the GSI carried out microscopic and chemical tests on the ossuary. Their results provided another seeming confirmation of the ossuary's authenticity: its stone is of the type commonly used in Jerusalem ossuaries and the patina that covers it "has a cauliflower shape known to be developed in a cave environment"—suggesting that it was naturally formed in a rock-cut burial chamber over hundreds of years. In sum, Rosenfeld

and Ilani concluded in their report, "No evidence that might detract from the authenticity of the patina and inscription was found."

The archaeological value of this potentially unique and precious relic was also plagued by nagging uncertainties about the date and place where it was obtained. According to current Israeli antiquities law, only artifacts that were discovered prior to 1978 can be privately owned or sold by officially licensed antiquities dealers. All subsequent finds belong to the state. In his October press conference, Shanks reported that the ossuary had been found "around fifteen years ago," which would therefore make it subject to confiscation by the Israel Antiquities Authority (IAA). But the collector, with whom Shanks was in close contact and whom he called "Joe" to preserve his anonymity, issued a clarification. "Joe" claimed he had obtained it as a sixteen-year-old—at a Jerusalem antiquities shop (but which one he could not exactly remember)—just a few years after the 1967 war. It was one of his earliest acquisitions and he had kept it at his parents' Tel Aviv apartment for many years. It was only fifteen years ago that he brought it to his own apartment. And why had the self-professed owner of "probably the largest and most important private collection of its kind in Israel" never recognized the ossuary's significance? Shanks quoted "Joe" as innocently admitting in one of their many conversations that "I never thought the Son of God could have a brother!"

The November/December 2002 issue of *Biblical Archaeology Review* carried

Lemaire's exclusive cover story on the ossuary with the bold headline "Evidence of Jesus Written in Stone." But this was only a part of a far wider publicity campaign. Shanks teamed up with Simcha Jacobovici, a Canadian film producer who believed the "James Ossuary" could be a huge media sensation all over the world. A deal was concluded with the Discovery Channel, which would air a nationwide prime-time documentary special during the Easter weekend. Negotiations also got underway with mass-market publisher Harper-Collins for a book that Shanks would coauthor with Ben Witherington III of the Asbury Theological Seminary in Kentucky, a staunch defender of the historicity of the gospels and an occasional columnist for Shanks' other publication, *Bible Review*. And as if that were not enough of a media overkill for a humble white bone box from Jerusalem, Shanks proposed (with the willing and by now enthusiastic cooperation of "Joe") that the ossuary would be the centerpiece of a highly publicized public exhibit at the prestigious Royal Ontario Museum (ROM) in Toronto, coinciding with the annual meetings of the Society of Biblical Literature.

Before the media uproar of the October 21 press conference, "Joe" reportedly insured the ossuary for $1 million and obtained

THE ARCHAEOLOGICAL VALUE OF THIS POTENTIALLY UNIQUE AND PRECIOUS RELIC WAS ALSO PLAGUED BY NAGGING UNCERTAINTIES

routine approval for the temporary export of an inscribed ossuary from the IAA. On October 25, while the media was still humming with excited speculation about the significance of the bone box, William Thorsall, ROM director and CEO, proudly announced in an official press release that the "ROM is honoured to receive the James Ossuary such a short time after its discovery," and that "we are delighted to be the first museum to display it and bring forth the various theories regarding its significance and archaeological history."

Yet for all the ballyhoo, hosannas, and lucrative negotiations, the journey of the James Ossuary to Toronto was ill-starred. When it arrived at the Royal Ontario Museum and was removed by the curators from its cardboard shipping box and bubble-wrap blanket, it was found to be severely damaged by a network of deep cracks. Desperate to recover from this public-relations debacle and launch their exhibition on time, ROM conservators began feverish work to repair the damage—discovering, in the meantime, carved rosette decorations on the side opposite the inscription that had apparently been overlooked by Lemaire. In the meantime, the identity of the owner was revealed by a reporter for the Israeli daily *Ha'aretz*. He was Oded Golan, a 51-year-old engineer, well known on the

Israeli antiquities collecting and dealing scene.

The IAA, for its part, was criticized (and embarrassed) by the ease with which it had issued the export permit. It demanded that Golan return the ossuary to Israel after the conclusion of the exhibition so that its legal status could be resolved and it could be examined by IAA experts. The whole affair of the James Ossuary was in danger of becoming a comedy of errors. But so many people were now caught up in the enthusiasm of the "first discovery that proved the historical existence of Jesus" that almost everyone forgot to laugh.

Or almost everyone. From the start there were some skeptical voices. In an op-ed piece in the *Los Angeles Times*, Robert Eisenman of University of California-Long Beach, a well-known, controversial scholar who had written extensively on James, termed the discovery "just too pat, too perfect." He suggested that the names of Jesus, Joseph, and James together "is what a modern audience, schooled in the Gospels, would expect, not an ancient one."

With the ossuary glued back together and dramatically illuminated in a main exhibit hall of the Royal Ontario Museum, the best possible light was cast on the celebrated discovery. Even proud owner Oded Golan had flown over to Toronto to be at the festive opening of the exhibition and to participate in the public lectures held in connection with it. Lemaire, basking in the media attention and scholarly acclaim of the moment, firmly defended his original conclusions about the inscription at a special session of the Society for Biblical Literature.

Standing at the lectern, he angrily dismissed claims that it was a modern forgery, misdated, or even written by two people. As a scholar of unquestioned reputation, Lemaire icily questioned the professional qualifications and expertise of those individuals who had come forward to challenge his reading.

Following Lemaire, in an impassioned rhetorical tour de force worthy of a skillful summation to the jury, Shanks also belittled the critics of the inscription as far less credible than the famous scholars who supported its authenticity. Addressing critics who found fault with the promotion of a privately owned artifact whose provenience was so uncertain, he railed against those who opposed the antiquities trade, suggesting that there are "bad" collectors who hoard their treasures and "good" collectors who share them with the world. Oded Golan was, by that definition, certainly good.

The doubters had been at least temporarily humbled. The sheer weight of skillful promotion, museum prestige, media attention, and scholarly reputation had lined up in favor of the authenticity of the James Ossuary and discouraged most from taking a closer look at the emperor's clothes.

Another Amazing Artifact

Hardly had Christmas come and gone when, in January, another amazing and unprecedented archaeological find, the so-called "Jehoash Inscription," was revealed to the world. It was rumored to have come from the construction rubble of recent, controversial building activities by the Muslim authorities on the Temple Mount in Jerusalem. According to another version, it was found lying face down, in the Muslim cemetery, down slope from the Temple Mount. Bearing fifteen lines of Hebrew-Phoenician script, this cracked gray stone slab was dated nine hundred years older than the James Ossuary and described repairs to the Temple in Jerusalem apparently overseen by Jehoash, son of King Ahaziah of Judah. It described how the ancient king of Judah collected contributions from his subjects and obtained the precious materials:

> *When the generosity of the men from the land and from the desert, and all the towns of Judah, was filled, to give much hallowed money to buy quarried stones, cypresses, and copper, meant to do the work faithfully. And I repaired the beaches of the Temple and the walls around, and the gallery, and the fences, and the spiral stairs, and the niches, and the doors. And this day would be a testimony that the craftsmanship would endure. May the Lord bless his people.*

This language was strikingly reminiscent of the account in 2 Kings 12. And at a time when the date of composition of the Hebrew Bible, like that of the Gospel accounts, had become a matter of disagreement among biblical scholars, the Jehoash Inscription offered a lapidary reply to those who would deny that the Hebrew Bible contained a reliable record of events. According to archaeologist Gabriel Barkay of Bar-Ilan University, this find, if authentic, would be "the most significant archaeological finding yet in Jerusalem and the Land of Israel. It would be a first-of-its-kind piece of physical evidence describing events in a manner that adheres to the narrative in the Bible." And Shanks, by now a familiar TV and newspaper presence when it came to assessing the significance of biblical discoveries, asserted that if authentic, the inscription would be "visual, tactile evidence that reaches across 2,800 years."

Photographs and feature stories about this find were quickly flashed around the world by a media hungry to relive the excitement of the James Ossuary. The circumstances of its discovery and ownership over the previous years were even murkier. Published reports in the Israel dailies *Maariv* and *Ha'aretz* suggested that it was owned by a Palestinian Arab antiquities dealer in Hebron. He had offered it for sale to the Israel Museum, which had declined. The museum had no comment. But the Jehoash Inscription had an additional, explosive effect in the turbulent world of Middle Eastern politics. It intensified an already fiery rhetorical battle between the Muslim religious authorities on the Temple Mount and those who sought full Israeli sovereignty there, at the site where the ancient temple stood.

The right-wing Israeli group The Temple Mount Faithful quickly posted photographs of the Jehoash Inscription on their website, declaring it "completely authentic" and noting that "people feel that the timing is no accident and that it is a clear message from the G-d of Israel Himself that time is short, the Temple should immediately be rebuilt...." A few days later, Abdullah Kan'an, secretary-general of Jordan's Royal Committee for Jerusalem Affairs, issued a press release asserting that extremist factions in Israel were using the claims of the discovered tablet to support their bid to destroy the Al-Aqsa Mosque and rebuild the Temple, and further warned that "if that happened, God forbid, a holy religious war will definitely inflame the whole region." This was dangerous territory for an archaeological artifact to be drawn into.

The process of recognition and authentication of the Jehoash Inscription seemed to duplicate the story of the James Ossuary in at least two important ways.

Once again the object had reportedly languished in a private collection for years until its true value was recognized. Its owner—though this time lacking a cute nickname—insisted on remaining anonymous and was represented in public by a prominent lawyer who zealously protected his anonymity. And once again Rosenfeld and Ilani of the GSI provided support for the artifact's authenticity through a series of seemingly conclusive scientific tests. Together with Michael Dvoracheck, another geologist, Ilani and Rosenfeld prepared a dramatic article for the GSI's scientific periodical, Current Research. Not satisfied with providing mere geological data, they also translated the inscription and—even though none of them was a trained historian, archaeologist, biblical scholar, or linguist-opined on its epigraphy, historical background, and biblical significance.

They identified the stone as arkosic sandstone, most likely originating in the area of southern Israel or Jordan. The chiseled letters seemed to be weathered (and thus most likely ancient) and the patina that covered the stone was produced over centuries by a natural process. Most intriguing, they found microscopic gold globules in the patina, which were not present in the stone itself. In addition, they noted that a carbon-14 dating of carbon particles within the patina performed by a laboratory in Florida had yielded a date of the third century B.C., by which time, it was suggested, the stone lay buried in the rubble around the Temple Mount.

The three geologists' interpretations were presented in a style more dramatic and speculative than usual for a geological journal. For example, they connected the presence of gold globules within the patina with the intense fire that melted the gold-lined walls of Solomon's Temple at the time of the Babylonian destruction of Jerusalem in 586 B.C.

A volunteer editor employed by the Geological Survey was so excited by the "discovery" that she shared galley proofs of the article with her son, a reporter at Ha'aretz, Nadav Shragai. Shragai broke the story in two headline-grabbing articles, and a new international media frenzy began.

Yet this time one important thing was different. The critical murmurings were earlier and louder than they had been with the James Ossuary—and they were from sources that could not be easily dismissed. In 1998, historian Nadav Na'aman suggested in a scholarly article that the text of the Books of Kings could have been based at least in part on public inscriptions. After he had first read the Jehoash Inscription in press reports, Na'aman told Ha'aretz, he assumed "one of two things—either I hit the nail on the head, and my theory was confirmed fantastically, or the forger read my theory and decided to confirm it."

Famed epigrapher Joseph Naveh of the Hebrew University subsequently revealed to the IAA and police investigators that he had secretly met with the owner's shadowy representatives in a hotel room in Jerusalem to evaluate the stone's authenticity. He immediately recognized it to be a crude forgery, haphazardly combining ninth-century Hebrew letter forms with seventh-century Aramaic and Moabite. And perhaps the most highly esteemed Semitic epigrapher in the world, Frank Cross of Harvard (who had been widely quoted as saying that if the James Ossuary was a forgery, "the forger was a genius") offered quite a different opinion about the Jehoash Inscription. He noted numerous errors of spelling, syntax, and terminology and declared without hesitation that it was a fake.

In the meantime, co-author Yuval Goren of Tel-Aviv University decided to confront the scientific conclusions of the GSI head-on. Through a controlled laboratory experiment, he demonstrated how it might be possible to manufacture a biblical relic like the Jehoash Inscription and obtain the same test results that Ilani and Rosenfeld had. After selecting an appropriate stone, incising the letters, and "weathering" them artificially by means of an abrasive airbrush, it was possible, Goren suggested, to cover it with an authentic-looking but totally artificial patina. If a modern forger ground some of the stone into powder, mixed it into a soup with microscopic gold globules and ancient charcoal samples, he or she could paint this "patina" over the entire surface

and fix it with heat.

So a negative verdict on the Jehoash Inscription was nearing. The present whereabouts of the stone were unknown—as was the owner's identity. But the James Ossuary was still capturing the world's attention. Startling developments would suddenly link the two together—and challenge the idea that the world's greatest, most celebrated scholars could infallibly distinguish valuable ancient inscriptions from worthless modern fakes.

A Storehouse in Ramat Gan

While Hershel Shanks and Ben Witherington III were about to embark on their cross-country authors' tour for their newly published book, James, the Brother of Jesus, proclaiming the spiritual and historical importance of the James Ossuary, the case of the Jehoash Inscription was finally on its way to being solved. *Maariv* correspondent Boaz Gaon reported that several months before, in response to rumors of an impending plot to defraud a wealthy collector in London by selling him a faked artifact, the IAA's Theft Unit had focused their attention on the Jehoash Inscription as possibly being the expensive bait for the impending sting.

Following a trail of leads to determine the identity of the shadowy "representatives" who had met with Professor Naveh in a Jerusalem hotel room, the investigators linked a phoney business card and a scribbled phone number to a Tel Aviv private detective who, confronted with some aggressive questioning, admitted that his employer was none other than Oded Golan-the innocent "Joe" of the James Ossuary saga. He said that Golan had hired him to bring the Jehoash Inscription to Naveh. Yet Golan repeatedly denied, in television and newspaper interviews, that he was the owner of the stone. He consistently claimed that the real owner was a Palestinian Arab antiquities dealer who lived in an area controlled by the Palestinian Authority and whose identity he had promised he would not reveal.

Then a stunning break in the story hit the headlines in Israel. A March 19 article in *Maariv* by Gaon reported that a court-authorized search warrant had been obtained by the police and Golan's apartment, office, and rented storage space were thoroughly gone over, yielding incriminating documents and photographs showing Golan posing proudly beside the Jehoash Inscription—which he still insisted he did not own. Reportedly, the police questioning continued for several days; Golan's offer—under-pressure of information about the stone's location in exchange for complete immunity from prosecution was refused. A surprise court-ordered search was then carried out by the police and by IAA investigators at a storage space Golan had rented in Ramat Gan (but that he had not voluntarily revealed to the police).

Gaon's *Maariv* article reported the discovery of some truly damning archaeo-logical evidence: scores of artifacts of unclear provenience, forged ancient seals and other inscriptions in various stages of production, epigraphic handbooks, engraving tools, and labeled bags of soil from excavation sites around the country. Handcuffed and taken to his parents' apartment for further questioning, Golan reportedly broke down and asked the police and the IAA officials to stop. He agreed to hand over the Jehoash Inscription to the proper authorities the following day.

> FRANK CROSS OF HARVARD ... NOTED NUMEROUS ERRORS ... AND DECLARED WITHOUT HESITATION THAT IT WAS A FAKE

Gold Dust and James Bond

And so, in March 2003, the James Ossuary and the Jehoash Inscription were finally together, now the subjects of an intensive, official examination by a multidisciplinary team of specialists gathered by the IAA and divided into epigraphic and scientific committees.

The Israeli Minister of Culture, Limor Livnat, had personally mandated the work of the scientific commission. She noted, particularly with regard to the Jehoash Inscription, that if it were found to be genuine, it would be "the most important archaeological discovery ever made in the State of Israel." Now both artifacts would be studied under controlled conditions, without personal ties to the owner or under the pressure of an upcoming museum exhibition.

The verdict of the epigraphers with regard to the Jehoash Inscription was unanimous: the numerous mistakes in grammar and the eccentric mixture of letter forms known from other inscriptions made it clear that this was a modern forgery. The James Ossuary was a different matter. The epigraphers were divided about the authenticity of the first part of the inscription but in light of the results of the patina committee, they unanimously agreed that the entire inscription must have been modern. In the case of the James Ossuary, it was geochemical and microscopic analysis, rather than scholarly erudition, that uncovered the truth.

Examination of the chalk from which the ossuary had been carved indicated that it was from the Menuha Formation of the Mount Scopus Group, consistent with the hundreds of other ossuaries found in the Jerusalem area. But the earlier geologists and the ROM conservators had mentioned only a single kind of "cauliflower"-shaped patina. Goren and Avner Ayalon of the GSI, however, identified three distinct coatings on the surface of the ossuary:

- A thin brown veneer of clay and other minerals cemented to the rock surface, presumably rock varnish created by living bacteria or alga over prolonged periods of time.

- A crusty natural coating of patina (this was the "cauliflower") that formed over the rock surface due to the absorption or loss of various elements and minerals.

- The "James Bond": a unique composite material nicknamed by Goren since it

was bonded onto the incised letters of the James Ossuary inscription but wasn't found at any other place on the ossuary surface-or on the three authentic inscribed ossuaries that the commission members had sampled for comparison.

The varnish covered large areas of the ossuary surface and the patina had burst through the varnish in many places. Both varnish and patina coated the rosettes on the other side of the ossuary. But microscopic analysis showed that the letters of the entire inscription "James, son of Joseph, brother of Jesus" were cut through the varnish, indicating that they were carved long—perhaps centuries—after the varnish-covered rosettes.

Strangest of all was the "James Bond," the chalky material that coated the letters. It contained numerous microfossils called coccoliths, naturally occurring as foreign particles in chalk, but not dissolved by water. Hence it was clear that this was not a true patina formed by the surface crystallization of calcite, but rather powdered chalk that was dissolved in water and daubed over the entire inscription. Thus, the forger's technique was apparent: the James Ossuary was an authentic, uninscribed artifact, on which decorative rosettes originally marked the "front" side. At some time long after the natural processes of varnish and patination in a damp cave environment had been completed, someone carved a series of letters through the natural varnish on the ossuary's "back" side. Then he or she covered the freshly cut letters with an imitation "patina" made from water and ground chalk.

Ayalon's study concentrated on a telltale clue to the nature of authentic ancient patina: its isotopic ratio of oxygen provides a distinctive indication of the qualities of the water with which the patina was produced.

Calcite (calcium carbonate, $CaCO_3$) is the primary component of naturally formed patina on buried archaeological artifacts in calcareous areas, such as the Jerusalem region. This is because calcite dissolves in ground water. With the loss of CO_2 from the ground water by evaporation, the calcite crystallizes again on the stone's surface (just like the "stone" that collects inside a tea kettle). The oxygen within this recrystallized calcareous coating—the patina—has the same isotopic ratio as the water from which it was produced. And that value can even be used to determine the temperature at which the crystallization took place.

Ayalon determined in his analysis that while the calcite of the patina from the uninscribed surface of the James Ossuary, and indeed the surfaces and inscriptions of other authentic ossuaries that he examined, had ratios that were normal for average ground temperature of the Jerusalem vicinity (64–68 degrees Fahrenheit), the ratios of the "James Bond" suggested that its crystallization took place in heated water (about 122 degrees), not the "cave environment" that the earlier geologists had claimed. The evidence pointed to an intentional faking of

> **BUT THE KEYSTONES OF THIS HASTILY CONSTRUCTED STONE WALL QUICKLY BEGAN TO CRUMBLE**

the patina over the letters of the "James, son of Joseph, brother of Jesus" inscription—and nowhere else.

And what of the two styles of handwriting on the James Ossuary that had been discerned by some early critics? The physical examination showed that the entire inscription was carved at the same time, so two different hands seemed unlikely in an inscription of only five words. An examination of the very same catalog of ossuaries that Lemaire had used as comparison for the letter forms in the James Inscription, L.Y. Rahmani's 1968 *A Catalogue of Jewish Ossuaries in the Collections of the State of Israel*, now seemed possibly to be their source. In an age of readily available scanning software it is entirely possible to make flawless copies of ancient letters as they appear on genuine artifacts. For example, taking the word "Jacob" (from catalog #396); the words "son of Joseph" (from catalog #573); "brother of" (from catalog #570); "Jesus" (common enough to have many examples) and resizing them and aligning them with Photoshop or PageMaker can create a puzzlingly authentic template for a faked inscription, that seemed to be carved by more than one hand.

In the case of the Jehoash Inscription, the geological verdict was as damning as the epigraphic one. The original GSI geologists had even misidentified the rock type. It was not arkosic sandstone from southern Israel or Jordan but low-grade metamorphic greywacke of a type found commonly in western Cyprus and areas still farther west.

Once again, there was a dramatic difference between the patina on the uninscribed back and sides of the stone from that found within and between the chiseled letters. Unlike the siliceous deposit everywhere else, this material was soft and made of pure clay mixed with powdered chalk. Within this artificial mixture were a few micron-sized globules of metal as well as carbonized particles. The isotopic ratios of oxygen for the calcite in this "patina" indicated again the crystallization was produced in hot water, not in the ground. Most obvious, the "patina" could be easily rubbed off the letters, revealing unmistakably fresh engraving marks.

Based on these results and a combination of epigraphic and historical considerations, the commission concluded in a packed press conference in Jerusalem on June 18 that both inscriptions were modern fakes, engraved on authentic artifacts and covered with a carefully prepared mixture to imitate patina and to make them look centuries old.

Lessons to Be Learned

The principal supporters and promoters of the dubious biblical relics quickly mounted a counterattack. "I am certain the ossuary is real," Oded Golan told *Ha'aretz*. Accusing the committee of having preconceived notions, Golan also asserted his confidence that the Jehoash Inscription was genuine.

Shanks, who had reaped enormous publicity for himself and his magazine from the promotion of the James Ossuary, was likewise reluctant to retreat. In a broadside quickly posted on the Biblical Archaeological Society website, he explained "Why I Am Not Yet Convinced the 'Brother of Jesus' Inscription is a Forgery." He once again summoned up the authority of the famous paleographers he had consulted, the results of the initial GSI examination, and the conclusion of the Royal Ontario Museum. He accused the IAA of stacking its committee with laymen who, according to Shanks, had all been convinced to come to their conclusion by Yuval Goren. He also launched a personal attack on IAA director Shuka Dorfman, suggesting that Dorfman's eagerness to see that the James Ossuary declared a forgery was because Dorfman "hates antiquities collectors, antiquities dealers, the antiquities trade, and would like to put Israeli antiquities dealers out of business."

But the keystones of this hastily constructed stone wall quickly began to crumble. On June 22, Amos Bein, director of the GSI, discredited the results of the initial ossuary examination by Rosenfield and Ilani, expressing confidence in Ayalon's new results, and stating unequivocally that it was "the official view" of the GSI that "the carbonate oxygen isotopic composition of the 'Jeoash Tablet' [sic] and the 'letters patina' of 'James Ossuary' reveals that the patina could not have formed under natural climatic conditions (temperature and water composition) that prevailed in the Judea Mountains during the last 2000 years."

Two days later, on June 24, even the epigraphical support, such as it was, seemed on the verge of collapse. Although Lemaire remained adamant that his original evaluation was correct, the biggest heavyweight in the world of ancient Semitic scripts, Harvard's Frank Cross, circulated a letter to colleagues around the world regretting Shanks' "continued persistence in making claims" for the authenticity of the James Ossuary, and declared that he now stood "wholly and unambiguously with those who believe the ossuary inscription to be a forgery, a good forgery, but a forgery."

As ARCHAEOLOGY'S September 2003 Issue went to press, the affair of the biblical sensations was finally reaching its conclusion. The most important unresolved issue was the decision of the IAA Fraud Unit and Israel Police as to which of the principals would be subjects of further criminal investigations—and which would be granted immunity as witnesses for the state. But this case was more than an instance of science and justice triumphing over charlatanism; it was something more like the passing of an age. In an era of digital scanning, even a teenager with average computer skills and the right software can resize and reproduce an ancient script more precisely than an expert scholar ever could do by hand. The age of the great sages of epigraphy with magnifying glasses and drawing paper would now have to give way to statistical studies of letter-form characteristics and detailed chemical and geological analysis.

There would also have to be a great change in the way that biblical finds are publicized and valued. The cases of the James Ossuary and the Jehoash Inscription showed that what was at stake is not mere collecting or celebrating relics but rather the integrity of archaeology itself.

Put simply, it is time for scholars to stop dealing with unprovenienced antiquities and work to outlaw the private antiquities trade. The respected scholar who publicizes or publishes a private artifact of dubious provenience is boosting its potential market value—and contributing to the general inflation of antiquities' monetary worth. The very serious question of the historicity of the Bible—with all its powerful implications for religious belief and identity—is not the sort of thing to be decided by staged public presentations of isolated artifacts from dubious sources. It is only by adopting a strict and uncompromising standard of evidence and rejecting temptation to simplistically trumpet a headline-grabbing relic or promote a high-visibility museum exhibition that our understanding of the Bible—and indeed all of the human past—will be advanced.

Sadly, the whole affair of the "greatest" archaeological discoveries of the century had precisely the opposite effect its passionate promoters intended. It made scholars outside the circle of true believers more skeptical of ever finding literal proof of the historicity of the Bible. And it made the wider public—to the extent that they were still paying attention—more doubtful that the biblical experts and university professors interviewed on TV about their latest sensation could ever be believed. The least that any of us concerned with the future of archaeology can now do is to persistently and aggressively attack sensational claims about artifacts of dubious origin, not help to construct them, and to recognize how dangerous and ultimately misleading this modern form of relic worship can be.

HOLLYWOOD HOLY LAND

THE PASSION OF THE CHRIST: CAN ANYONE EVER KNOW THE FACTS ABOUT THE DEATH OF JESUS?

by SANDRA SCHAM

By now, millions of people have seen the online film trailer for *The Passion of the Christ*, Mel Gibson's epic drama on the death of Jesus, which opens in theaters on Ash Wednesday. It shows powerful images: Jesus's blood-drenched face, the scourging, the trail of blood on the stones, the nailing of his palms to the cross. Millions have also seen in print the arguments from various quarters concerning the movie's alleged anti-Semitic overtones. One of the film's more intriguing aspects, however, has been all but lost in the hype surrounding it.

The film drew the attention of scholars because of Gibson's claim that it represents the "facts" about Jesus' death. "I wanted to bring you there and I wanted to be true to the Gospels," he has said of the movie. "That has never been done." Thus, we can surmise that what makes *The Passion* unique among the many embattled Jesus pictures, such as *The*

Last Temptation of Christ, is its claim to portray the truth. But few scholars today would defend the Gospels as history.

William Fulco, a Jesuit priest, archaeologist, and professor of ancient Mediterranean studies at Loyola Marymount University, translated the script of *The Passion* into Aramaic (the other language spoken in the movie is Latin). He is quite aware of the lack of archaeological evidence supporting the events described in the Gospels, and he has categorically denied that historical verisimilitude was an aim of the movie. He says that "tremendous efforts were expended" to insure that location, costumes, and languages in the movie had an authentic aura, but that when it came to the archaeological record, "we really have no known buildings related to this story." But Paula Fredricksen, a professor of biblical studies at Boston University and a member of a group of scholars who first raised the anti-Semitism issue, contends that the filmmakers are promoting the film as "historically accurate—when it's really nothing of the sort." She says that some of the movie's nods to historical accuracy, such as the use of Aramaic by the region's inhabitants, are undermined by dubious elements, such as the use of Latin by the Romans when addressing the locals. Greek was the lingua franca of the Roman Empire in Palestine.

In the long run, *The Passion* may be judged to have only the most tenuous relationship to history or archaeology, but that probably won't diminish its appeal. "There is a desire that modern folks have for a sort of visual impression of this stuff-psychologically, it is very important," says Adam Porter, an archaeologist at Illinois College who specializes in Jewish and Gentile relations in antiquity. "It gives you the sense of being there."

In that respect at least, the movie will represent no less truthful a picture of Jesus' life than what is now on offer to Christian tourists in the streets of Jerusalem. Although the sites that are supposed to represent the "true" setting for New Testament events are largely uncorroborated, and even refuted, by archaeological data, pilgrims still flock to the Holy Land to physically "verify" the facts of Jesus' life.

If they are at all attuned to their historical surroundings, tourists retracing the route of the Passion in Jerusalem will quickly realize that what they are seeing has little to do with the life and times of Jesus. Following the sequence of events outlined in the Bible, their first stop will be the Mount of Olives and the Garden of Gethsemane. Although the Mount itself has been well known since early antiquity, the garden has proven a bit more difficult to locate. In Hebrew, Gethsemane means "oil press," so the site might have been anywhere on the olive tree-covered hill. Modern tourists are taken to the place where the fourth-century Gethsemane Church, since replaced by two other churches, was built. This, they are told, is the spot where Jesus was arrested.

The next stop on the itinerary is likely to be the place where Pontius Pilate condemned Jesus. Unfortunately for those who wish to make a historical as well as religious identification, archaeologists have suggested three possible sites for this event. Traditionally, most tourists have begun their pilgrimages at the Antonia Fortress, which was a defensive tower built by Herod to protect the Temple Mount (on top of an earlier tower erected during Nehemiah's time). Archaeologists and historians, however, favor either the Hasmonean Palace, built prior to Herod's time to house the rulers of Judea and probably located in what is today the Jewish Quarter, or Herod's Palace, the remains of which are under the Citadel at Jaffa Gate. These two sites, however, would require a substantial rerouting of the Via Dolorosa, or the Way of the Cross-Jesus' path from condemnation to entombment that snakes through Jerusalem's Old City. The path was laid out in the thirteenth or fourteenth century A.D. but was based on pilgrim sites originally identified by Empress Helena in the fourth century A.D. (Helena, mother of Constantine, visited Jerusalem around A.D. 330 and "discovered" many of the Christian sites still recognized today.) Consequently, most tourists will begin their journey at the northwestern corner of the Temple Mount, where the Antonia Fortress once stood.

In the immediate area of the Antonia Fortress is the Ecce Homo Arch, where Pilate, showing Jesus to the crowd, is said to have uttered this famous phrase. (Ecce Homo is Latin for "Behold the Man.") As the arch was built by the Roman emperor Hadrian (A.D. 76 to 138), the story presents certain difficulties for historians. Near the arch is the Sisters of Zion Convent, under which were found Roman pavings identified as the Lithostratos, the place of Jesus' judgment. In recent years, archaeologists have identified this structure as also dating to the time of Hadrian. The Sisters remain undeterred, however, in presenting it as the pavement where Jesus stood before Pilate. Mark Chancey, an archaeologist from Southern Methodist University, says this

reflects "a legitimate religious phenomenon, even though it is not a legitimate historical enterprise." The sisters, he argues, are motivated by faith, not a desire to fudge history, and through this faith have infused the spot with true religious resonance-however lacking it may be in historical veracity. Chancey sees such an act as the "creation of sacred space by regarding some place as holy and by allowing people to connect with what they see as holy."

Continuing along the Via Dolorosa, tourists will find the Church of the Flagellation and the Church of the Condemnation and Imposition of the Cross—built on medieval foundations in 1927 and 1903, respectively—which mark those events of the Passion. With the exception of these churches, however, the Via Dolorosa is lined with small shops, most of which sell items related to all three religions in the city, including crucifixes, olive-wood nativity scenes, menorahs, candlesticks, and prayer rugs. This commercialism can be a source of consternation for Christian visitors who will likely be reminded of the story of Jesus driving the merchants from the Temple. The Via Dolorosa leads directly to the Church of the Holy Sepulchre. Although it was built in the Middle Ages on a Byzantine foundation, Chancey says this may be the closest we get to Jesus in archaeology, because the tomb in the church dates to the first century, when it was outside the city walls near a gate to Jerusalem—a likely place for a crucifixion. The Holy Sepulchre is yet another sacred site discovered by Empress Helena.

The huge Holy Sepulchre complex will probably be the Christian tourist's last stop, as it incorporates the end of the Passion route at

Golgotha, or Calvary, the place of Jesus' crucifixion. Today Golgotha is a hall divided between the Catholic and Greek Orthodox churches. The place where Jesus' cross supposedly stood—most likely identified by the Empress Helena—is a glass-encased depression in the bedrock foundation.

One of the harsh realizations Christian travelers to the Holy Land may face is the fact that many of the sites sacred to them have seen violence more recent than that inflicted upon Jesus. The Church of the Nativity in Bethlehem was the focus of daily newscasts when armed Palestinian militants seized it in 2002 and were subsequently besieged by the Israeli army, while the Church of the Holy Sepulchre is the scene of regular conflict between various Christian factions that have laid claim to the Church. An uneasy truce exists that is often disrupted by riots, particularly at Easter. No one Christian community has been given keys to the church, which instead have been entrusted for centuries to two Muslim families in Jerusalem.

The location of a Christian traditional sites has always been based upon the presence of an early church either from the Byzantine or the Crusader period, and still is to this day. Archaeologists and historians follow this lead, describing early church sites in terms of the New Testament events they are supposed to commemorate rather than as sites representing the periods in which they were actually built. In all of the countries with putative Christian associations, tourism officials recognize that Christians are the most loyal visitors to the Holy Land, coming in times of instability when others refuse to do so. In the 1990s, in anticipation of an influx of Christian tourists

for the turning of the millennium, the antiquities departments of both Israel and Jordan engaged in a competition of sorts to locate more Christian sites—in spite of the fact that neither the year 2000 nor the designation "Holy Land" have much meaning for the majority Jewish and Muslim populations of these two countries. Among the important finds from this very recent period are the famous Baptismal Site of Jesus in Jordan, evidenced by the foundations of a fourth-century church, and the site of Mary and Joseph's Rest on the Road to Bethlehem, also determined by the foundations of a church, this one dating to the fifth century.

Because of the craving for physical evidence of the Bible by devout tourists, and the strong religious, nationalist, and commercial investments in the old stories, the lack of demand for critical scholarship on the life of Jesus is hardly surprising. Archaeologists and historians are rapidly coming to the conclusion that, for most people, the past is a sort of theme park—and they want the themes to be familiar ones. "Everybody already thinks they know the story of Jesus," says Fredricksen. "A truly ancient Jesus is just too different for audiences to deal with."

Fulco agrees. Without depending overly much on archaeology and history, which provide little enough support for the dramatic reconstruction of *The Passion*, the story must pull the audience "into the past but also convey some sort of familiarity," he says. "You are not brought back to Jesus—Jesus is brought up to your time."

Like the many tours of Jerusalem that give tourists the chance to walk in Jesus' footsteps, The Passion is likely to find a large,

"TWO THUMBS WAY UP!
A GREAT EPIC FILM."
-Ebert & Roeper

"POWERFULLY MOVING!"
-Peter Travers, ROLLING STONE

A
M E L   G I B S O N
F I L M

THE
PASSION
OF THE CHRIST

J I M   C A V I E Z E L

A movie poster released for The Passion of The Christ, *which was promoted as faithful to the gospels.*

authentic, there was no reason to associate it with Jesus," says Chancey. "The scholars who were promoting the ossuary seemed to belittle that problem from the start." Certain kinds of artifacts continue to garner great publicity because people make the leap from an object or site dating from the right period to Jesus. A New Testament-period wooden craft discovered in 1986 on the mud flats of the Sea of Galilee was immediately dubbed the "Jesus Boat."

Despite all of the much-touted and soon forgotten "stupendous" finds, the historical Jesus and his disciples remain elusive to scholars: The archaeological evidence for Jesus's life just isn't there. Chancey says, "It's very hard to locate one individual, particularly one from the masses. Nobody doubts that Jesus existed, but finding evidence in the archaeological record is really an impossibility."

Where archaeology fears-or is unable-to tread, however, Hollywood has always displayed a willingness to rush in and, despite the lack of evidence relating to Jesus's life and ministry, his story will continue to capture the imaginations of filmmakers. And tourists to the Holy Land will continue to be guided to places where the events of the Bible "actually" took place, because, as Chancey says, that way "everybody wins-the pilgrims get to walk where Jesus walked, and the tourism industry gets the money."

receptive, and emotionally engaged audience-as does anyone who claims to have a new or different insight on the Jesus historical narrative. This eagerness was apparent with the quick acceptance by scholars and the public alike of the "Jesus Box," now largely discredited. "Even if the inscription [had been]

ABOUT THE
AUTHORS

SUSAN E. ALCOCK is John H. D'Arms Professor of Classical Archaeology and Classics at the University of Michigan. Recent books include *Archaeologies of the Greek Past: Landscape, Monuments and Memories* (2002). She is a 2001 winner of a MacArthur Fellowship from the John D. and Catherine T. MacArthur Foundation.

ANTHONY F. AVENI is the Russel B. Colgate Professor of Astronomy and Anthropology at Colgate University. Receiving his Ph.D. in astronomy from the University of Arizona, he helped develop and is now considered one of the founders of archaeoastronomy. He was voted 1982 National Professor of the Year, the highest national award for teaching.

ŞENGÜL AYDINGÜN, an art historian and archaeologist based in Istanbul, is a former curator at the Hagia Sophia Museum.

PATRICIA M. BIKAI received her Ph.D. in biblical archaeology from the Graduate Theological Union at Berkley. Currently, she is the Associate Director of the American Center of Oriental Research (ACOR).

RICHARD J. CLIFFORD, a Jesuit priest, is Professor of Biblical Studies at Weston Jesuit School of Theology in Cambridge, MA, where he has taught since completing doctoral studies at Harvard. He has served as General Editor of the *Catholic Biblical Quarterly* for five years and was president of the Catholic Biblical Association in 1991.

TRUDE DOTHAN is a Professor of Archaeology at the Hebrew University of Jerusalem. He directed the Tel Miqne-Ekron excavations for 14 seasons between 1981 and 1996, with Seymour Gitin. Both professors are currently working on the final Ekron excavation reports.

ISRAEL FINKELSTEIN is the Director of the Sonia and Marco Nadler Institute of Archaeology at Tel Aviv University. The author of many books discussing the Holy Land, one of his most recent includes *The Bible Unearthed*, co-authored with Neil Asher Silberman.

SEYMOUR GITIN is Dorot Director and Professor of Archaeology at the W.F. Albright Institute of Archaeological Research, which is affiliated with the American School of Oriental Research in Jerusalem. He directs the Tel Miqne-Ekron excavation with Professor Trude Dothan, and has excavated at Gezer, Jebel Qa'aqir, and Dor.

YUVAL GOREN is the Associate Professor of Archaeology in the Jacob M. Alkow Department of Archaeology and Ancient Near Eastern Cultures at Tel-Aviv University.

BARUCH HALPERN is Chaiken Family Chair in Jewish Studies, Professor of Ancient History, Classics and Mediterranean Studies, Religious Studies and Social Thought at Penn State. Among his books are *The First Historians* and *David's Secret Demons*.

SPENCER P.M. HARRINGTON is a former senior editor at ARCHAEOLOGY magazine.

ELIZABETH J. HIMELFARB is a former associate editor at ARCHAEOLOGY magazine.

RICHARD A. HORSLEY (BA, MDiv, PhD, Harvard University) is Distinguished Professor of Liberal Arts and the Study of Religion at the University of Massachusetts Boston. Among his books is *The Message and the Kingdom* (with Neil Asher Silberman). He is regularly interviewed for documentaries on Jesus, Paul, and other biblical figures on PBS, ABC, BBC, Discovery, and A&E.

PATRICK E. MCGOVERN is a Senior Research Scientist in the Museum Applied Science Center for Archaeology (MASCA) of the University of Pennsylvania Museum of Archaeology and Anthropology in Philadelphia, and an Adjunct Associate Professor of Anthropology.

A specialist in Phoenician art and trade, **GLENN MARKOE** received his masters and doctoral degrees in Ancient History and Mediterranean Archaeology from the University of California at Berkeley. The recipient of a Fulbright Fellowship for Cyprus in 1987, he has served as Curator of Classical and Near Eastern Art at the Cincinnati Art Museum since 1988, where he has produced a number of major exhibitions, most recently, "Petra: Lost City of Stone," which is currently touring North America through 2006.

ERIC M. MEYERS received his Ph.D. in 1969 from Harvard University specializing in Hebrew Bible/Old Testament, archaeology of the ancient Near East, and Jewish History of the Greco-Roman period. He has authored or co-authored nine books. Meyers is Bernice and Morton Lerner Professor of Judaic Studies and is currently Director of the Graduate Program in Religion at Duke University.

JOSEPH NAVEH is a Professor of Archaeology at the Hebrew University of Jerusalem.

ABRAHAM RABINOVICH is the author of the recently published *The Yom Kippur War* (Schocken). Born in New York, he has resided in Israel since 1967. He is a former feature writer with *The Jerusalem Post* and is presently a Jerusalem-based freelance journalist.

KRISTIN M. ROMEY is deputy editor at ARCHAEOLOGY.

MARK ROSE received his doctorate from the Program in Classical Archaeology, Indiana University. He is ARCHAEOLOGY's executive and online editor.

SANDRA SCHAM is a Lecturer and Research Development Specialist in the Department of Anthropology at the University of Maryland. She is also the coordinator for the Negev Bedouin Identity Project at Howard University.

NEIL ASHER SILBERMAN is a historian with the Ename Center for Public Archaeology in Berlin. His most recent book, with Israel Finkelstein, is *The Bible Unearthed*. Silberman is a contributing editor at ARCHAEOLOGY.

A former senior editor at ARCHAEOLOGY, **ANDREW L. SLAYMAN** is a professional photographer (www.slayman.com).

SUSAN STANLEY was an editorial intern at ARCHAEOLOGY.

ROBERT STIEGLITZ, PH.D. (Brandeis University, 1971), has excavated in the U.S., Greece and Israel, and has surveyed through-

out the Mediterranean world. Having taught at universities in Greece and Israel, he is now the Associate Professor of Hebraic Studies and director of the program in Ancient and Medieval Civilizations at Rutgers University, Newark, NJ.

DAVID USSISHKIN, a Professor at Tel Aviv University, was a director of the 1999 Megiddo Expedition, which also included Loyola Marymount, the University of Southern California, Vanderbilt University, and the University of Rostock. Israel Finkelstein and Baruch Halpern were his co-directors.

HAIM WATZMAN is a freelance science and academic affairs writer in Jerusalem.

L. MICHAEL WHITE received his doctorate from Yale in 1982. Currently the Ronald Nelson Smith Endowed Chair in Classics, he teaches at the University of Texas at Austin, and has taught at Yale and Indiana University, Bloomington. He is both the founder and Director of the Institute for the Study of Antiquity and Christian Origins (ISAC).

Further Reading

S.E. Alcock, *Graecia Capta: The Landscapes of Roman Greece* (Cambridge: Cambridge University Press, 1993).

S.E. Alcock, *Archaeologies of the Greek Past: Landscape, Monuments and Memories* (Cambridge: Cambridge University Press, 2002).

M. E. Aubet, *The Phoenicians and the West: Politics, Colonies and Trade* (Cambridge: Cambridge University Press, 1993).

A.F. Aveni, *Empires of Time: Calendars, Clocks, & Cultures* (New York: Colorado University Press, 2002).

A.F. Aveni, *Conversing with the Planets: How Science and Myth Invented the Cosmos* (New York: Colorado University Press, 2002).

M. Balmuth, ed., *Hacksilber to Coinage* (New York: American Numismatic Society, 2001).

D. Clark and V. Matthews, eds., *One Hundred Years of American Archaeology in the Levant: Proceedings of the American Schools of Oriental Research Centennial Celebration* (Washington, DC, Atlanta: ASOR Publications, 2000).

Creation Accounts in the Ancient Near East and in the Bible (Washington, DC: Catholic Biblical Association, 1994).

Eerdmans Dictionary of the Bible (Grand Rapids, MI: Eerdmans, 2000).

I. Finkelstein and N.A. Silberman, *The Bible Unearthed, Archaeology's New Vision of Ancient Israel and the Origins of Its Sacred Texts.* (New York: Free Press, 2001).

B.M. Gittlen, ed., *Sacred Time, Sacred Space: Archaeology and the Religion of Israel* (Winona Lake, IN: Eisenbrauns, 2001).

E. Gubel and E. Lipinski, ed., *Phoenicia and its Neighbors* (Leuven 1985).

D. B. Harden, *The Phoenicians* (Harmondsworth 1971).

R.A. Horsley, *Archaeology, History, and Society in Galilee: The Social Context of Jesus and the Rabbis* (Harrisburg, PA: Trinity Press International, 1996).

R.A. Horsley and N.A. Silverman, *The Message and the Kingdom* (New York: Grosset/Putnam, 1997; Minneapolis: Fortress, 2002).

R.A. Horsley, *Jesus and the Spiral of Violence: Popular Jewish Resistance in Roman Palestine* (Minneapolis: Fortress, 1992)

R.A. Horsley, *Jesus and Empire: The Kingdom of God and the New World Disorder* (Minneapolis: Fortress, 2003).

E. Lipinski, ed., *Phoenicia and the Eastern Mediterranean in the First Millennium B.C.* (Leuven 1987).

E. Lipinski, ed., *Phoenicia and the Bible* (Leuven 1991).

G. Markoe, *Peoples of the Past. Phoenicians* (London: British Museum Press, 2000, 2002).

G. Markoe, *Phoenicians* (Folio Society of London, 2004).

G. Markoe, *Phoenician Bronze and Silver Bowls from Cyprus and the Mediterranean* (Berkeley: Berkley University Press, 1985).

S. Moscati, ed., *The Phoenicians* (New York 1988).

S. Parpola and R.M. Whiting, eds., *ASSYRIA 1995: 10th Anniversary Symposium of the Neo-Assyrian Text Corpus Project* (Helsinki: University of Helsinki, 1997).

G. Pisano, *Phoenicians and Carthaginians in the Western Mediterranean* (Rome, 1999).

INDEX